iPhone™ SDK Programming:
A Beginner's Guide

James A. Brannan

New York   Chicago   San Francisco
Lisbon   London   Madrid   Mexico City
Milan   New Delhi   San Juan
Seoul   Singapore   Sydney   Toronto

The McGraw·Hill Companies

Cataloging-in-Publication Data is on file with the Library of Congress

McGraw-Hill books are available at special quantity discounts to use as premiums and sales promotions, or for use in corporate training programs. To contact a representative, please e-mail us at bulksales@mcgraw-hill.com.

iPhone™ SDK Programming: A Beginner's Guide

1234567890   FGR FGR   019

ISBN   978-0-07-162649-1
MHID   0-07-162649-2

Sponsoring Editor   Roger Stewart
Editorial Supervisor   Patty Mon
Project Manager   Harleen Chopra, International Typesetting and Composition
Acquisitions Coordinator   Joya Anthony
Technical Editor   Billy Meyers
Copy Editor   Lisa McCoy
Proofreader   Eina Malik, International Typesetting and Composition
Indexer   Robert Swanson
Production Supervisor   Jean Bodeaux
Composition   International Typesetting and Composition
Illustration   International Typesetting and Composition
Art Director, Cover   Jeff Weeks
Cover Designer   Jeff Weeks

For Timothy Hill and Doctor Ronald Holt. This book is not some lofty political or anthropological treatise, but it was fun writing.

About the Author

By day, **James A. Brannan** works as a Java SOA engineer. By
night, he writes computer books. This is his second book, and
he has a third on the way. By necessity, he programs using Java
during the day, but likes Objective-C much more. He has two
kids, a wife, two Macs, and a bicycle, but no dog. He lives in
Gaithersburg, Maryland.

About the Technical Editor

Billy Meyers has been programming for about 15 years, and his
most recent work of note is his task manager program for the
iPhone called To Do's by AustinBull Software, which is one of
the most popular free task managers available in Apple's App
Store. He began writing code in junior high and high school,
and is now working on completing a second degree in Computer
Science at Texas A&M University in Commerce, Texas.

Contents

Acknowledgments

Thanks to the technical editor, Billy Meyers, and everybody at McGraw-Hill, particularly Roger Stewart, Joya Anthony, Patty Mon, Harleen Chopra, and Lisa McCoy.

I really put you all through a wringer a couple times, but it all worked out. Special thanks to Everaldo and his Crystal Project Icons licensed under the LGPL. These icons have made my examples much more visually appealing in both this book and others. Thanks to Vimeo for providing such a great platform for hosting high-definition video. And of course, thanks to Neil Salkind, my book agent, who introduced me to this computer book writing and kept the ship navigating straight despite some stormy moments. Finally, thanks to the iPhone SDK Forum (www.iphonesdk.com). In no small part, the idea for a tutorial-based approach for this book came directly from your video tutorials offered on your site.

Introduction

The response to the iPhone is overwhelming. The App Store has captured the hobbyist's imagination like no other platform in recent memory. Hobbyists have made—and will continue making—money from their creations sold on the App Store. And we aren't necessarily talking about high-minded technical innovations. The media has reported that apps that make your iPhone pass gas have made folks hundreds of thousands of dollars. Rival farting App developers have even gone so far as suing one another over the App Store's precious revenue. The iPhone and the App Store are here to stay—well, at least until the next big thing comes along.

As proof of the iPhone's popularity, since posting a few tutorial videos on Vimeo, people from Asia, Europe, and South America have contacted me about the videos. So, when I decided upon writing this book, I remembered this international appeal of the iPhone. I tried making this book as accommodating as possible for as wide an audience as possible. I have kept colloquialisms to a minimum, for instance. But more importantly than avoiding colloquialisms, the book relies upon discrete, numbered steps that illustrate each major concept. Rather than a lot of prose describing the iPhone SDK, I show you the iPhone SDK.

The Book's Focus

This book has two goals. The first goal is getting you comfortable with using the iPhone's user interface controls in Interface Builder. Interface Builder is a useful tool that removes much complexity from creating and laying out user interface controls. It is this book's premise that once you master this tool, building a graphical user interface (GUI) using Interface Builder is quicker and more intuitive than using code.

The other goal this book has is brushing up your C and introducing you to Objective-C. Most likely you haven't used C since college. After refreshing your memory on C, the book moves to Objective-C, the language of choice for Mac OS X and iPhone OS applications.

The book also provides a two-chapter Objective-C tutorial. Based on the number of jobs listed on www.DICE.com for Objective-C programmers nationwide (fewer than 100), chances are you have never used Objective-C. But Objective-C is the language used for Cocoa and Cocoa Touch, so you must understand Objective-C if you wish to program for the iPhone. This book provides two chapters on Objective-C and tries sneaking Cocoa topics into the book where appropriate.

NOTE

This book's code examples can be downloaded at www.mhprofessional.com/ computingdownload. The book's code examples are also available at the author's website: www.jamesabrannan.com. Videos accompanying each Try This example are available on the author's website.

The Book's Content

The book assumes no prior C or Objective-C knowledge. Although not comprehensive, chapters on C and Objective-C should provide enough detail to understand the book's remaining chapters. The book starts with the prerequisites. Both C and Objective-C are prerequisites to programming iPhone applications. You don't need to be a C expert to use Objective-C, but you should remember C's basics. After providing a C refresher, the book has two chapters on Objective-C. These chapters are somewhat cumbersome, and not nearly as exciting as the remaining chapters, but Objective-C is the language used for Cocoa Touch, so you'd be advised to learn it. After learning Objective-C, the book provides a chapter on installing an iPhone application on an iPhone or iPod touch. It also provides a tutorial on debugging and testing your application.

Chapter 6 finally begins the book's UIKit coverage. Chapters 6 through 10 discuss the UIView subclasses you use when laying out an iPhone application. Chapter 11 discusses alerts, action sheets, and application badges. Chapters 12 and 13 discuss the many controls available for an iPhone user interface. Chapter 13 also discusses how to use an iPhone's camera.

After learning about the UIKit, the book then moves to discussing several other essential iPhone application-programming topics. Chapter 14 discusses setting your application's preferences using the Settings application. Chapter 15 discusses file I/O, property lists, and archiving objects. Chapter 16 discusses using the iPhone's built-in database, SQLite. And Chapter 17 discusses Core Data, by far the easiest persistence framework you can use while programming an iPhone. Chapter 18 discusses using iTunes music in your application.

Chapter 1

The iPhone Software Development Kit (SDK)

Key Skills & Concepts

- Understand the App Store
- Understand how to obtain Xcode and the iPhone SDK
- Understand if this book is right for you
- Understand Xcode's help and Apple's online documentation
- Understand this book is about User Interface controls and using Interface Builder

I am mostly a loner—nobody calls me—so why do I pay over 100 dollars a month for an iPhone? It is a darn useful toy—I mean tool. The last time I got lost, I started the Maps application, and within seconds, it had located my position and provided me with a map. I can check my e-mail anywhere, and the last time I needed to impress my friends, I bought and installed the iFart application. I use the iPod app to listen to music, and every once in a long while, someone calls.

As well as being mostly a loner, I am also an old guy and not the best candidate for expounding the iPhone's many virtues. For instance, I think texting is a time-waster. But my 14-year-old nephew, here on vacation the other week, certainly didn't think so. He spent the majority of his time texting friends back home. About what, who can guess, but he did it, and my brother was paying for it. I should also mention he downloaded apps from the App Store, and my brother was paying for those, too.

If you want some of my nephew's money—I mean my brother's money—you can get some by writing and selling an iPhone application on the App Store. Unfortunately, the sure path to riches, iPhone pornography and iPhone gambling, is off limits on the App Store, but there are plenty other applications you might write.

The App Store

The App Store is a unique concept. The App Store is an Apple application on iPhones and iPod touches. You use the App Store to browse and download applications from Apple's iTunes Store. Some applications are free, while others have a (usually) nominal charge. Using your iTunes account, you can download applications directly to your iPhone or iPod Touch. What I like is that I can use an iTunes Gift Card that I can buy at my local grocery store; no credit card needed.

Don't know what to buy? You can go to one of the many Web sites dedicated to reviewing applications on the App Store. For instance, www.appstoreapps.com (Figure 1-1) provides reviews of both free and paid applications. Most applications are junk, but some are quite good.

Downloading applications from the App Store is both easy and inexpensive. That makes it a lucrative market for independent developers wishing to take advantage of the iTunes Store's large user base. Independent developers can develop applications for the App Store by

Figure 1-1   The appstoreapps.com Web site reviews most App Store applications.

downloading the iPhone SDK, developing an application, and joining the iPhone Developer Program. Apple then reviews your application, and if it passes the review process, it is added to the iTunes Store.

The Software Development Kit (SDK)

So you have decided to try your hand at developing applications for the App Store. The first thing you must do if you wish being an iPhone developer is register as a member at the iPhone Dev Center at http://developer.apple.com/iphone. Membership is free and allows downloading the SDK.

The second thing you must do, arguably the first, is install Xcode and the iPhone SDK by downloading it from Apple's Developer Connection. Step-by-step installation instructions are available on Apple's Web site. After installing the iPhone SDK, the absolute next thing you should do is start Xcode and download the documentation—all the documentation (Figure 1-2). It will take awhile, but it is well worth it.

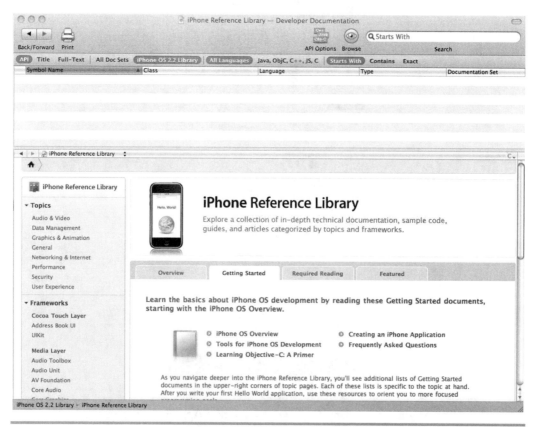

Figure 1-2 The iPhone Reference Library in Xcode

NOTE
You will find Apple's documentation surprisingly complete and well written. I refer to this documentation often in this book, so it is best to download it before continuing.

Paid Membership

Testing applications on an iPhone or iPod touch and selling applications on the App Store require that you register with the iPhone Developer Program. This membership is different from membership to the iPhone Dev Center. The iPhone Developer Program for individuals costs $99 and entitles you to the tools needed to test on an iPod touch or iPhone. It is also how you submit and distribute your application to the App Store, and Apple distributes any profit you might earn through your iPhone Developer Program membership.

Objective-C, Foundation Framework, Cocoa Touch, and UIKit

Apple describes the iPhone's technology as layers. The base layer is the Core OS layer. On top of that layer is the Core Services. On top of the Core Services is the Media layer. The topmost layer is Cocoa Touch (Figure 1-3).

You can simplify the iPhone operating system (OS) even more; think of it as two layers—a C layer and a Cocoa layer (Figure 1-4). The C layer comprises the operating system's layer. You use BSD UNIX–style C functions to manipulate this layer. This layer consists of things like low-level file I/O, network sockets, POSIX threads, and SQLite. The Media layer is also rather low-level and contains C application programming interfaces (APIs) like OpenGL ES, Quartz, and Core Audio. The Cocoa layer overlays the C layer, and it simplifies iPhone programming. For instance, rather than manipulating C strings, you use the Foundation framework string, NSString.

Cocoa Touch

On the iPhone, Cocoa is called Cocoa Touch, rather than simply Cocoa, because the iPhone OS contains touch events. If you have ever tapped, flicked, swiped, or pinched your iPhone's display, you know what touch events are. Touch events allow you to program responses to a user's touching the screen with his or her fingers.

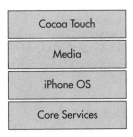

Figure 1-3   The iPhone's technology layers

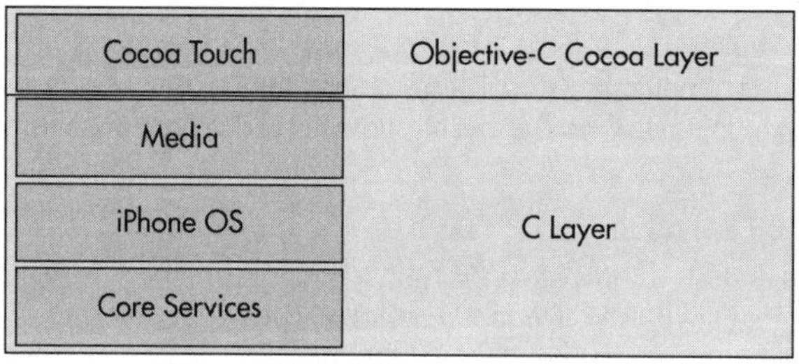

Cocoa Touch	Objective-C Cocoa Layer
Media	
iPhone OS	C Layer
Core Services	

Figure 1-4 The iPhone's programming layers

Cocoa Touch also provides the primary class libraries needed for iPhone development. The two Cocoa Touch frameworks you will use in every iPhone application you write are the Foundation framework and the UIKit framework. A framework is collection of code devoted to a similar task. The Foundation framework is dedicated to standard programming topics, such as collections, strings, file I/O, and other basic tasks. The UIKit is dedicated to the iPhone's interface and contains classes such as the UIView. In this book, you spend most your time learning the UIKit.

Foundation Framework

The Foundation framework contains Objective-C classes that wrap lower-level core functionality. For instance, rather than working with low-level C file I/O, you can work with the NSFileManager foundation class. The Foundation framework provides many useful classes that you really should learn if you wish programming robust iPhone applications. The Foundation framework makes programming using collections, dates and time, binary data, URLs, threads, sockets, and most other lower-level C functionality easier by wrapping the C functions with higher-level Objective-C classes.

TIP

See Apple's Foundation Framework Reference for a complete listing of the classes and protocols provided by the Foundation framework.

NOTE

If you are a Java programmer, think of the iPhone's programming environment like this: Objective-C is equivalent to Java's core syntax. The Foundation framework is equivalent to Java's core classes, such as ArrayList, Exception, HashMap, String, Thread, and other Java Standard Edition classes, and the UIKit is the equivalent of SWING. I realize it's a simplification, but it works for me.

The iPhone Frameworks

Table 1-1 lists the frameworks available to you as an iPhone developer. Of these frameworks, this book dedicates itself to the UIKit rather than trying to cover a little bit of every framework.

Framework	Purpose
AddressBook	Accessing user's contacts
AddressBookUI	Displaying Addressbook
AudioToolbox	Audio data streams; playing and recording audio
AudioUnit	Audio units
CFNetwork	WiFi and cellular networking
CoreAudio	Core audio classes
CoreFoundation	Similar to Foundation framework, but lower level (don't use unless you absolutely must)
CoreGraphics	Quartz 2D
CoreLocation	User's location/GPS
Foundation	Cocoa foundation layer
MediaPlayer	Video playback
OpenAL	Positional audio library
OpenGLES	Embedded OpenGL (2-D and 3-D graphics rendering)
QuartzCore	Core animation
Security	Certificates, keys, and trust policies
SystemConfiguration	Network configuration
UIKit	iPhone user interface layer

Table 1-1   Frameworks on the iPhone

It is this book's premise that once you understand how to create an iPhone application using the UIKit classes, you should learn the other frameworks.

iPhone Limitations

If you have never programmed for a small device like an iPhone, there are some limitations you should be aware of before you begin programming. Memory and processor speed are constrained, and the screen is small. Security is also tight on an iPhone, and applications are limited in what they can do.

Memory and Processor Speed

An iPhone's memory is constrained. Chances are, you have a Mac with a dual-core and 2GB of memory. Not so on the iPhone. Although Apple hasn't divulged this information, according to hacker Craig Hockenberry of furborg.org, he has estimated that an iPhone has about a 600 MHz processing speed with 128MB of available physical memory. The memory of the device is limited compared to your desktop.

CAUTION
If your application uses too much memory, the iPhone OS X may abruptly terminate your application to prevent a system crash.

Small Screen

An iPhone screen is 480 × 320 pixels. There is not much room to work with. Of course, controls such as buttons are smaller on an iPhone, but the layout space is still significantly constrained. If you are accustomed to programming user interfaces on a 1280 × 800 pixel display, you must adjust your thinking. Screen size is limited.

The small screen size also results in only one window being visible at a time. In fact, every application you develop in this book consists of one window. There will rarely be any reason to create another window when programming an iPhone application. Instead, what you do is swap views into and out of an application's window. But only one view is visible at a time—no exceptions. This restriction is sensible, as the screen is so small.

Security

You can only read or write to directories that are part of your application's bundle. Areas accessible to your application are said to be in your application's sandbox. You cannot read files created by other applications. You also cannot write to anywhere outside your application's sandbox. Applications written by SDK users cannot share resources, period.

Short-Lived Applications

Another iPhone application limitation is that it cannot be memory-resident. A memory-resident application can run in the background while a user runs other applications. Forget about memory-resident applications when programming for the iPhone. You can't do it.

An iPhone can only have one program running at once. This restriction puts your application in constant danger of the OS terminating it. Think about it: Allegedly, an iPhone's primary purpose is still that of a cellular phone. A phone call might arrive while your application is running. In this situation, the OS asks a user if he or she wishes answering the call. If the user chooses to answer the call, the iPhone OS terminates your application.

Because of this constant probability of sudden termination, you should program defensively and anticipate abrupt terminations. You will see that the UIKit makes this easy by providing event handlers you can implement whenever your application is about to terminate.

NOTE
Before you rail against Apple on this limitation, consider the alternative. Suppose you develop a long-running and battery-eating application that is memory-resident. Your application's users notice a short battery life for their iPhone. Who do they blame, you or Apple? Apple.

Manual Memory Management

One of the big improvements in Objective-C 2.0 is garbage collection. Garbage collection frees developers from having to worry about memory management, as the system does so automatically. But the iPhone, with its limited resources, does not include Objective-C 2.0 garbage collection. You must still manage memory yourself. You can use something called autorelease, which makes memory management a little easier, but even autorelease is not recommended. Instead, you should manage memory manually. Although not a huge limitation, it is a pain, as forgetting to release an object is all too easy a mistake to make. Of course, as you will see in Chapter 5, there are tools to help you track down and fix these errors.

Relevant Documentation

Apple has considerable online documentation. You have access to that documentation through both your Developer Connection membership and through Xcode's help. You should refer to that documentation often. Most documentation is also available as PDF documents. The first two documents you should download and print are the iPhone Application Programming Guide and iPhone Development Guide. You might then consider downloading and printing Cocoa Fundamentals Guide. You will also find documents on Objective-C and various Cocoa classes. If you followed this chapter's earlier recommendation and downloaded the documentation, you will find that all this information is at your fingertips using Xcode's help. This book tries not to duplicate these online and desktop sources, but rather complement them by providing step-by-step examples illustrating how to do things. Once you understand how, the online documentation shows you more options to expand upon this book's tutorial.

Try This   Getting a Quick Start on iPhone Development

This chapter ends with a quick-start example to whet your appetite. The next four chapters cover prerequisites that you should have prior to learning the iPhone's UIKit and Cocoa Touch. But you are probably ready to start programming using these frameworks now, so this chapter ends with a simple iPhone application. This quick start also familiarizes you with the IBOutlet and IBAction keywords and their use, and it familiarizes you with Xcode and Interface Builder.

NOTE

Almost every Try This example in this book has an accompanying video available at my Web site (www.jamesabrannan.com). The first video—this Try This application—has accompanying audio explaining the steps taken. The remaining videos have no sound; however, they follow their corresponding Try This application's numbered steps exactly, so you can follow the video by referring to the book.

(continued)

Figure 1-5 New Project dialog

1. Open Xcode. From the menu select File | New Project and the New Project dialog appears (Figure 1-5).

2. Select View-based Application and click Choose. In the Save As dialog, give the application the name QuickStart (Figure 1-6).

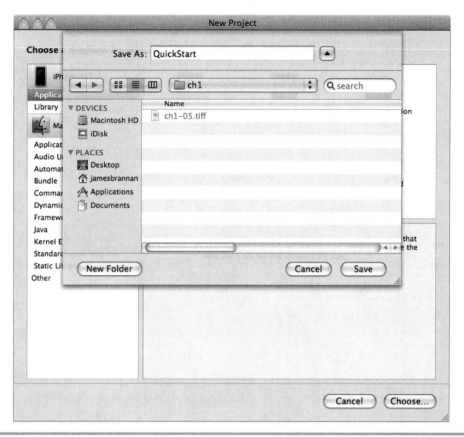

Figure 1-6 Save As dialog

3. Xcode should create the project. In the Groups & Files pane, expand the Classes and Resources folders (Figure 1-7).

4. Double-click QuickStartViewController.xib to open it in Interface Builder.

(continued)

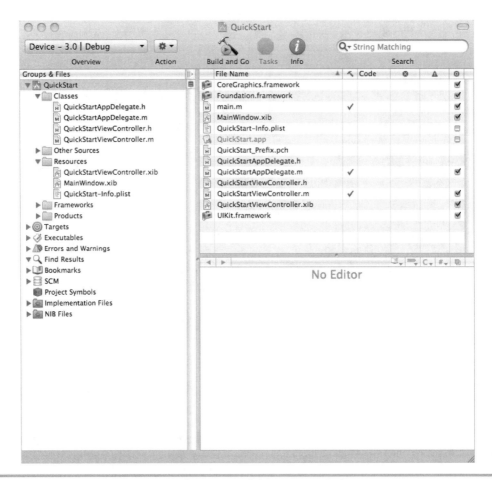

Figure 1-7   Xcode with Classes and Resources folders expanded

5. If a canvas like the one shown in Figure 1-8 is not visible, double-click View in the document window (Figure 1-9).

6. Ensure the library is visible by selecting Tools | Library from Interface Builder's main menu. Ensure the library shows all Cocoa Touch classes by going to the library's top pane, expanding Library, and clicking Cocoa Touch (Figure 1-10).

Figure 1-8 A view's canvas in Interface Builder

Figure 1-9 The document window

(continued)

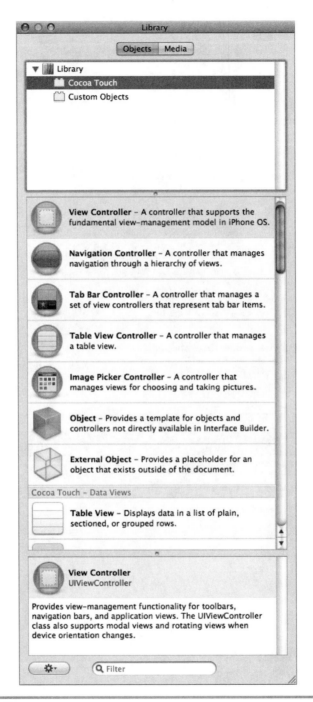

Figure 1-10 The library

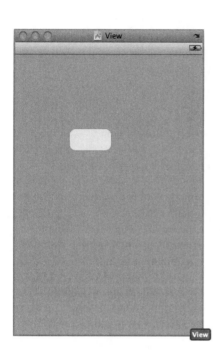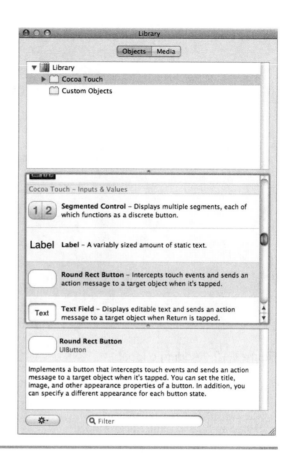

Figure 1-11   Adding a button

7. Scroll through the controls until you find a Round Rect Button. Drag-and-drop the button to the canvas (Figure 1-11).

8. Double-click the button on the canvas, and give the button a title.

9. Drag a label from the library to the canvas (Figure 1-12).

(continued)

Figure 1-12 Adding a label

10. Save and exit Interface Builder.

11. Select QuickStartViewController.m in the Classes folder in Groups & Files. Xcode should display the file in the editor pane (Figure 1-13).

12. Change QuickStartViewController.m so it matches Listing 1-1.

13. Open QuickStartViewController.h and modify the file so it matches Listing 1-2.

14. Select Build | Build from Xcode's main menu to build the application.

15. Open QuickStartViewController.xib in Interface Builder.

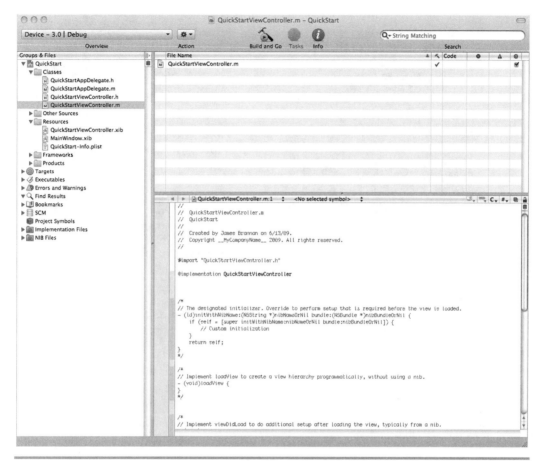

Figure 1-13   Xcode displaying QuickStartViewController.m

16. Select the button. Select Tools | Inspector from Interface Builder's main menu to show the Inspector (Figure 1-14). Open the Button Inspector by clicking the inspector's second tab (Figure 1-15).

17. Next to Touch Up Inside, click and hold on the little circle. Move your cursor to File's Owner in the document window and release. Select sayHello: from the pop-up window (Figure 1-16).

(continued)

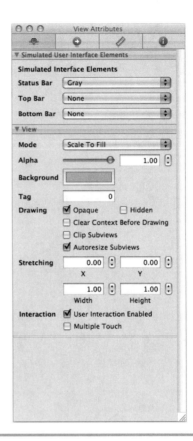

Figure 1-14   The Inspector

Figure 1-15   The button's Button Inspector

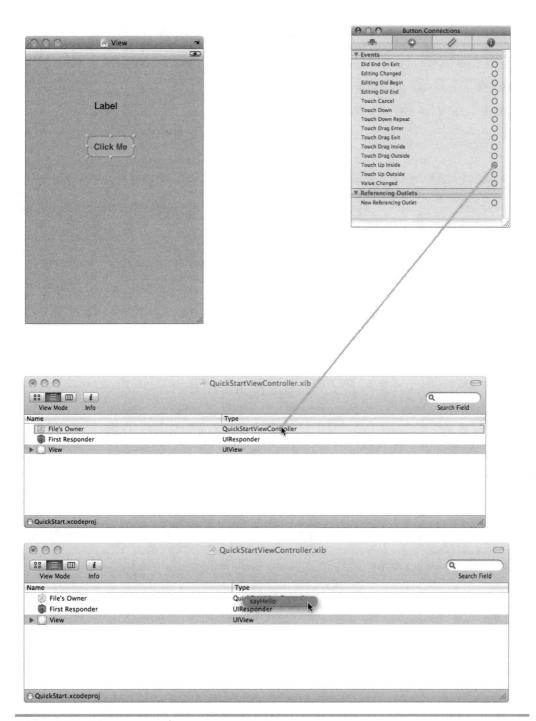

Figure 1-16   Connecting a button to an IBAction   *(continued)*

18. Click the label on the canvas, and the Inspector's content should change to match the label. Click the circle next to New Referencing Outlet, and drag-and-drop on the File's Owner. Select myLabel from the pop-up window. Be careful not to select View.

19. Save and exit Interface Builder.

20. In Xcode, ensure the Active SDK shows the Simulator and Debug options selected (Figure 1-17).

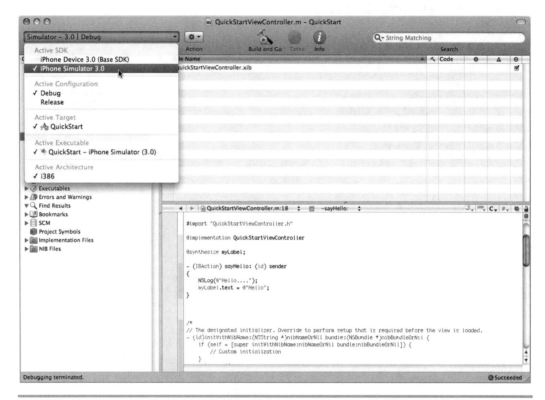

Figure 1-17 Ensuring Active SDK shows Debug and the Simulator selected

Figure 1-18 The application running in the iPhone Simulator

21. From Xcode's main menu, select Build | Build And Run. Xcode should start the simulator, install your application in it, and start your application (Figure 1-18).

22. Select Run | Console to show the Debugger Console.

23. Click the button, and the label's text changes to Hello and the console displays the log (Figure 1-19).

Listing 1-1 QuickStartViewController.m

```
#import "QuickStartViewController.h"
@implementation QuickStartViewController
@synthesize myLabel;
- (IBAction) sayHello: (id) sender {
 NSLog(@"Hello....");
```

(continued)

```
    self.myLabel.text = @"Hello";
}
- (void) dealloc {
 [super dealloc];
 [myLabel release];
}
@end
```

Listing 1-2 QuickStartViewController.h

```
#import <UIKit/UIKit.h>
@interface QuickStartViewController : UIViewController {
 IBOutlet UILabel * myLabel;
}
@property (nonatomic, retain) IBOutlet UILabel * myLabel;
- (IBAction) sayHello: (id) sender;
@end
```

Figure 1-19 The application after clicking the button

You just did a lot of steps with no explanation. But what you did in this Try This will be second nature by this book's end. The biggest concept you must take from this simple example is using the IBAction and IBOutlet keywords.

IBAction and IBOutlet are covered several times in this book. IBActions are how you connect methods in classes in Xcode to events fired by components created using Interface Builder. IBOutlets are how you connect properties in classes in Xcode to graphical components created using Interface Builder.

These graphical components reside in a nib file, so a more correct explanation would be that IBActions and IBOutlets connect code to components in a nib file. For instance, you connected the button's Touch Up Inside event to the sayHello: action. The button lives in the nib, while the sayHello method lives in the compiled class. Making the sayHello method an IBAction connects the two. Like the button, the label also lives in the nib, while the myLabel property lives in the compiled class. Making the myLabel property an IBOutlet in the class file and then connecting the two in Interface Builder allows the class to manipulate the label via the myLabel property. Don't worry if this is still somewhat confusing—it won't be by the book's end. If you must know more now, Chapter 7 has a more "official" explanation of IBOutlets and IBActions.

Summary

This chapter introduced you to this book's content. Anyone with basic programming skills can write and release an application on Apple's App Store. Moreover, he or she can make money selling the application. Although the easy applications have all been released, there is room for high-quality applications on the App Store. All it takes is for Apple to feature your application on its Web site, and you are looking at a few thousand dollars for your efforts.

I love iPhone programming, and I find Objective-C a beautiful, elegant language. I am certain that by this book's end, you shall, too.

Chapter 2

A C Refresher

Key Skills & Concepts

- Creating simple C command-line programs

- Using C comments

- Understanding headers, import, and include

- Understanding preprocessor statements

- Reviewing data types and operators

- Understanding C functions, basic C syntax, and using pointers

Like every modern operating system, language, and programming tool of any importance, Mac OS X and the iPhone's operating system (also OS X) were built using the C programming language. Not the Objective-C programming language and Cocoa framework, not the C++ programming language, but C. Objective-C is an object-oriented language built using C. Cocoa is a framework that hides difficult C programming tasks with easy-to-use objects programmed in Objective-C. But behind every Cocoa object you construct, you find C code defining the construct.

NOTE
The computer scientists Dennis Ritchie and Brian Kernighan developed C at Bell Laboratories in 1978.

You must know at least some C if you want to program using Objective-C. In this chapter, you review basic C. This chapter assumes some programming experience—for instance, I assume you know what a method, an integer, a function, and other basic programming constructs are. Ideally, you have had at least one university course using Java or an year's experience using Java. Experience using C# also suffices, as the language is remarkably similar to Java.

C Command-Line Programs

Like Java, C programs start with a main method. The C main method takes an integer and a pointer to a character array as inputs and returns an integer.

```
int main (int argc, const char * argv[])
```

The returned integer typically indicates the program's success or failure. Zero usually indicates success, while a number indicates failure. Often programmers return different values as error codes. Program users can then determine what went wrong by looking up the error code in the application's documentation.

Main can only be implemented once in your program. When your program runs, OS X finds the main method and uses it as your program's starting point.

Try This Creating a Simple C Program Using Xcode

1. Open Xcode, and create a new project. Select Command Line Utility | Standard Tool, and click the Choose button. Name the project C Main Project (Figure 2-1).

2. Open main.c and note the method created by Xcode. It even created the "Hello World" message for you (Listing 2-1). Click Build And Go, and review the Debugger Console's logging.

Listing 2-1   The main method in a C program

```
#include <stdio.h>
int main (int argc, const char * argv[]) {
  // insert code here...
printf("Hello, World!\n");
return 0;
}
```

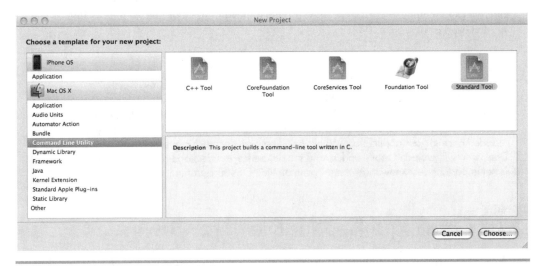

Figure 2-1   Xcode New Project dialog

C Comments

C's comment syntax is the same as Java's. A double forward slash indicates everything following on the same line is a comment. A slash followed by an asterisk indicates everything following until the next asterisk and slash is a comment. For instance, the following are both comments. The first is a single-line comment, while the second is a multiline comment.

```
// This is a comment in C code.
/* This is a multiline comment in C Code.
This comment can be multiple lines. */
```

Comments are, of course, ignored by the compiler, and are ways for you to provide code explanation for future programmers who might debug or modify your code.

Understanding Headers, Import, and Include

A header file ends with an .h file extension and contains method prototypes and preprocessing statements. A prototype is a function's signature. A signature is a method name, return type, and parameters, with no body. Compilers use prototypes so methods in other files can "see" the function.

You can also say a header file declares methods. Declaring a method means you are telling the compiler you intend to define a method with the same signature as the declaration.

Code including or importing a header file declares to a compiler it might use that header file's functions. Through the compiler's magic, the compiler combines all files and resolves references to methods in different files; provided they all play fair and include or import the needed header files.

TIP

In standard C programs, you usually see headers included in other files. You use the #include directive when including a file in another file. In Objective-C, you typically see headers imported in other files. You use the #import directive when importing a file in another file. When importing a header file, the compiler ensures the header is only included once in your application. When including a file, no such protection is provided. Don't worry if you don't really understand the difference—understanding the difference is not important. Just know that when iPhone or Mac OS X programming, use import.

Try This Creating a Header File

1. Create a view-based iPhone application using the View-based Application template. Name the application CreateHeaderFile.

2. In Groups & Files, create a new folder named c_code. Add a C file to the folder using the New File dialog (Figure 2-2). Be certain the Also Create "cwork.h" check box is selected, name the file cwork.c, and add it to the project.

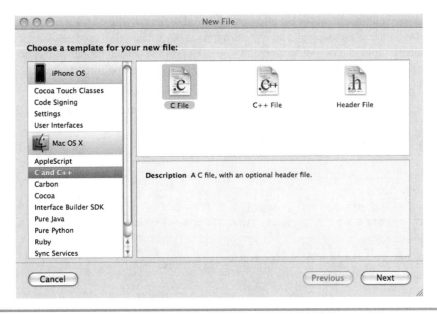

Figure 2-2   Adding a C file to Groups & Files using New File dialog

NOTE

You use a view-based iPhone application to illustrate using C in an iPhone application. You can freely mix Objective-C and C in iPhone programs, as Objective-C is a superset of C.

3. Type the code in Listing 2-2 into the cwork.c file. Be certain you add the method's signature to cwork.h (Listing 2-3).

Listing 2-2   The sayHello method defined in cwork.c

```
#include "cwork.h"
void sayHello() {
  printf("hello programmer....\n");
}
```

Listing 2-3   The sayHello method declared in cwork.h

```
#include <stdio.h>
void sayHello();
```

(continued)

The sayHello method is declared in cwork.h and defined in the cwork.c file. The sayHello method returns no value and so its return type is void. The printf method is declared in the standard input and output header, and so you import the stdio.h header file. Note the angle brackets; you import system libraries using angle brackets. You import headers exclusive to your project using double quotes.

4. Open main.m, import cwork.h, and add the sayHello method to the file (Listing 2-4).

Listing 2-4   The sayHello method added to main.m in the sample project

```
#import <UIKit/UIKit.h>
#import "cwork.h"
int main(int argc, char *argv[]) {
 NSAutoreleasePool * pool = [[NSAutoreleasePool alloc] init];

 sayHello();

 int retVal = UIApplicationMain(argc, argv, nil, nil);

 [pool release];

 return retVal;
}
```

5. Click Build And Go, and "Hello World" outputs on the console.

Preprocessor Statements

The #include and #import statements are preprocessor statements. When compiling a program, the compiler processes all statements with a # sign before compiling the program; hence, the term preprocessor statement. The compiler replaces the preprocessor statements with their values.

Try This   Using Preprocessor Statement

1. Open the cwork.h header file from the previous section's project, CreateHeaderFile.

2. Type #define MYNUMBER 20 in cwork.h and save the file.

3. Modify the sayHello method to the code as in Listing 2-5. Notice that you change the sayHello method to return an integer. You must also change the cwork.h file (Listing 2-6).

4. Compile and run the application. The console should now echo the message with the number defined in cwork.h.

Listing 2-5 The sayHello method modified to include a preprocessor statement

```
int sayHello() {
  printf("hello programmer....%d\n", MYNUMBER);
  return 0;
}
```

Listing 2-6 The cwork.h file

```
#include <stdio.h>

#define MYNUMBER 20

int sayHello();
```

NOTE

You define constants in header files using the #define preprocessor directive. You don't include a constant's type when defining a constant.

You defined a constant in cwork.h; then when you compiled, the compiler first resolved any defined constants, replacing the constant with the literal value.

Data Types and Operators

C's basic data types are the same as Java's and should appear familiar (Table 2-1).

C's common operators should also appear familiar (Table 2-2). Note the table excludes the less commonly used bitwise and shift operators.

Data Type	Description
char	An 8 byte ASCII character
short	A small integer
int	An integer
long	Large integer
float	Floating point number, single precision
double	Floating point number, double precision

Table 2-1 C's Basic Data Types

Operator	Operator Character(s)
Assignment	=
Addition	+
Subtraction	-
Division	/
Multiplication	*
Remainder (mod)	%
unary ++ and --	x++ or x-- ++x or --x
Equal	==
Not Equal	!=
Greater Than	>
Less Than	<
Greater Than or Equal	>=
Less Than or Equal	<=
Boolean Not	!
Boolean And	&&
Boolean Or	||

Table 2-2 C's Basic Operators

Control, Functions, and Conditional Statements

Control statements, functions, and conditional statements all have the same syntax as their Java counterpart. Conditional if statements are the same as used in Java (Listing 2-7).

Listing 2-7 Using if statements in C

```
if(myInt < 2) {
  printf("the value is not equal");
  myOtherInt = 3;
}
else if (myInt == 5) {
  myOtherInt = 7;
}
else {
  myOtherInt = 3;
}
```

Switch statements are also equivalent to a Java switch statement (Listing 2-8).

Listing 2-8   C's switch statement

```
switch (myInt) {
  case 1:
    myOtherInt = 3;
    printf("case one");
    break;
  case 2:
    myOtherInt = 5;
    break;
  default:
    myOtherInt = 4;
}
```

Loops should prove familiar if you know Java, as should the do-while loop and the for loop (Listing 2-9).

Listing 2-9   The while, do-while, and for loops using C

```
int i = 0;
while(i < 20) {
  printf("loop%d", i);
  i++;
}
do {
  printf("loop%d", i);
  i--;
} while(i > 0)
for(int i =0; i < 20; i++) {
  printf("loop%d", i);
}
```

Arrays and Structures

C arrays are similar to Java arrays. You declare arrays the same, but C has no new keyword; you simply start using the array (Listing 2-10).

Listing 2-10   Using a C array

```
int myArray[100];
myArray[0] = 1;
myArray[1] = 2;
```

C has structs; Java doesn't have a struct data type. In C, a struct is similar to a class, but has no methods or inheritance (Listing 2-11).

Listing 2-11   A C struct

```
struct myBox {
   int length;
   int width;
}
```

Arrays can hold structures; for instance, you might declare an array to hold 100 myBox instances (Listing 2-12).

Listing 2-12   Using a C struct in an array

```
struct myBox myBoxes[100];
myBoxes[0].length = 10;
myBoxes[0].width = 2;
```

Functions

You declare functions the same way using C as you do using Java, only C does not restrict a function's visibility. C has no public or private functions. Like Java, you declare a C function with a return type, a name, and argument list. You write function declarations in header files. You write function definitions in C source files. Functions that don't return anything use void as their return type. If a function takes no arguments, you can optionally list the arguments as void.

```
void sayHello(void);
```

Although you can't declare a function private, you can declare a function static. But a static function in C is very different from a static function in Java. In C, declaring a function static is similar to declaring a function private in Java. In C, only functions declared in the same file can use a function declared static. Static functions are useful for utility functions that won't be used elsewhere in a program.

```
static void sayHello(void){ printf("hello\n");}
```

Note that you don't declare the static method's prototype in a header file. You simply write the method in the source file using the method.

The printf Method

C uses the printf function for outputting to the standard output stream. Its declaration is as follows:

```
int printf( const char *format, arg1, arg2, ..., argn);
```

The function takes a pointer to the characters you wish sending to the standard output stream and zero or more items for formatting. For instance consider the following printf statement.

```
printf("Hello world...%d times", 22);
```

This statement results in the following output.

```
Hello world...22 times
```

Another common argument is %s for character strings. For instance, the following code illustrates a character array and then prints it.

```
char * hello = "hello turkey";
printf("%s\n", hello);
```

Pointers

Java does away with pointers; however, Objective-C relies extensively upon pointers. A pointer is a reference to another variable, or more technically, a pointer is a variable that references another variable's memory space. Think of your computer's memory as one large cubbyhole block. A variable occupies a cubbyhole. A pointer points to the particular cubbyhole, but the pointer's value is not the value in the cubbyhole; the pointer's value is the cubbyhole's address.

In Figure 2-3, the cubbyhole n is located in row 2, column 5 and its value is 12. Cubbyhole n's value is 12 and address is second row, fifth column. Pointer p points to n's location, which is second row, fifth column. Pointer p's value is not 12, but rather, second row, fifth column. This is an important distinction.

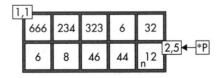

Figure 2-3 Pointers as cubbyholes

You indicate pointers using the asterisk (*). Pointers point to a location in memory of another variable. The ampersand (&) indicates a variable's address in memory.

Try This Using Pointers

1. Create a new C command-line application, name the application Using Pointers.

2. Modify main.c file so it appears like Listing 2-13.

3. Click Build And Go.

Listing 2-13   C program illustrating pointers

```
#include <stdio.h>
int main (int argc, const char * argv[]) {
  int avalue = 10;
  int *pavalue = &avalue;
  printf("address:%p value:%d", pavalue, *pavalue);
  return 0;
}
```

In the previous statement, avalue's value is 10, pavalue points to avalue's memory address, and the printf command prints avalue's address followed by avalue's value, as pavalue points to avalue's address while *pavalue is avalue's value.

NOTE
If you are following along in Xcode, realize your address values will be different from those listed in this chapter's example code results.

```
address:0xbfffff628 value:10
```

4. Modify main so the first two lines appear as follows:

```
//int avalue = 10;
  int avalue;
```

5. Add the following line to just before the method's return statement:

```
printf("value's actual value:%d", avalue);
```

6. Compile and run. Listing 2-14 contains the incorrect output.

Listing 2-14   Output from C command-line program

```
[Session started at 2008-09-05 21:35:14 -0400.]
address:0xbffff628 value:-1073744308 value's actual value:-1073744308
The Debugger has exited with status 0.
```

The results are not as expected. Although the second printf statement works, the first doesn't. Initializing a variable only reserves memory space; it does not assign the variable a value. When you refer to an uninitialized variable using a pointer, you get an incorrect result. You must initialize a variable with a value before using it.

7. Change the method so that avalue is initialized to 10 and then click Build And Go. The debugger console echoes 10, as expected.

Dereferencing a Pointer

You can also dereference a pointer by assigning the pointer's location a new value. You do this through what's called dereferencing the pointer. Consider the code in Listing 2-15.

Listing 2-15   Dereferencing a pointer

```
int a = 10;
int *b = &a;
*b = 52;
printf("value:%d value:%d",*b,a);
```

The third line sets the content of the memory at the address pointed to by the pointer b to the integer value 52. The address pointed to by pointer b happens to be the variable a, so changing the content changes a's value too, as a is the location pointed to by b. Running this code results in both values printing as 52.

Pointers and Arrays

One place, where pointers are useful in C programming is arrays. A common technique is to iterate through an array using a pointer as an iterator to the array's elements. The following project illustrates this technique.

Using an Array with Pointers

1. Create a new command-line application called C Pointer Array.

2. Modify main in main.m to appear like Listing 2-16.

Listing 2-16   A C program iterating through an pointer array

```c
#include <stdio.h>
int main (int argc, const char * argv[]) {
  int values[10];
  int *iterator;
  for(int i = 0; i < 10; i++) {
    values[i] = i * 2;
    printf("value: %d  ", values[i]);
  }
  iterator = values;
  for(int i = 0; i < 10; i++) {
    printf("value(%d):%d ", i, *(iterator+i));
  }
  *(iterator+4) = 999;
  printf("\nvalue of element at 4: %d", values[4]);
  return 0;
}
```

3. Click Build And Go. Listing 2-17 is the debugger's output.

Listing 2-17   Debugger Console output

```
[Session started at 2008-09-05 21:57:35 -0400.]
value: 0  value: 2  value: 4  value: 6  value: 8  value: 10  value: 12
value:14  value: 16  value: 18  value(0):0  value(1):2  value(2):4
value(3):6
value(4):8  value(5):10  value(6):12  value(7):14  value(8):16
value(9):18
value of element at 4: 999
The Debugger has exited with status 0.
```

What you did in this example was use a pointer to iterate through an array. The iterator points to the array's address. The iterator first points to the array's element at the zero position. The iterator + 1 points to the first position's element. The iterator + n points to the nth position's element. As you iterate through the array's values, you can use the value at the address to which the iterator points.

Summary

This chapter did not provide enough detail to completely learn C. In fact, this chapter hardly scratched C's surface. But it did provide you with enough information to understand the rest of this book. You must know basic C to understand Objective-C and iPhone programming. Hopefully this chapter refreshed your memory enough to begin the next chapter. If you are familiar with Java's basic programming structures, C header files, and C pointers, you should have no trouble understanding the next two Objective-C chapters. If you are still uncertain, you can find many free online C tutorials using Google. But don't worry—C is kept to a minimum in this book.

NOTE

If new to programming and C programming, you should buy the book:
The C Programming Language, by Brian W. Kernighan and Dennis M. Ritchie.

Chapter 3

Just Enough Objective-C—Part One

Key Skills & Concepts

- Understanding Objective-C classes and objects

- Understanding an interface and an implementation

- Understanding simple messaging

- Understanding alloc and init

- Managing memory using retain and release

- Managing memory using autorelease

iPhone applications use Cocoa classes, and these classes use the Objective-C programming language. So you must know Objective-C if you wish to program iPhones. At first glance, Objective-C's syntax might seem strange and difficult. But don't worry—the language is easy and its strangeness will give way to an elegance I'm sure you will appreciate. In this and the next chapter you learn enough Objective-C to begin iPhone programming.

CAUTION
If coming from a .NET or Java background, pay particular attention to the sections on memory management. Unlike these languages, memory management is not automatic on the iPhone. You must manage memory manually.

Objective-C Classes and Objects

Objective-C classes are the same as classes in any other object-oriented programming language. A class encapsulates both state (properties) and behavior (methods), and forms an object-oriented program's basic building blocks. An object-oriented application functions by objects sending messages between each other. For instance, in a typical Java command-line application, you begin the program by calling a static method called main in a class. This main method instantiates one or more objects, and the application's remaining functionality consists of messages between those objects instantiated in the main method, as well as any objects they might in turn instantiate.

Class Interface and Implementation

Objective-C separates a class into an interface and an implementation. An interface declares instance variables and methods. It is a standard C header file and doesn't provide any method implementations. The implementation contains the class's method implementations. It is a file with its own .m extension rather than a .c extension.

Try This Generating an Objective-C Class's Interface and Implementation

1. Create a new View-based Application and name it ChapThree.

2. In Groups & Files, right-click Classes and select Add | New Group from the pop-up menu. Name the group Objective-C.

3. Right-click the newly created Objective-C folder and select Add | New File from the pop-up menu. From the New File dialog, highlight Cocoa Touch Class and select Objective-C class. Ensure the Subclass says NSObject (Figure 3-1). Click Next.

4. On the next dialogue screen, name the class Simple. Be certain to also check the checkbox asking if you wish to generate a header file for the class.

The template generated Simple for you, writing its interface in Simple.h (Listing 3-1) and its implementation in Simple.m (Listing 3-2).

Listing 3-1   Objective-C interface

```
#import <Foundation/Foundation.h>
@interface Simple : NSObject {
}
@end
```

Listing 3-2   Objective-C implementation

```
#import "Simple.h"
@implementation Simple
@end
```

The @interface and @implementation Compiler Directives

In Simple.h, note the @interface compiler directive. In the Simple.m file, note the @implementation compiler directive. These directives distinguish a class's interface from its implementation. Code within the @interface and @end compiler directives in Simple.h comprise Simple's interface, while code within the @implementation and @end compiler directives comprise Simple's implementation.

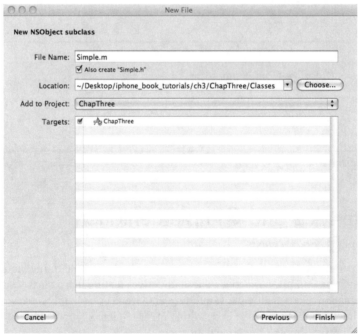

Figure 3-1 Selecting a new Objective-C class using Xcode's New File dialog

Method Declaration and Definition

You declare a class's methods and instance variables in its interface. You define a class's methods and instance variables in its implementation. Declaring a method means you tell the compiler that a class will have a method, with a certain signature, but you don't provide the actual code for the method. For instance, consider the following method declaration.

```
- (void) sayHello: (NSString*) name;
```

The declaration tells the compiler to expect a method called sayHello that returns nothing (void) and takes an NSString as an argument. The declaration says nothing about the method's content.

You provide the compiler with a method's implementation by defining the method. Defining a method means you provide a method declaration's actual behavior, or its implementation. For instance, the sayHello method in Listing 3-3 provides the sayHello method declaration's behavior.

Listing 3-3   A simple Objective-C method implementation

```
- (void) sayHello: (NSString*) name {
  NSMutableString *message = [[NSMutableString alloc] initWithString:
@"Hello there "];
  [message appendString:name];
  NSLog(message);
  [message release];
}
```

Try This ## Adding sayHello to the Simple Class

1. Open the last section's project, ChapThree. Add the sayHello method from Listing 3-3 to Simple.m (Listing 3-4). Don't forget to add the method's declaration to Simple.h (Listing 3-5).

2. Open main.m and import Simple. Then in main, create a Simple instance and call it sayHello method (Listing 3-6).

3. Build and run the program, and the hello message appears in the debugger console.

Listing 3-4   Simple.m modified to declare sayHello

```
#import "Simple.h"
@implementation Simple
- (void) sayHello: (NSString *) name {
```

(continued)

```
    NSMutableString *message = [[NSMutableString alloc] initWithString:
@"Hello there "];
    [message appendString:name];
    NSLog(message);
    [message release];
}
@end
```

Listing 3-5 Simple.h modified to declare sayHello

```
#import <Foundation/Foundation.h>
@interface Simple : NSObject {
}
-(void) sayHello: (NSString *) name;
@end
```

Listing 3-6 The file main.h modified to call the sayHello method

```
#import <UIKit/UIKit.h>
#import "Simple.h"
int main(int argc, char *argv[]) {
  NSAutoreleasePool * pool = [[NSAutoreleasePool alloc] init];
  Simple * mySimple = [[Simple alloc] init];
  [mySimple sayHello:@"James"];
  [mySimple release];
  int retVal = UIApplicationMain(argc, argv, nil, nil);
  [pool release];
  return retVal;
}
```

Interface Anatomy

A class's interface consists of import statements, a class declaration, any instance variables, and method signatures. Review Simple's interface in the Simple.h file. Objective-C classes import or include other libraries and headers just like C (just a reminder, always use import, as this assures you won't include the header file twice). The following line declares to the compiler an Objective-C class named Simple that extends NSObject.

```
@interface Simple : NSObject
```

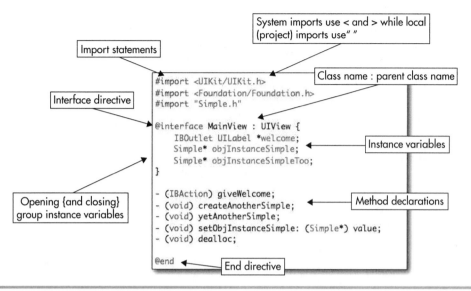

Figure 3-2   An Objective-C interface summary

An opening and closing brace follows the class declaration. Instance variables go between these braces. Below the closing brace, you add class method declarations. Following any method declarations, the interface ends with the @end directive, which signifies the interface's end. Figure 3-2 summarizes an Objective-C interface's anatomy.

Implementation Anatomy

An interface is only half an Objective-C class, though. A class's implementation is as important as its interface. Review Simple's implementation in the Simple.m file. This file begins by importing the class's interface. Simple's implementation then begins with the @implementation compiler directive.

```
@implementation Simple
```

Simple's implementation ends with the @end compiler directive. Method definitions go between the two directives. Figure 3-3 summarizes an Objective-C class implementation.

Public, Private, and Protected Instance Variables

Class's can set instance variables to be private, protected, public, and package. You use the compiler directives @private, @protected, @public, and @package to declare instance variable visibility. The private directive ensures variables marked as private are only visible

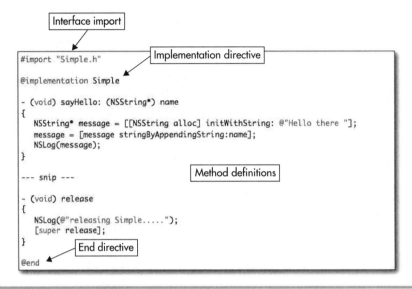

Figure 3-3 An Objective-C implementation summary

to the class that declares the instance variable. The protected directive ensures protected variables are only visible to the declaring class and its descendants. The public directive allows any class access to the public variables. The package directive is applicable only to 64-bit systems, and is a little more involved than the other directives. Refer to Apple's documentation for more information on the package directive.

Consider the interface code snippet in Listing 3-7.

Listing 3-7   Public and private methods

```
@public
  NSString* groupName;
  int intGroupSize;
@private
  NSString* otherGroupName;
  int intOtherGroupSize;
```

In this interface declaration, the instance variables groupName and intGroupSize are public, while otherGroupName and intOtherGroupSize are private.

Understanding Simple Messaging

Objective-C methods look substantially different from Java methods. Although the syntax is confusing at first, it's not difficult once you become used to it. Note that you don't say that you "call a method" when using Objective-C. Instead, you "send a message to a receiver." For instance, using Java you might type the following:

```
objMyObject.getFooUsingID(33);
```

When describing this line, I write that I am calling objMyObject's getFoo method and passing the argument 33. In Objective-C, the same message appears as follows:

```
[objMyObject getFooUsingID : 33];
```

When describing this line, I write that I am sending a getFooUsingID message, passing the argument 33, and objMyObject is the receiver.

The difference between calling a method and sending a message isn't Objective-C's only difference from Java, C++, and other dot-notation languages. Objective-C uses what's called infix notation. Infix notation mixes operands and operators. You don't really need to fully understand infix notation, other than it means Objective-C looks substantially different from Java and C++. An Objective-C message begins with an opening square brace and ends with a closing square brace followed by a semicolon. The object's name follows the opening brace, followed by a space, followed by the message. Arguments passed to the message follow a colon. You can, of course, have multiple-argument methods, as you will see in the next chapter. For now, though, just consider single-argument methods. Figure 3-4 summarizes an Objective-C message with a single argument.

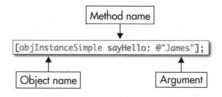

Figure 3-4   A simple Objective-C message

Using self in a Message

The term self refers to an object when sending a message, and it is also the receiver. For instance, you might make a mental note to yourself to pick up milk on the way home from work (Listing 3-8).

Listing 3-8   A method using the self keyword

```
-  (void) goHome {
    [self pickupMilk];
}

-  (Milk*) pickupMilk {
}
```

Both methods are in the same object, and so the goHome method sends the message pickupMilk to itself, or self.

Nested Arguments

Like Java, you can nest Objective-C messages. For instance, using Java, you might write the following:

```
objMyObject.getFoo(objMyFooIdentifier.getID());
```

In Objective-C, you would write the same statement as follows:

```
[objMyObject getFoo: [objMyFooIdentifier getID]];
```

Using Java, you might nest an object's constructor in another method.

```
objTester.testFubar(new Fubar(33));
```

In Objective-C, you can also nest object constructors in other methods.

```
[objTester testFubar[[Fubar alloc] initWithInteger : 33]]];
```

In this method, a new Fubar instance is first allocated and then initialized with 33, and the resulting object reference is sent as an argument to the testFubar message.

Class and Instance Methods

As discussed earlier, you declare methods in a class's interface and define methods in a class's implementation. Just like C, a method declaration consists solely of the method's signature, while the definition is the method's actual implementation. In both files, there are two method types: instance and class methods. Instance methods begin with a minus sign, while class methods begin with a plus sign. A class method is similar to a Java static method, meaning you don't need to create a class instance to use the method. For instance, the following is an instance method.

```
- (void) sayHello: (NSString*) name
```

Using the method requires creating a class instance first. Although not required, you should also initialize the class. Remember, all classes extend NSObject, which has an init method, so every Objective-C class is guaranteed to implement init.

```
Simple *objSimple = [[Simple alloc] init];
[objSimple sayHello:@"James"];
```

Now consider class methods. Class methods begin with a plus sign.

```
+ (id) sayGoodBye;
```

A class method doesn't require creating a class instance before using the method. For instance, when first allocating space for an object instance, you call a class's alloc method. If the class doesn't implement the alloc method, the runtime traverses up the class's inheritance hierarchy until it finds an alloc method or it reaches NSObject's alloc method and calls it.

```
Simple *mySimple = [Simple alloc];
[mySimple init];
```

This alloc method is a class method example. You don't instantiate a class instance before calling alloc; rather, you call alloc directly using the class. You create and use class methods just like Java static methods. And like Java static methods, you have the same restrictions. You can't reference that class's instance variables from a static method, as the instance variables haven't been initialized. You also can't refer to other instance methods from the same class as the class method. Remember, like a Java static method, you are using an uninitialized class, not an initialized object. If your class method relies upon a class being initialized, runtime errors will result.

Try This Adding sayGoodBye as a Class Method to Simple

1. Open the last example's project in Xcode. Open Simple.h and add the sayGoodBye method declaration to it (Listing 3-9). Be certain to use a + and not a – in the method's signature.

2. Add the method's definition to Simple.m (Listing 3-10).

3. Have main.m call the sayGoodBye method as in Listing 3-11.

4. Build and run the application, and "Goodbye..." is written to the debugger console (Listing 3-12).

(continued)

Listing 3-9   Simple.h modified to include sayGoodBye declaration

```
#import <Foundation/Foundation.h>
@interface Simple : NSObject {
}
+ (void) sayGoodBye;
-(void) sayHello: (NSString *) name;
@end
```

Listing 3-10   Simple.m modified to include sayGoodBye definition

```
#import "Simple.h"
@implementation Simple
+ (void) sayGoodBye {
  NSLog(@"Goodbye...");
}
- (void) sayHello: (NSString *) name {
  NSMutableString *message = [[NSMutableString alloc]
initWithString:@"Hello there"];
  [message appendString:name];
  NSLog(message);
  [message release];
}
@end
```

Listing 3-11   The main.h file modified to call sayGoodBye

```
int main(int argc, char *argv[]) {
  NSAutoreleasePool * pool = [[NSAutoreleasePool alloc] init];
  Simple * mySimple = [[Simple alloc] init];
  [mySimple sayHello:@"James"];
  [mySimple release];
  [Simple sayGoodBye];
  int retVal = UIApplicationMain(argc, argv, nil, nil);
  [pool release];
  return retVal;
}
```

Listing 3-12   Debugger console after running ChapThree

```
[Session started at 2008-12-17 21:33:38 -0500.]
2008-12-17 21:33:40.498 ChapThree[851:20b] Hello there James
2008-12-17 21:33:40.501 ChapThree[851:20b] Goodbye...
```

The alloc and init Methods

The alloc method is how you create class instances for all Objective-C classes. This method allocates memory space for the new object instance. It is inherited from the NSObject class, so you don't really need to implement this method yourself.

The init method is how you initialize a class once allocated. Unlike the class method alloc, the init method is an instance method. The init method is also a method in NSObject. If a class has no specific initialization requirements, you don't need to override int, nor are you required to call it when instantiating a class. However, if you have specific initialization requirements, you should override this method. Good programming practice, though, is to always call init, usually on the same line as the allocation.

The init method returns an id. An id is an Objective-C type that is a pointer to the object instance's address. The id is weakly typed, though, and the runtime treats all ids the same. Overriding an init method should always call the class parent's init method (Listing 3-13).

Listing 3-13   A simple init implementation

```
- (id) init {
  if (self = [super init]){ magicNumber = 5;}
  return self;
}
```

In Listing 3-13, the method assigns itself to its parent's id. If the parent's init method fails, it returns a nil value and the if statement fails. If it succeeds, the evaluation is true and the instance variable, magicNumber, is set to five. The init method ends by returning itself.

You can also initialize an object by passing arguments. By convention, initialization methods that take arguments are named init, followed by the data type of the argument. For instance, you could modify the init method in Listing 3-13 to Listing 3-14 if you wanted to initialize with an integer passed as a parameter.

Listing 3-14   A simple init method

```
- (id) initWithInt : (int) value {
  if (self = [super init])
    magicNumber = value;
  return self;
}
```

Managing Memory Using Retain and Release

Unlike Java or C#, when programming for the iPhone, you manage memory manually; there is no garbage collection on the iPhone. Although as of OS X 10.5, Cocoa includes an option to use automatic garbage collection, this option is not available on the iPhone. Table 3-1 summarizes Objective-C's memory management methods.

Memory Related Method	Description
+alloc	Allocate memory for new object and assign object reference count of one.
−autorelease	Add receiver to autorelease pool.
−dealloc	Deallocate memory for an object with zero reference count.
−release	Decrease object's reference count by one.
−retain	Increase object's reference count by one. Returns the object as an id.
−copy	See documentation.

Table 3-1 NSObject Memory Management Related Methods

Objective-C uses reference counts to determine if memory should be released or retained. When you create a class instance, the runtime allocates memory for the object and assigns that object a reference count of one. For instance, suppose you had a class named Simple. You first allocate space for it using NSObject's alloc method.

```
Simple *objSimple = [[Simple alloc] init];
```

You then use the object.

```
[objSimple sayHello:@"James"];
```

When finished, you call its release method. If no release method is found, the runtime moves up the classes' inheritance hierarchy until it finds a release implementation. As all classes extend NSObject, if no release instance is found, the runtime calls NSObject's release method.

```
[objSimple release];
```

When an object's reference count reaches zero, the runtime calls the object's dealloc method to deallocate the object. As with retain, if the runtime doesn't find a dealloc method, it moves up the inheritance hierarchy until it finds one. If no dealloc method is found, the runtime calls NSObject's dealloc method and the object is deallocated so the memory can be reclaimed.

You've already seen how alloc, release, and dealloc work; you allocate memory for an object and assign it a reference count of one using the alloc method, and you decrement the reference count by one when calling release. When an object's reference count reaches zero, the program calls NSObject's dealloc method.

The retain method increments an object's reference by one and returns the object reference as an id. Unlike Java, this referencing isn't automatic; you must explicitly call retain to increase an object's reference count. For instance, consider the following Objective-C code (Listing 3-15).

Listing 3-15   Using retain

```
Simple *objSimple = [[Simple alloc] init];
Simple *objSimpleTwo = objSimple;
NSLog(@"retaincount: %d", [objSimple retainCount]);
[objSimple release];
//this causes an error because objSimpleTwo is released
[objSimpleTwo sayHello:@"James"];
```

NOTE
Typically, there is no reason to call retainCount. In this chapter, I use retainCount to illustrate Objective-C memory management.

The first line allocates objSimple, and the runtime assigns the object a reference count of one. The second statement creates a new pointer to the objSimple object; both objSimple and objSimpleTwo point to the same physical object in memory. But because the code doesn't call retain, the physical object's reference count is not incremented. When the object is then released, the reference count is decremented by one and the reference count for the object becomes zero. The object is deallocated, so the next line fails, as objSimpleTwo is pointing to deallocated memory space.

Instead, the code should have explicitly retained objSimpleTwo.

```
[objSimpleTwo retain];
```

Retaining objSimpleTwo would have incremented the object's reference count by one, bringing it to two. Then, when objSimple was released, the object's reference count would still be one and the object would not be deallocated. The subsequent call to sayHello would work just fine, as the object that objSimpleTwo pointed to would still exist. Note, this is a somewhat unrealistic example, as you will never write code like Listing 3-15, but it illustrates retain and release.

You can override the NSObject's retain, release, dealloc, and alloc methods. But if you do, be certain to call the object's super method version. The method call for these methods must make it up the inheritance hierarchy to NSObject for memory management to function correctly.

Try This Using Manual Memory Management

1. Open the previous Try This project and implement dealloc, retain, release, and alloc in Simple.m (Listing 3-16). Note that retain returns an id, and that all these methods are declared in NSObject and don't require you adding their signatures to Simple.h.

2. Modify main.m to write log statements of the Simple's retaincount (Listing 3-17).

3. Build and run the application. The debugger includes the logging added in Listing 3-16 (Listing 3-18).

Listing 3-16 Simple.m modified to include memory management methods

```
#import "Simple.h"
@implementation Simple
+ (void) sayGoodBye {
  NSLog(@"Goodbye...");
}
- (void) sayHello: (NSString *) name {
  NSMutableString *message = [[NSMutableString alloc]
initWithString:@"Hello there"];
  [message appendString:name];
  NSLog(message);
  [message release];
}
- (void) dealloc {
  NSLog(@"deallocating Simple....");
  [super dealloc];
}
- (id) retain {
  NSLog(@"retaining Simple.....");
  return [super retain];
}
- (void) release {
  NSLog(@"releasing Simple.....");
  [super release];
}
+(id) alloc {
  NSLog(@"allocating Simple....");
  return [super alloc];
}
@end
```

Listing 3-17   The main.h file modified to include retainCount logging

```
#import <UIKit/UIKit.h>
#import "Simple.h"
int main(int argc, char *argv[]) {
  NSAutoreleasePool * pool = [[NSAutoreleasePool alloc] init];
  Simple * mySimple = [[Simple alloc] init];
  NSLog(@"retaincount: %d", [mySimple retainCount]);
  [mySimple sayHello:@"James"];
  [mySimple release];
  [Simple sayGoodBye];
  int retVal = UIApplicationMain(argc, argv, nil, nil);
  [pool release];
  return retVal;
}
```

Listing 3-18   Debugger console echoing memory management logging

```
[Session started at 2008-12-17 22:30:02 -0500.]
2008-12-17 22:30:03.894 ChapThree[1062:20b] allocating Simple....
2008-12-17 22:30:03.895 ChapThree[1062:20b] retaincount: 1
2008-12-17 22:30:03.899 ChapThree[1062:20b] Hello there James
2008-12-17 22:30:03.903 ChapThree[1062:20b] releasing Simple.....
2008-12-17 22:30:03.904 ChapThree[1062:20b] deallocating Simple....
2008-12-17 22:30:03.904 ChapThree[1062:20b] Goodbye...
```

In main.m, the main method first allocates a new Simple instance and assigns the pointer (mySimple) to point to the newly allocated and initialized object.

```
Simple *mySimple = [[Simple alloc] init];
```

The reference count to the object mySimple points to is one, and the debug statement in Listing 3-17 prints a retain count of one.

Instance Variables and Memory

In Chapter 4, you will learn about properties. You should use them and their accessor methods. If you do, you avoid this section's complications. But you should still understand a little about instance variables and how they are handled in memory. Suppose you have an instance variable, personName, you wish to set, as in Listing 3-19.

Listing 3-19 An instance variable in Simple.h

```
#import <Foundation/Foundation.h>
@interface Simple : NSObject {
  NSString * personName;
  }
  -(void) sayGoodBye;
  - (void) sayName;
  -(void) sayHello: (NSString *) name;
@end
```

Now suppose you modified sayHello to set personName, as in Listing 3-20. You must
retain the variable; otherwise, it goes away at the method's end.

Listing 3-20 Retaining an instance variable

```
- (void) sayHello: (NSString*) name {
  NSMutableString *message = [[NSMutableString alloc] initWithString:
@"Hello there "];
  [message appendString:name];
  NSLog(message);
  personName = [name retain];
  [message release];
}
```

Note that by retaining name, you are increasing its reference count by one, returning
it, and then setting personName to it. Thus, retaining name is retaining personName. Not
retaining a variable when assigning it to another variable, as in Listing 3-20, is a good
example of the type of problem you might encounter when not using properties. The name
variable pointer is passed to sayHello. Assume there is only one other pointer pointing to
name (a retainCount of one). Then, after assigning personName to name, the retain count
remains one. The personName pointer is now at the mercy of the pointer that originally
pointed to name outside the sayHello method. When the pointer external to Simple releases
the object name points to, the object is deallocated. So the personName pointer now points
to deallocated memory space and an error occurs. To correct this problem, you call retain
on the instance variable as in Listing 3-20. Anytime you set an instance variable, you should
retain it. That way, you ensure that it will not reach a zero reference count while the instance
variable still points to the object. Of course, the better solution is to always use accessor
methods combined with properties. You learn about accessor methods and properties in the
next chapter.

NOTE

You could have written the code in Listing 3-20 using one of NSString's class methods. But using stringWithString would not illustrate using retain.

```
personName = [NSString stringWithString:name];
```

Managing Memory Using Autorelease

Managing reference counts manually is tiresome and error-prone. NSObject's autorelease method manages an object's reference count for you. The autorelease method uses what's called a release pool to manage an object's references. Refer to Listing 3-17 and note that this method's first step is allocating an NSAutoreleasePool. Its second-to-last step is releasing that pool. Calling autorelease adds the object to the pool, and the pool retains the object for you. Consider the sayHelloTom method in Listing 3-21.

Listing 3-21   A method using autorelease

```
- (void) sayHelloTom {
  Simple *objSimple = [[[Simple alloc] init] autorelease];
  [objSimple sayHello:@"Tom"];
}
```

The method allocates a Simple instance and then calls autorelease, assigning objSimple to the autorelease pool. When the method finishes executing, the autorelease pool is deallocated and the Simple instance is subsequently released.

NOTE

The iPhone Cocoa Touch framework creates an autorelease pool for every event loop and releases it when the loop completes.

Using autorelease and accepting the default autorelease pools makes memory management easy. However, the problem is that there's a penalty: The objects persist for the release pool's lifetime. There is one solution, and that is to manage the NSAutoReleasePool yourself. For instance, you could modify Listing 3-22 to manage its own autorelease pool.

Listing 3-22   The sayHelloTom method managing its own autorelease pool

```
- (void) sayHelloTom {
  NSAutoreleasePool *pool = [[NSAutoreleasePool alloc] init];
  Simple *objSimple = [[[Simple alloc] autorelease] init];
  [objSimple sayHello:@"Tom"];
  [pool release];
}
```

When the pool is released and deallocated, the pool releases the object pointed to by objSimple. When the physical object pointed to by objSimple is released, the reference count is zero, so the runtime deallocates the object. You should note, though, that in this example, the results are exactly the same as if you had used the default autorelease pool. Unless creating many objects, it's probably best to stick to the default NSAutoreleasePool rather than trying to manage it yourself. After all, how long does an event loop last? Of course, if you are doing an intensive process, involving many objects or unusually large objects, you might consider managing the autorelease pool manually.

Summary

You're not finished with Objective-C yet. You still haven't learned about properties, multiple-argument messages, Objective-C's dynamic binding and typing, inheritance, composition, categories, protocols, or handling exceptions. This might seem like many topics still to learn, and it is, but Objective-C is a full-featured object-oriented language. Despite the length of this and the next chapter, realize you are only scratching the surface of Objective-C.

Chapter 4

Just Enough Objective-C—Part Two

Key Skills & Concepts

- Using properties

- Understanding multiple-argument messages

- Understanding the id variable type, dynamic typing, and dynamic binding

- Understanding inheritance

- Using composition

- Using categories

- Using protocols

- Handling exceptions

In the last chapter, you learned about Objective-C classes, simple message syntax, and managing memory. In this chapter, you learn about properties, multiple-argument messages, dynamic binding, polymorphism, the id type, and inheritance. You also learn about categories and protocols. And finally, you learn about Objective-C exception handling.

Properties

In the last chapter, you had to manage memory when setting an object's instance variable. For instance, if using retain and release, you would write a setter method that explicitly retained the passed value (Listings 4-1 and 4-2).

Listing 4-1   Writing a method that sets an instance variable (interface)

```
@interface MyClass : NSObject {
 Simple * objInstanceSimple;
}
-(void) setObjInstanceSimple: (Simple*) newValue;
@end
```

Listing 4-2   Writing a method that sets an instance variable (implementation)

```
@implementation MyClass
- (void) setObjInstanceSimple: (Simple*) newValue {
 [newValue retain];
```

```
 [objInstanceSimple release];
 objInstanceSimple = newValue;
}
@end
```

Remember, when using Objective-C objects, you are simply manipulating pointers. Pointers point to memory space. When changing an instance variable whose type is inherited from NSObject, you are changing the memory space it points to. Changing the memory space a variable points to without using retain or release almost always results in errors. In Listing 4-2, you explicitly set MyClass's instance variable, objInstanceSimple. The method first retains newValue. The method does this to prevent newValue from being deallocated, should the object later release the newValue. The method then releases objInstanceSimple. It does this to prevent a memory leak when changing objInstanceSimple to point to the memory space pointed to by newValue. After releasing objInstanceSimple, it changes objInstanceSimple to point to newValue.

Managing memory when getting and setting an object's instance variables is a pain. Objective-C 2.0 makes instance variables easier by using properties. Properties are shortcuts for creating instance variable accessors. You create properties using compiler directives. The @property directive declares a property, @synthesize tells the compiler to generate accessors, and @dynamic tells the compiler you will provide the accessor methods. A property directive also has one or more attributes. Table 4-1 summarizes the most common attributes.

The readonly attribute indicates the property is read-only, and the synthesize directive only creates a getter for the property. Retain instructs the compiler to create the setter so it retains the object.

NOTE

This chapter only covers a few basic principles of properties. Refer to Apple's documentation for a more complete discussion about properties.

Property Attribute	Description
assign	Setter assigns instance variable to object.
copy	Setter copies object to instance variable.
nonatomic	Return value without calling retain and autorelease on object.
readonly	Instance variable is read-only; cannot set its value.
readwrite	Instance variable has a getter and setter (default).
retain	Setter assigns instance variable to object and calls retain.

Table 4-1   Property Attributes Covered in this Chapter

Retain

When using a property with retain and managing memory yourself, you must release the temporary variable. For instance, suppose you set an instance variable called objSimpleRetain and this instance variable's property had a retain attribute.

```
@property(retain) Simple objSimple;
```

When setting this property, you must release whatever temporary instance you might create. Consider the following method that sets objSimpleRetain.

```
- (IBAction)giveWelcome {
 Simple* temp1 = [Simple alloc];
 self.objSimpleRetain = temp1;
 [objSimpleRetain sayHello:@"Mike"];
 NSLog(@"retaincount (mike): %d", [objSimpleRetain retainCount]);
 [temp1 release];
}
```

The temp1 reference is released at the method's end. If you ran the giveWelcome method, NSLog would print two as the retain count. The retain count of two is because the method first allocates temp1, which sets the object's retain count to one, and then the method sets the property; because the property specified retain, the object's retain count becomes two. Finally, the method releases temp1 and the retain count returns to one.

Note that you could have just as easily used autorelease and let the runtime release the temporary object at the event loop's end by writing the method as follows:

```
- (IBAction)giveWelcome {
 Simple* temp1 = [[Simple alloc] autorelease];
 self.objSimpleRetain = temp1;
 [objSimpleRetain sayHello:@"Mike"];
 NSLog(@"retaincount (mike): %d", [objSimpleRetain retainCount]);
}
```

Assign

You can also specify a property use assignment by using the assign attribute.

```
@property(assign) Simple objSimple;
```

Specifying assign is equivalent to simply assigning a pointer to an object without increasing its retain count. You must take care to not call autorelease or release a temporary object, as the assigned property simple points to the temporary object. I generally avoid using assign for objects.

Where assign is appropriate is for creating primitive properties. For instance, you might make an integer a property of a class. An integer is a primitive, and so you assign values to the property; you do not assign a pointer to the integer.

```
@property (assign) int myInteger;
```

Copy

Sometimes you might wish to obtain an independent object copy. You accomplish this using the copy attribute. When you use the copy attribute, the setter creates a new object and the original object is duplicated. This property is an independent object, not related to the original. There are two copy types: shallow and deep.

A shallow copy is when you only duplicate an object's references to its instance variables, while a deep copy is when you make a copy of those instance variables as well. Making a shallow copy is easy—a deep copy, not so much.

To copy your own custom class, your class must implement the NSCopying protocol. You learn more about protocols later; a comprehensive discussion on writing your own class that implements the NSCopying protocol is beyond this chapter's scope and would needlessly complicate it. However, in Chapter 15, this book does briefly discuss the NSCopying protocol. Look up the NSCopying online documentation for more information.

However, copying a Cocoa class that already implements the NSCopying protocol is not beyond this chapter's scope. For instance, copying an independent string copy seems a reasonable enough requirement. Consider the class, Foo, in Listings 4-3 and 4-4, and a method that uses Foo (Listing 4-5).

Listing 4-3   Foo's interface

```
#import <Foundation/Foundation.h>
@interface Foo : NSObject {
 NSString * myString;
}
@property(copy) NSString *myString;
@end
```

Listing 4-4   Foo's implementation

```
#import "Foo.h"
@implementation Foo
@synthesize myString;
@end
```

Listing 4-5   A method that uses Foo

```
- (IBAction)giveWelcome {
 Foo * myFoo = [[Foo alloc] autorelease];
 NSString* message = [[[NSString alloc] initWithString: @"A copied
 string."] autorelease];
 myFoo.myString = message;
```

```
message = @"A Changed string.";
NSLog(myFoo.myString);


}
```

The giveWelcome method creates a Foo instance (myFoo), a new string (message), and then sets myFoo's myString property to message. Because Foo's interface declared that myString uses copy, myFoo creates a copy of the new string when giveWelcome sets myString. When giveWelcome changes the message to a different string, myFoo.myString remains the same value. Had you used retain or assign, the myFoo.myString's value would have changed as well.

Releasing Properties

Remember, every class you define should ultimately inherit from the NSObject class. The NSObject class contains a dealloc method. You use this method to release any instance variables and perform other cleanup tasks. When you declare properties in your class, you should always override this method by declaring your own dealloc method in your class. You will see this over and over again in the remainder of this book. In fact, to avoid memory leaks, remember this one rule: when using properties with the attributes nonatomic and retain, always release the properties in a dealloc method. For instance, in Listing 4-3 you declare a property named myString in the class Foo. To prevent a memory leak, Foo should have a dealloc method like Listing 4-6. As you progress through this book, the dealloc method should become second nature.

Listing 4-6   A simple dealloc method

```
- (void) dealloc {
   [super dealloc];
   [myString release];
}
```

Multiple-Argument Messages

As with Objective-C's other language constructs, multiple arguments will probably appear strange at first; however, once you become accustomed to it, I am confident you will find the syntax easier than Java, C++, and other dot-notation languages. Why am I so confident that you will love Objective-C's syntax for multiple arguments? In a word, readability. How many times have you seen code like this in a Java program?

```
objMyClass.startPlay("Adventures of Tom Thumb", 44, new CherryPie( ),
 "Jack Sprat", 77);
```

What exactly do the arguments mean? What are you sending to the startPlay method in objMyClass? Now consider the same method using Objective-C.

```
[objMyClass startPlay: @"Adventures of Tom Thumb" audienceMembers:44 pie:
  [[CherryPie alloc] init] supportingActor:@"Jack Sprat" extrasNeeded:77];
```

You know exactly what the arguments sent to the method mean when using Objective-C. You are starting a play entitled "Adventures of Tom Thumb" that has 44 members in the audience, needs a cherry pie, has a supporting actor named Jack Sprat, and requires 77 extras.

The signature of the method called in the previous message has a syntax as follows:

```
- (void) startPlay: (NSString*) title audienceMembers: (int) value pie:
  (CherryPie*) pievalue supportingActor: (NSString*) actorvalue
  extrasNeeded: (int) extrasvalue;
```

The first argument is unnamed. The second and any further arguments are distinguished by a space followed by an argument name and colon, followed by the type in parentheses, followed by a parameter name to hold the value.

Now, here's the tricky part: When referring to a multiple-argument method, when calling the method, you refer to its named arguments. An argument's named argument is the name prior to the argument's data type. When using the argument within the method's implementation that the argument is a part of, you refer to the actual parameter name, not the argument name. So, for instance, in the startPlay method's implementation, you refer to title, value, pievalue, actorvalue, and extrasvalue. When calling the method, you refer to startPlay's named arguments: audienceMembers, pie, supportingActor, and extrasNeeded.

Try This Creating A Simple Multiple-Argument Message

1. Create a new View-based Application. Name the project SimpleMultiArg.

2. Create a new NSObject subclass called Simple. Xcode generates the Simple.h and Simple.m files.

3. Open Simple.h and add a method declaration for startPlay (Listing 4-7).

4. Open Simple.m and add the method's implementation (Listing 4-8).

5. Modify main.m to use Simple so it appears like Listing 4-9.

6. Build and run the application. The Debugger Console should echo the same logging as Listing 4-10.

(continued)

Listing 4-7   Simple's interface

```
#import <Foundation/Foundation.h>
@interface Simple : NSObject {
}
- (void) startPlay: (NSString*) title audienceMembers: (int) value
supportingActor: (NSString*) actorvalue
 extrasNeeded: (int) extrasvalue;
@end
```

Listing 4-8   Simple's implementation

```
#import "Simple.h"
@implementation Simple
- (void) startPlay: (NSString*) title audienceMembers: (int) value
supportingActor: (NSString*) actorvalue extrasNeeded: (int)
extrasvalue {
 NSLog(@"The title: %@", title);
 NSLog(@"Audience: %d", value);
 NSLog(@"Supporting actor: %@", actorvalue);
 NSLog(@"Extras needed: %d", extrasvalue);
}
@end
```

Listing 4-9   The main.m file modified to call Simple's startPlay method

```
#import <UIKit/UIKit.h>
#import "Simple.h"
int main(int argc, char *argv[]) {
 NSAutoreleasePool * pool = [[NSAutoreleasePool alloc] init];
 Simple * objSimple = [[[Simple alloc] init] autorelease];
 [objSimple startPlay:@"Peter Pan" audienceMembers:500
supportingActor:@"John Doe" extrasNeeded:55];
 int retVal = UIApplicationMain(argc, argv, nil, nil);
 [pool release];
 return retVal;
}
```

Listing 4-10   Debugger console output from running program

```
[Session started at 2008-12-29 18:49:55 -0500.]
2008-12-29 18:49:57.242 SimpleMultiArg[3132:20b] The title: Peter Pan
```

```
2008-12-29 18:49:57.243 SimpleMultiArg[3132:20b] Audience: 500
2008-12-29 18:49:57.244 SimpleMultiArg[3132:20b] Supporting actor:
John Doe
2008-12-29 18:49:57.245 SimpleMultiArg[3132:20b] Extras needed: 55
```

NOTE

The method startPlay is not the method's true name. In Objective-C, if more than one parameter, the method's parameters (other than the first parameter) are part of the method's name. For instance, the startPlay method's name is actually the following. By this book's end, you should be familiar with this naming convention, as many of the methods you use have multiple parameters.

```
startPlay:audienceMemebers:supportingActor:extrasNeeded:
```

Understanding the id Variable Type, Dynamic Typing, and Dynamic Binding

Objective-C is a dynamically typed language. Like Java, when using Objective-C, object types can be determined dynamically at runtime rather than statically at compile time. Objective-C accomplishes this dynamic typing using the id data type.

The id Type

The id variable is a data type that represents an object's address. Because it's just an address, id can be any object, and because its type is a pointer, you don't need to include the * symbol, as the * symbol signifies a pointer to a specific type. For instance,

```
Foo * myFoo;
```

is a pointer to a Foo object. The compiler knows the pointer points to an address that contains a Foo type. However, the following,

```
id myFoo;
```

provides no such information to the compiler. The compiler only knows that myFoo is a pointer—the compiler knows where the pointer is pointing, but doesn't know the data type of what myFoo points to. Only at runtime can it be determined what myFoo actually points to.

Dynamic Binding and Dynamic Typing

Objective-C accomplishes dynamic behavior using what's called dynamic typing and dynamic binding. Dynamic typing means that an object's type is not determined until runtime. For instance, a method that takes an id or an instance variable of type id has no way of knowing the object's type until the object is actually sent to the method or assigned to the instance variable.

Dynamic binding means that a method to invoke is not determined until runtime. And, unlike Java, Objective-C often doesn't require casting an object to its specific data type before being used.

Understanding Inheritance

You have already seen how Objective-C classes inherit from parent classes. In the interface, you specify that a class inherits from another class by placing the parent's name after the class's name and a colon.

```
@interface SimpleChild : Simple
```

Like any object-oriented language, Objective-C classes extend ancestors further up its hierarchy, with new methods and instance variables. Objective-C child classes can also redefine an ancestor's method. But, like Java (and unlike C++), an Objective-C class can only inherit from one parent; Objective-C doesn't support multiple inheritance.

Overriding Methods

Objective-C inheritance allows overriding methods, but not instance variables. You already saw an example of overriding methods when you overrode NSObject's dealloc, retain, and release methods in the class Foo.

```
#import "Foo.h"
@implementation Foo
- (void) dealloc {
 NSLog(@"deallocating Foo....");
 [super dealloc];
}
---snip---
@end
```

Instead of calling NSObject's methods, the runtime first calls Foo's, but since the methods in Foo all call its parent's version of each method, the runtime looks in Foo's inheritance hierarchy for a version of the method until it finds NSObject's version.

NOTE

The term "super" refers to the class's parent. For instance, you might have a method called doIt that matches the parent's doIt method. But doIt might add functionality and not replace functionality, so you should call the parent doIt method as well.

```
- (void) doIt {
 [self doMyStuff];
 [super doIt];
}
```

Overloading Methods

Unlike Java, you cannot overload methods when using Objective-C. In Java you overload a method when you provide a method with the same name but a different signature in the same class. For instance, you could define two methods like the following. The two methods are treated as distinct methods by the Java runtime.

```
public void myMethod(String name);

public void myMethod(int age);
```

Not so when using Objective-C, when faced with two methods like below, the compiler issues an error and will not compile your class.

```
- (void) myMethod: (NSString *) name;

- (void) myMethod: (int) age;
```

Because Objective-C does not support overloading, in the Objective-C programming community, it is common practice to add the argument's name to the method name.

```
- (void) myMethodString: (NSString *) name;

- (void) myMethodInt: (int) age;
```

Finally, you should note that for multiple argument methods, Objective-C's lack of method overloading is not problematic if any argument other than the first is different. Remember, a method's name includes its argument names. The following two method names are not the same.

```
- (void) myMethod: (int) age name: (NSString *) theName;

- (void) myMethod: (NSString *) name age: (int) theAge;
```

The compiler treats these methods as distinct because their names are actually myMethod: name: and myMethod:age: and not simply myMethod. Get used to this naming convention, it might seem strange at first, but it honestly makes Apple's documentation much easier to use.

Using Categories

Categories allow other classes to be extended without requiring inheritance. A category can contain both new methods and methods that override a class's methods. Categories are most useful when you find yourself in a situation where a supplied class doesn't provide functionality you want. To use a category, you create an interface and an implementation that specifies the class you wish to add a category to, followed by the category's name in parentheses. For instance, if you wished to add a category named FooCategory to NSString, you would type the following in the FooCategory.h file.

```
@interface NSString (FooCategory)
```

In the FooCategory.m file, you would type the following:

```
@implementation NSString (FooCategory)
```

followed by whatever methods you wished to add to NSString. Then, in the class you wished to use the category's methods, simply import the category and the runtime automatically resolves calls, such as,

```
[objMyString aReallyDumbMethod];
```

to the category rather than NSString.

NOTE
You can't add instance variables to a class using a category.

NOTE
In the category's header file, you must import the header file containing the class the category is extending.

Using Protocols

Protocols are similar to Java interfaces. In Java, an interface specifies the methods that a class that implements the interface must have. This is often called a contract. A class claiming to implement an interface should implement that contract—the class is promising it contains implementations for all of the interface's method declarations. So when you write a method like the following, you can rest assured the object has the called method implementation.

```
- (void) handleDoIt : (id <DoerProtocol>) objADoerImpl {
  [objADoerImpl doSomething];
}
```

The method handleDoIt takes an id specified to implement the DoerProtocol as an argument. Then when handleDoIt calls doSomething (a method declared in DoerProtocol), the runtime automatically, using dynamic binding, finds the correct object method implementation and calls it. Incidentally, when completing the task in the dynamic binding and dynamic typing section, you created a method that took an id and then called a specific method on an object, called play.

```
- (void) doIt: (id) value {
  [value play];
}
```

Although the code compiled and worked, this is not the best way to implement a method such as this in my opinion. Instead, you should have used a protocol—that way, it's explicit that the method's argument must be an object that implements the play method (assuming play is declared in the protocol).

```
- (void) doIt: (id <PlayerProtocol>) value {
  [value play];
}
```

The code in the method that takes a protocol as an argument can then call protocol methods, knowing that the class that adopts the protocol has the specified methods. It's not until runtime that the actual class method is dynamically bound to the interface method.

Consider a method that takes a protocol as an argument. At compile time, the compiler only knows that the method takes an instance of the protocol. The compiler doesn't know the actual object's data type. If the method calls a protocol method, the compiler only assumes the method is declared by the protocol. The compiler doesn't know the method definition. At runtime, though, you pass an actual object to the method. When the object is passed to the method, it is dynamically typed. Then, when the method calls the protocol's method, the protocol's method is dynamically bound to the object's method. Thus, just like Java, you can specify generic methods that take a protocol as an argument and then let the runtime dynamically type and bind the object when running the application.

You define a protocol using the @protocol compiler directive combined with an @end directive. You define method declarations between the two directives. For instance, the following code defines a protocol named MyProtocol.

```
#import <Foundation/Foundation.h>
@protocol MyProtocol
- (NSNumber*) myMethod;
@end
```

You specify a class conforms to a protocol by adding the protocol's name in the class's declaration in its header file.

```
@interface Foo : NSObject <MyProtocol>
```

Specifying a protocol in a class's declaration guarantees that class implements the methods declared in the MyProtocol protocol.

Protocols allow adding optional method declarations in addition to required method declarations. You specify optional methods using the @optional compiler directive and required methods using the @required compiler directive. The default for methods is required. For instance, you could modify MyProtocol to have an optional myMethodTwo method.

```
#import <Foundation/Foundation.h>
@protocol MyProtocol
- (NSNumber*) myMethod;
@optional
- (void) myMethodTwo;
@end
```

Of course, having a Java programmer's perspective, I question the logic behind a contract with an optional method declaration—if I write code against a protocol, I darn sure want the method to be there. Of course, this is Objective-C, so unlike Java, if the method isn't there, you don't get an exception. Remember, in Objective-C, you send a message and if nobody can handle the message, nothing happens.

You use the protocol similar to a class, only there is a subtle difference. When passing a class, you aren't actually passing the class, but rather a pointer. For instance, in the sayHello method, you are not passing a string called name as a parameter, but rather a pointer to a string.

```
- (void) sayHello: (NSString*) name;
```

But a protocol isn't a class; it's merely a header file with declarations (not definitions). Instead, you must either pass just the protocol itself (and the id is automatically understood) or you must pass an id.

Using a protocol rather than an id, you would specify something similar to the following in the interface of the class using your protocol. Suppose you wished defining a protocol for thermometers. There are many different ways a thermometer might be implemented. However, they all must tell the user his or her temperature. So if you created a Doctor class, although you know it should tell the patient his or her temperature, you do not know the specific type of thermometer the Doctor will use. So you use a protocol.

```
- (void) sayTemp : (<ThermProtocol>) objTherm;
```

You declare that a method takes a protocol as an argument. You don't specify the object's class, though. For instance, in the sayTemp method, you only know objTherm adopts the ThermProtocol. You do not know objTherm's actual class type.

When using an id—incidentally, this is the preferred syntax you see in Apple's documentation—you would specify something similar to the following.

```
- (void) sayTemp : (id <ThermProtocol>) objTherm;
```

In this example, you declare that sayTemp takes any class that implements the ThermProtocol. Actually, the first method signature without the id is also stating that sayTemp takes any class that implements the ThermProtocol, only the id is left implicit. Both method signatures work equally well, but by convention the second signature is what most programmers write.

Handling Exceptions

Objective-C's exception handling is similar to Java's and C++'s. Like Java and C++, you use a try-catch block. Code that might raise an exception is wrapped in a try block, followed immediately by a catch block. The @try compiler directive defines a code block that might throw an exception. The @catch directive defines a code block that handles the immediately preceding try block. The @finally directive defines a code block that is always executed, regardless if an exception was thrown.

```
@try {
}
@catch(NSException *e) {
}
@finally {
}
```

The most general exception is an NSException. All exceptions inherit from this Cocoa class. Like Java, you can throw an exception. In Objective-C, you use the @throw compiler directive.

NOTE

Apple recommends using the NSError Foundation Framework class rather than NSException for handling expected errors. See Apple's "Introduction to Error Handling Programming Guide for Cocoa" and also "Introduction to Exception Programming Topics for Cocoa" for more information on both classes. Scattered through this book's examples, you will see instances of NSError and NSException.

Summary

This chapter covered many topics in not very many pages, so it is okay if you're slightly confused. If you understood half of this chapter's topics, you should do okay for the book's remainder. If you wish, you might consider reading Apple's "Object-Oriented Programming with Objective-C," available from the iPhone Developer's site. It's terse and provides a good introduction to object-oriented programming concepts using Objective-C. Because you already know Objective-C's basic principles, understanding the document should prove easier than reading it without knowing Objective-C. Also, although produced by a different publisher, I must recommend the book *Programming in Objective-C 2.0* by Stephen G. Kochan (Addison-Wesley Professional, 2009). This book is clear, concise, and will teach you Objective-C. However, these two chapters should provide you with everything you need to know so that you can understand this book's remainder. If you buy this book after the Winter of 2010, I should have a book written on Objective-C entitled *Objective-C for iPhone Programmers: A Beginner's Guide*. For now, continue reading this book and then before pursuing advanced iPhone topics, consider quickly working through an Objective-C book. Objective-C is not hard once you get past the different syntax. If you understand properties, protocols, and releasing instance variables in the dealloc method and also Objective-C's basic syntax, then you should feel comfortable moving to this book's next chapter. If you have a basic understanding, trust me when I say that, by this book's end, Objective-C's syntax will seem natural.

Chapter 5

Deploying to an iPhone, Debugging, and Testing

Key Skills & Concepts

- Registering for iPhone developer membership

- Obtaining a certificate and provisioning

- Debugging an iPhone application

- Using zombies to debug

- Finding memory leaks

This book isn't covering the iPhone's UIKit or Cocoa Touch yet, but have patience, you begin these topics in the next chapter. Do not skip to the next chapter though; this chapter is important. In this chapter, you become familiar with many basic tasks required for compiling, debugging, and installing your App on your iPhone or iPod Touch. This chapter is not comprehensive, but it does show you the debugger, Xcode's and Interface Builder's major features, and how to get your App on your device for debugging. If you are not a registered, paid, iPhone developer, you should do so now. Go to the iPhone Dev Center now (http://developer.apple.com/iphone) for complete instructions. You cannot debug Apps on your device until you register.

This chapter covers two topics: installing applications on an iPhone or iPod touch and debugging iPhone applications. Although you can perform basic debugging using the iPhone Simulator on your computer, truly debugging and testing your application requires installing and running it on an iPhone or iPod touch. For instance, consider memory limitations. On your desktop computer, memory is virtually unlimited. Moreover, you probably have a dual-core, blazing-fast processor. Not so on your iPhone. An iPhone and iPod touch have fewer resources available than the iPhone Simulator, so you should test your applications on an actual device.

NOTE

You must have an iPhone Developer membership to complete some tasks in this chapter. If you do not, you can follow along, but I'd recommend getting membership as soon as possible.

This chapter briefly reviews obtaining membership to the iPhone Developer's program. It then covers obtaining a certificate and provisioning for your application. This chapter's coverage is not comprehensive, though, as the iPhone website practically holds your hand through the certificate and provisioning process, and there is no need to duplicate its hand-holding here. After installing an application on an iPhone or iPod touch, you can truly debug and test the application. This chapter's second half introduces you to debugging in Xcode and testing for memory leaks using Instruments. As with the certificate and provisioning discussion, this chapter's debugging and testing coverage is not comprehensive, but it should be enough to make you comfortable with performing both tasks.

Ask the Expert

Q: Why should I care about getting my App on my device right now? Shouldn't I wait until I know how to develop before I get iPhone Developer Program membership?

A: No. You should obtain membership as soon as possible. Some code will work on the iPhone Simulator but not on actual device. Moreover, the converse is also true. For instance, as of Summer 2009, the MPMediaPlayer, the Framework you use to access a device's iTunes media collection, functions only on a device and not the simulator. I also find it tremendously fulfilling to see my App running on my iPod and iPhone. And you can show off your development efforts to friends and family. Besides, it can take Apple awhile to process and approve your membership request. So do it now.

Installing Applications on an iPhone

Installing an application on an iPhone or iPod touch requires iPhone Developer membership. After you have a membership, installing an application is not difficult, as Apple's Developer Portal provides step-by-step instructions.

NOTE

Apple's "iPhone Development Guide," available online, provides a good introduction to installing applications on an iPhone or iPod touch. The examples here illustrate installing an application as of May 2009. Undoubtedly there will be differences in the web application by the time you read this chapter. The process's fundamentals remain the same, though.

Membership

Membership in the iPhone Dev Center on the Developer Connection Web site is a prerequisite to downloading the iPhone SDK. However, to install applications and eventually sell applications on the App Store requires membership in the iPhone Developer Program. Apple offers two membership types: corporate and individual. You must apply, pay a $99 fee, and receive acceptance before becoming a full individual member. After becoming a member, you are granted access to the iPhone Developer Program's Program Portal. This site is where you obtain certificates, assign new devices, create application IDs, and create provisioning profiles.

Certificates, Devices, Application IDs, and Provisioning

A certificate is the first thing that is required. You obtain your certificate by following the instructions on the How To tab in the portal's Certificates tab (Figure 5-1).

After obtaining the certificate, you must register the devices you wish to use for debugging. I own an iPod touch and an iPhone, so I registered both (Figure 5-2). As with certificates, complete instructions are provided on the How To tab.

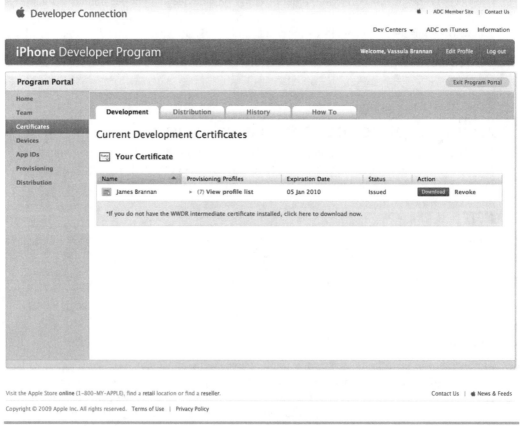

Figure 5-1 The Certificates tab

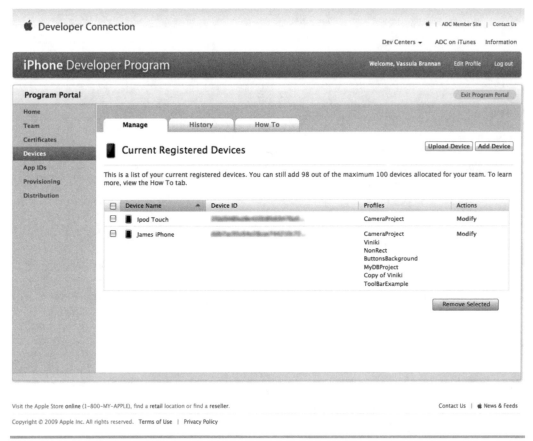

Figure 5-2 The Devices tab

After registering your devices, you can obtain application IDs and provision them. Any application you wish to test on a device must have an App ID (Figure 5-3). After obtaining the App ID, you must obtain a provisioning profile (Figure 5-4). A provisioning profile is installed on your device. An application is tied to a provisioning profile, so, a provisioning profile allows you to install a particular application on a particular device.

Apple's Developer Portal has a complete discussion of the provisioning process; the process is not difficult. What I did when learning the process was open two browser windows, one where I muddled through the steps and one where I skimmed the instructions. It helped that I have two monitors. In the following example, I take you through registering and installing a simple application on my iPhone.

Figure 5-3 The App IDs tab

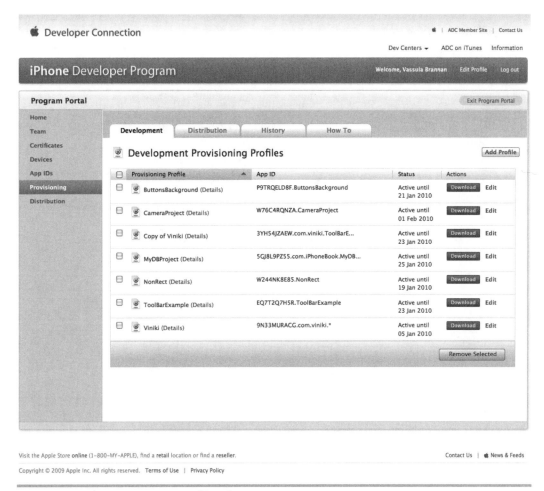

Figure 5-4 The Provisioning Profile tab

Try This Deploying an Application to iPhone

1. Create a new View-based Application named OnMyPhone.

2. Log in to the iPhone Developer Program Portal.

3. Click the Certificates tab. If you haven't installed your certificate, do so now. These steps assume a certificate (see Figure 5-2).

4. Click the Devices tab. If you haven't installed your devices, do so now. These steps assume a registered device (see Figure 5-3).

(continued)

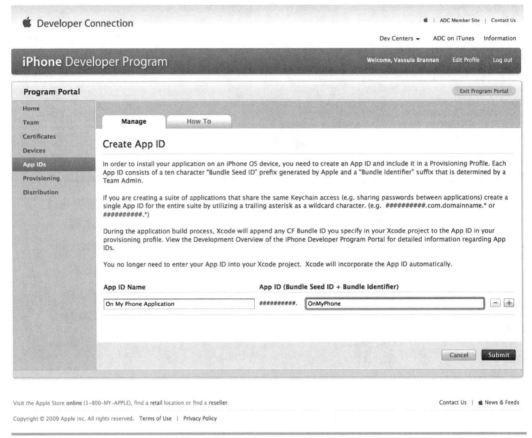

Figure 5-5 Adding an application to the App IDs

5. Click the App IDs tab and add the application (see Figure 5-3). Click the Add ID button on the page's right, and add the OnMyPhone application (Figure 5-5).

6. Click the Provisioning tab and click the Add Profile button on the page's right (see Figure 5-4). Complete the form; be certain you select the certificate and the device you want to provision (Figure 5-6).

7. Click Submit, and you return to the Provisioning page. The Provisioning Profile's status for My On My Phone Profile should say "Pending." Refresh the page until the status has an "Active until" date. You are usually quickly granted a profile.

8. Download the profile by clicking the Download button next to the profile. The profile should have a title like "My_On_My_Phone_Profile.mobileprovision." Move it to a safe location.

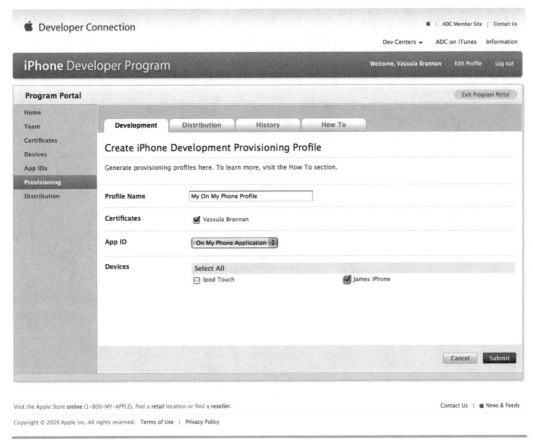

Figure 5-6 Provisioning the OnMyPhone application

9. Ensure your device is connected to your computer.

10. Return to Xcode. From the Windows menu, select Organizer. If your device is attached, it should appear under DEVICES (Figure 5-7).

11. Drag the provision file to the Provisioning list.

12. Change the application's Active SDK to Device – 3.0 | Debug.

NOTE
Select the latest SDK on your computer, not necessarily 3.0.

(continued)

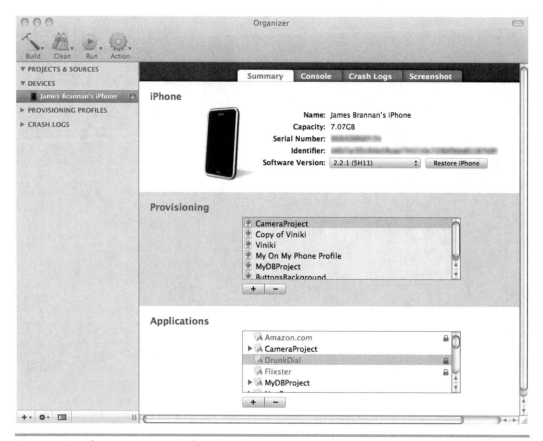

Figure 5-7 The Organizer window

13. You might receive an error the first time (Figure 5-8). Don't despair; the error is often easily fixed.

14. Open the project's Project Info window and navigate to the Build tab. Change the code signing identity to the provision just installed (Figure 5-9).

15. Close the Project Info window and open Info.plist. Change the bundle identifier to OnMyPhone.

16. Click Build And Go, and the application installs and runs on your device. You should see logging in the Debugger Console similar to Listing 5-1.

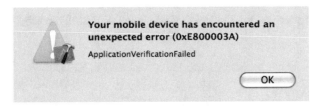

Figure 5-8 Error message

Figure 5-9 Changing the code signing identity

(continued)

Listing 5-1   Debugger Console logging when running on iPhone

```
Program loaded.
target remote-mobile /tmp/.XcodeGDBRemote-1193-51
Switching to remote protocol
mem 0x1000 0x3fffffff cache
mem 0x40000000 0xffffffff none
mem 0x00000000 0x0fff none
sharedlibrary apply-load-rules all
run
Running…
```

NOTE

For more information on provisioning, obtaining App IDs, and other program portal topics, refer to Apple's "iPhone Developer Program User Guide."

Debugging

Debugging and testing your application is paramount if you wish to provide users with a robust application. Xcode provides several excellent tools for debugging and testing your applications. In this section, you explore basic debugging using Xcode's graphical front-end to the GNU debugger.

NOTE

For a more complete introduction to debugging, refer to Apple's "Xcode Debugging Guide," available online.

Using the Debugger

Xcode's visual debugger overlays the command-line GNU debugger. The open-source GNU debugger has a long pedigree and is the industry standard when it comes to C and C++ debuggers on UNIX and Linux. Figure 5-10 shows the debugger window's panes. The top left pane is the Thread list, also sometimes called the call stack. This tells you where your application is currently at in any point in the application's processing. Below the stack pane is the Text editor pane. The right pane is the Variable list. This pane lets you see the current function's local variable values, argument values, and constant variables.

Along the debugger window's top, notice the Build And Go, Tasks, Restart, Continue, Step Over, Step Into, Step Out, and Deactivate buttons. Also notice the Breakpoints and Console buttons to the right of the other buttons. Table 5-1 summarizes each button's purpose.

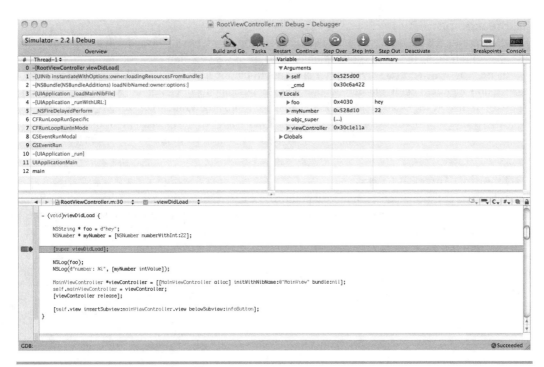

Figure 5-10   The debugger window

Button	Function
Build And Go	Builds the application and launches it in the debugger.
Tasks	Stops any tasks currently running.
Restart	Stops and starts the application running in the debugger.
Pause/Continue	Pauses the application running in the debugger. Note, when the application is paused, this button says Continue. Continue "un-pauses" the application and resumes processing.
Step Over	Processes the next line of code. If the next line is a function call, it skips over the function, proceeding to the next line.
Step Into	Processes the next line of code. If the line is a function call, it jumps to the code in the function.
Step Out	Processes until the function exits.
Deactivate	Disables the current breakpoint.
Breakpoints	Opens the Breakpoints window.
Console	Opens the Debugger Console window.

Table 5-1   Debugger Window Buttons

Breakpoints

Breakpoints tell the debugger where to pause. If you set no breakpoints and then run the application in the debugger, nothing unusual happens, as you didn't tell the application to pause. There are several ways to set a breakpoint, but the easiest is to click in the Editor window's gutter next to the line of code you wish the debugger to stop at (Figure 5-11). If you wish to disable the breakpoint, click it again and it turns light blue, indicating it is disabled. If you wish to remove the breakpoint, CTRL-click and select Remove Breakpoint from the pop-up menu. Alternatively, you can drag the breakpoint off the gutter to remove it. When you run the application in the debugger, it will pause processing at the first encountered breakpoint.

Stepping Through Code

When an application pauses at a breakpoint, you can step through your code's execution. Step Over moves directly to the next line, skipping over any functions. Step Into also moves to the next line, but if the next line is a function, it jumps to the function's first line, and you can

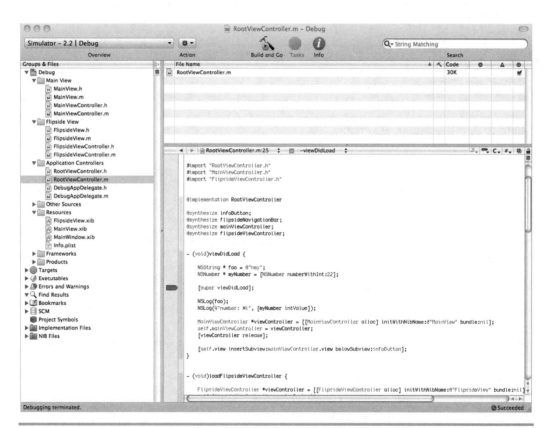

Figure 5-11 Setting a breakpoint

either step through the function line-by-line or step out of the function. If you choose Step Out, the debugger jumps to the first line after the function call.

Debugger Datatips

One thing you can do while debugging is obtain a variable's value and modify it while debugging. You can move your cursor over the variable, and a datatip appears with the variable and its value (Figure 5-12). You can even modify the value if desired.

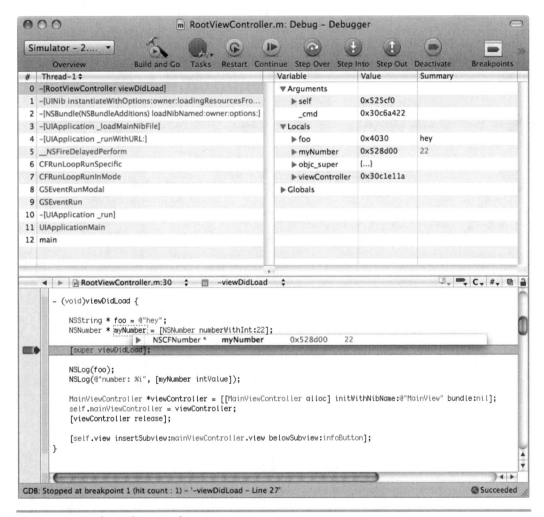

Figure 5-12   The Debugger datatips

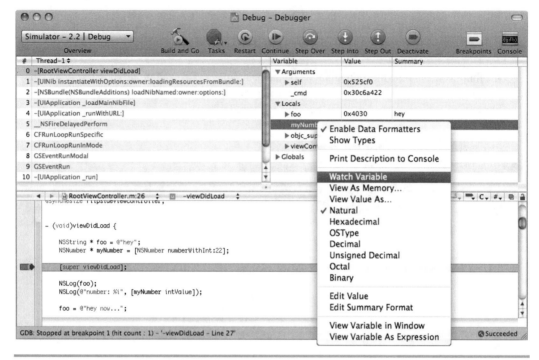

Figure 5-13 Setting a watchpoint

Watchpoints

Sometimes you might be interested in having the program pause when a value changes. A watchpoint pauses the program when the watched item's value changes. Setting a watchpoint is tricky the first time, but is then easy. To set a watchpoint, start the application in the debugger, and when the application pauses at a breakpoint, select the variable in the debugger window's variable list. Right-click it and select Watch Variable from the shortcut menu (Figure 5-13). After clicking Continue, if the value changes, the debugger notifies you and pauses (Figure 5-14).

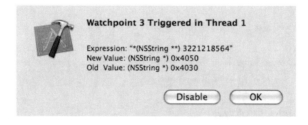

Figure 5-14 The debugger notifies you when a watchpoint's value changes.

Try This Debugging an Application

1. Create a new Utility Application named Debug.

2. Open FlipsideView.xib in Interface Builder and remove the File's Owner's outlet connected to the view (Figure 5-15).

3. Select Build and Run from the Build menu to run the application. Click the Info button, and the application crashes. Although the console displays the exact error message, suspend disbelief and pretend like it didn't.

4. Quit the iPhone Simulator and return to Xcode.

5. Open MainViewController.m and add a breakpoint at the second line in showInfo (Figure 5-16).

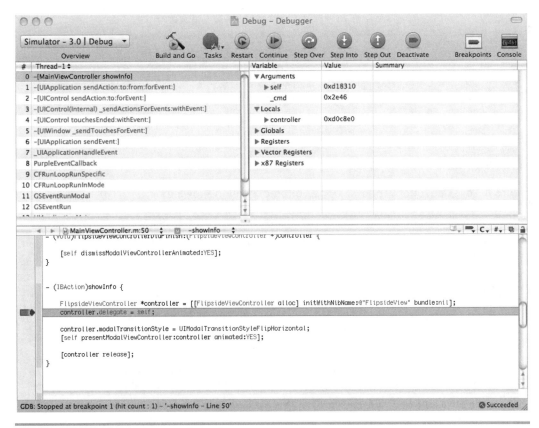

Figure 5-15   Remove the view from the view controller.

(continued)

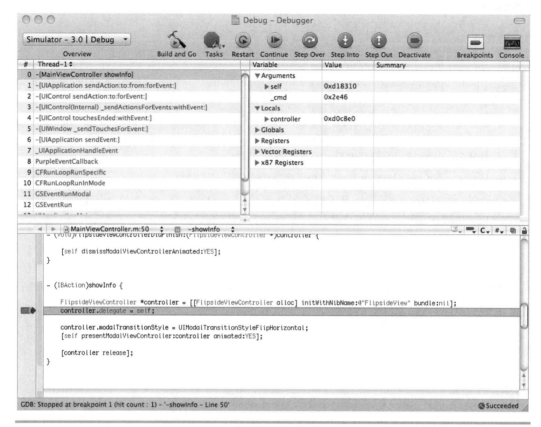

Figure 5-16 Debugger window stopped at breakpoint in showInfo

6. Select Build and Debug from the Run menu to run the application in the debugger. If the debugger window is not visible, from the Run menu select Debugger.

NOTE

Build and Go builds an application and then either runs or debugs the application, depending upon your previous choice.

7. Try stepping over the next few lines and the application crashes. You now know exactly which line in your code causes the application to crash. Something about presenting the FlipsideViewController caused the crash.

TIP

Forgetting to set a File's Owner view outlet is a common mistake.

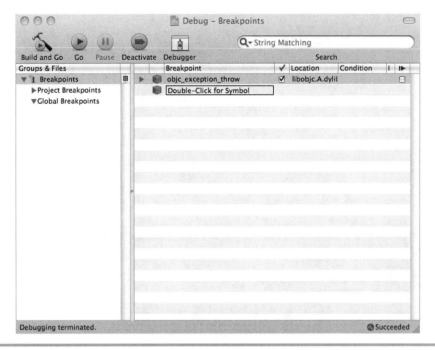

Figure 5-17 Adding objc_exception_throw as a breakpoint

8. Stop the iPhone Simulator and return to Xcode. Remove the breakpoint.

9. From the Run menu, select Show | Breakpoints.

10. On the Debug-Breakpoints window, double-click Double-Click For Symbol and add a new breakpoint at the objc_exception_throw method by entering this method to the list (Figure 5-17).

11. Click Build And Go on the Debug-Breakpoints window to launch the application in the debugger.

12. Click the Info button, and the application halts at the newly set breakpoint. Open the debugger window, if it is not already open (Figure 5-18).

13. Notice the upper-left window. This contains the stack listing. Follow the stack down several items, and you see the last thing to occur prior to an NSException is loading the view from the nib. Follow the stack to row 6, and you see the last line of code in the view controller that was executed in the lower pane (Figure 5-19). So you know trying to load the view from the nib caused the crash.

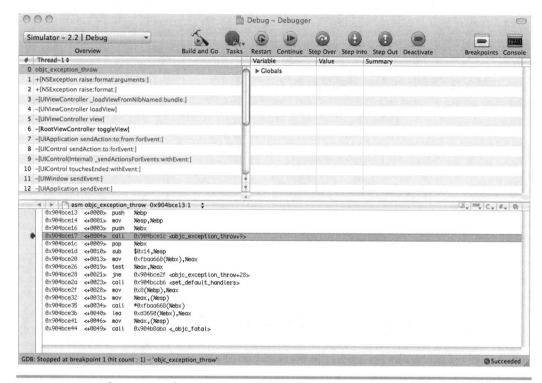

Figure 5-18   Debugger window paused at objc_exception_throw breakpoint

NSZombieEnabled

When an object is deallocated, if there are any objects with a reference to the deallocated object, they are no longer referencing a valid object. Any messages sent to the deallocated object result in errors. Often, the error is rather cryptic. For instance, the following code fragment is obviously an error.

```
FooBar * myFooBar = [[FooBar alloc] init];
NSMutableArray * myArray = [[NSMutableArray alloc] initWithObjects:
myFooBar,nil];
[myFooBar dealloc];
[[myArray objectAtIndex:0] sayHello];
```

FooBar is allocated, initialized, and added to myArray. There are two references to myFooBar, so its retainCount is two. However, deallocating myFooBar makes both references invalid, pointing to deallocated memory space. The sayHello message is sent to the first object in myArray—the problem is that the object no longer exists. Although in this simple example

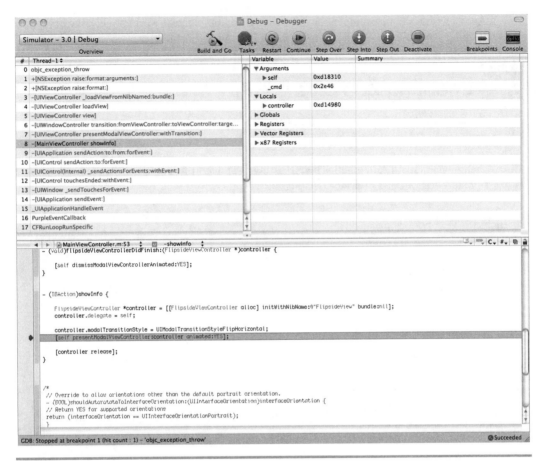

Figure 5-19   Following the stack trace takes you to an error's source.

it is easy enough to surmise the cause of the error message, in a real application, finding this type of error's source is often difficult.

```
objc[1289]: FREED(id): message sayHello sent to freed object=0x521a90
Program received signal: "EXC_BAD_INSTRUCTION".
```

Zombies help avoid this nebulous error, helping you track down an error's source. You enable zombies by setting the NSZombieEnabled environment variable in Xcode. Then, when debugging the application, rather than releasing an object, the debugger creates a zombie object. The zombie knows its original identity before joining the undead. The result, though, is you usually receive a more descriptive error message.

```
2009-02-28 12:28:38.749 Zombie[1316:20b] *** -[FooBar sayHello]:
message sent to deallocated instance 0x52c6a0
```

Again, in this simple example, the difference is trivial; in a real-world project, the difference is not trivial. The following task illustrates using NSZombieEnabled.

Try This Enabling Zombies

1. Create a new View-based Application named Zombie.

2. Create a new Objective-C class called FooBar.

3. Create one method called helloThere (Listing 5-2). Don't forget to put the method's signature in FooBar's interface (Listing 5-3).

Listing 5-2 FooBar.m

```
#import "FooBar.h"
@implementation FooBar
- (void) sayHello {
 NSLog(@"Hello there...");
}
- (void) dealloc {
 [super dealloc];
}
@end
```

Listing 5-3 FooBar.h

```
@interface FooBar : NSObject {
- (void) sayHello;
 @end
```

4. Modify applicationDidFinishLaunching in ZombieAppDelegate (Listing 5-4). Don't forget to import FooBar.

Listing 5-4 ZombieAppDelegate.m

```
#import "ZombieAppDelegate.h"
#import "ZombieViewController.h"
#import "FooBar.h"
@implementation ZombieAppDelegate
@synthesize window;
@synthesize viewController;
- (void)applicationDidFinishLaunching:(UIApplication *)application {
  FooBar * myFooBar = [[FooBar alloc] init];
```

```
    NSMutableArray * myArray = [[NSMutableArray alloc]
    initWithObjects:myFooBar,nil];
    [myFooBar dealloc];
    [[myArray objectAtIndex:0] sayHello];
    [window addSubview:viewController.view];
    [window makeKeyAndVisible];
}
- (void)dealloc {
    [viewController release];
    [window release];
    [super dealloc];
}
@end
```

5. Select Build And Debug on the Run menu to build and debug the application.

Notice the first time you run the application the error description is not all that descriptive (Listing 5-5). The debugger only knows the sayHello message was sent to an object already freed. The debugger doesn't know the object's identity. To change this, you must enable zombies.

Listing 5-5   Debugger Console error logging when zombies are not enabled

```
Attaching to program: `/Users/jamesbrannan/Library/Application
Support/iPhone
Simulator/User/Applications/05688B53-AF22-4F21
-95D3AFFE2682A6EA/Zombie.app/Zombie', process 1351.
objc[1351]: FREED(id): message sayHello sent to freed object=0x521bd0
Program received signal: "EXC_BAD_INSTRUCTION".
```

6. In the Groups & Files pane, expand Executables and double-click Zombies. This should open the Executable Info window (Figure 5-20).

7. Click the Arguments tab and add the NSZombieEnabled variable to the variable list. Assign it the value YES and ensure it is selected.

8. Build and debug. Now the error message is more descriptive (Listing 5-6).

Listing 5-6   Debugger Console output after zombies are enabled

```
Attaching to program: `/Users/jamesbrannan/Library/Application
Support/iPhone Simulator/User/Applications/F8340D01-C5D8-45AF-96A4-
512660FD2380/Zombie.app/Zombie', process 1387.
2009-02-28 12:40:08.812 Zombie[1387:20b] *** -[FooBar sayHello]:
message sent to deallocated instance 0x52c6a0
```

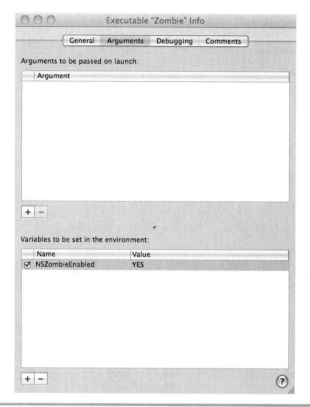

Figure 5-20 The Executable Info window

Instruments—Leaks

Instruments is a powerful suite of debugging and testing tools. This chapter cannot possibly cover it adequately. Tools include Activity Monitor, CPU Sampler, Leaks, Object Allocations, Core Animation, OpenGL ES, and System Usage (Figure 5-21).

NOTE

For more information on Instruments, refer to Apple's documentation "Instruments User Guide," available online or via the Instruments' Help menu.

However, one tool worth introducing you to here is Leaks. You can use Leaks without knowing much about it. The Leaks instrument allows you to easily find memory leaks in your application. It tells you how many leaks occurred, each leak's size, the address of the leak, and

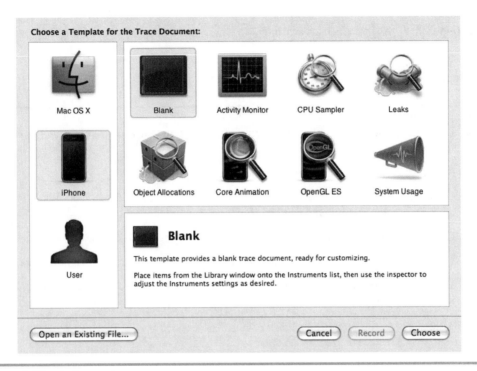

Figure 5-21   Instruments

the leaked object's type. Using Leaks is fairly intuitive—rather than explaining, let me simply explain by example through the following application.

Try This Find a Memory Leak

In the following task, you find memory leaks using the iPhone Simulator and on an actual device. If you didn't do the OnMyPhone exercise in this chapter's beginning, do so now.

Find a Memory Leak on iPhone Simulator

1. Create a new Utility Application named Sieve.

2. Create a new Objective-C class named FooBar.

3. Open FlipsideViewController.m and implement the viewDidAppear method (Listing 5-7). Don't forget to import FooBar.

(continued)

Listing 5-7　The viewDidAppear method

```
- (void) viewDidAppear:(BOOL) animated {
 FooBar * myFooBar = [[FooBar alloc] init];
}
```

---

4. Build the application. Ignore the warning informing you that you never use the FooBar instance in viewDidAppear.

5. Select Run | Start With Performance Tool | Leaks.

6. Click the Info button and the Done button repeatedly for about 30 seconds. When finished, click Stop in the Instruments window (Figure 5-22).

7. Click Leaks, and a detailed list of the leaked objects appears. Click one of the leaks.

8. Click View | Extended Detail, and a call stack appears on the window's right (Figure 5-23).

9. Double-click the viewDidAppear call, and the debugger opens to the line allocating and initializing FooBar.

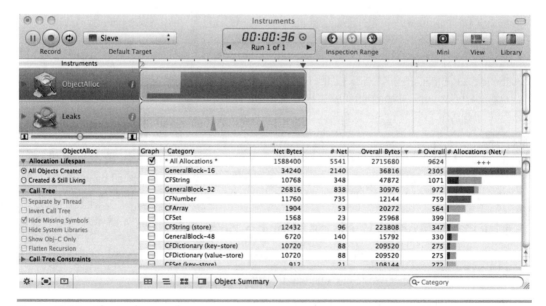

Figure 5-22　The Leaks panel

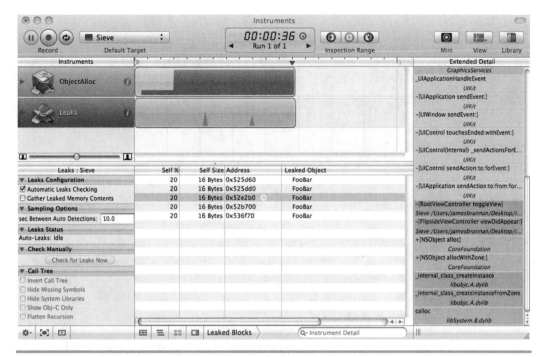

Figure 5-23   The Leaks panel showing extended details

10. Close the debugger and return to the Instruments window. Select a leak. Below the listing, click the button that has three indented lines (Figure 5-24). Instruments shows the leak's call tree.

11. Select Invert Call Tree, Hide System Libraries, and Show Obj-C Only. Select the leak. You might have to click a few times. Leaks shows only the method written by you in the application (Figure 5-25).

Figure 5-24   Button that changes view to call tree

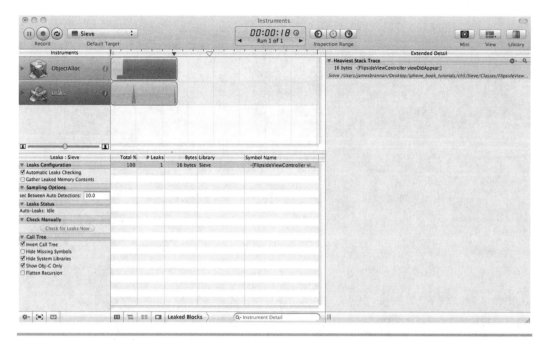

Figure 5-25   Leaks showing only method with corresponding Objective-C source code

Deploying and Distributing Your Application

After debugging and testing, you deploy your application for release. But building your application for release requires several steps beyond this book's scope. However, they are briefly summarized here. For comprehensive instructions, refer to several of the documents referenced throughout this chapter.

Deploying Your Application

All the nifty things you accomplished in this chapter were because compiling for debugging adds these nifty symbols so the debugger can run. You don't want this extra stuff in your released application; it will slow it down or worse. For instance, suppose you left the NSEnableZombie environment variable set to YES. Now when the application ran, zombies would overrun it rather than the objects being released properly. The application would be sluggish and probably be abruptly terminated by the device's operating system.

To modify your application for release, the first thing you must do is ensure your application's active configuration is set to Release (Figure 5-26). Of course, be certain to build for device and not the iPhone Simulator. You must then ensure the build configuration is correct (Figure 5-27). But note, this build configuration should still be seen as testing, as to truly build for release there are some other steps you must do.

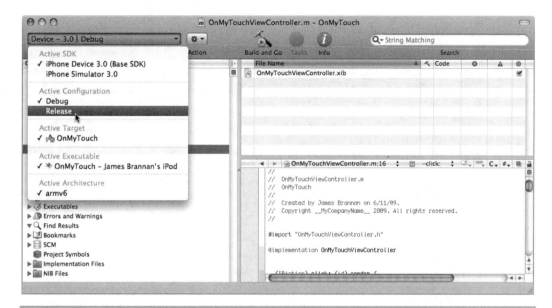

Figure 5-26   Setting the Active Configuration to Release

NOTE

A good comprehensive book on Xcode is *Xcode 3 Unleashed* by Fritz Anderson. Although the book does not cover iPhone development, it discusses debugging, testing, deployment, and many other Xcode topics in great detail. Another document you should often refer to is Apple's "Xcode Build System Guide."

Distributing Your App

To really build your App for release to the world at large, you must follow Apple's instructions for distributing Apps. Complete instructions can be found in Apple's "iPhone Developer Program User Guide" and are not repeated here. You must have an iTunes Connect Account if you wish selling your App on the App Store. If you wish distributing your application directly to others, you must create and download an iPhone Distribution Certificate and a Distribution Provisioning Profile. After installing these in Xcode, you can then build your application for release and have the application distributed to others.

After obtaining the necessary credentials, you must then create a new Xcode build configuration. Apple's "iPhone Developer Program User Guide" provides step-by-step instructions on how to do this. The instructions are not repeated here, as presumably, by the time you are ready to release an App on the App Store you will be a more advanced developer and can find the documentation yourself. For now, just realize that when you are ready to distribute your application to others, or on the App Store, you will have to create a new build configuration in Xcode, and instructions on doing that are in the manual referenced.

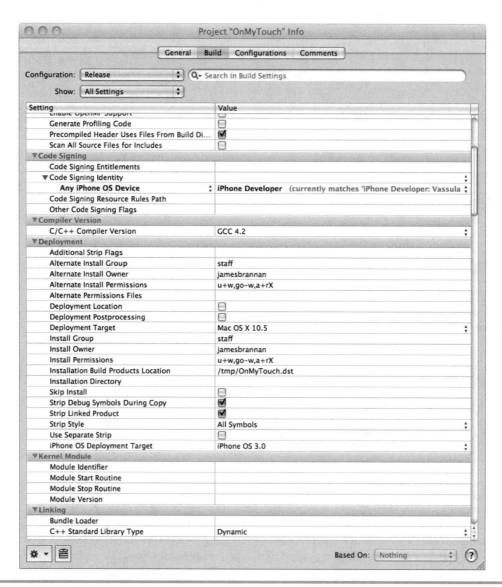

Figure 5-27 The Build Configuration's settings

NOTE

Remember, installing and debugging on registered test devices do not require anything other than what was covered in the beginning of this chapter. You are not required to create a different build configuration to debug and test on your devices.

Summary

Debugging and testing your application requires installing it on a test device. Besides, it is much more rewarding seeing your App run on a bona fide iPod touch or iPhone. But getting your application on a device requires you becoming an iPhone Developer Program member. You must then follow the instructions to getting the proper credentials so you can install on your device. Trust me when I say you can muddle through the online instructions, they are easy to follow.

Many iPhone errors are cryptic at best. Rather than running and rerunning an application aimlessly until you eventually find the error, take some time to learn the debugging tools Xcode has available to you. Refer to the documents referenced throughout this chapter. Use the debugger to find errors. After debugging your application, test its memory usage on the iPhone Simulator. After testing on the iPhone Simulator, install the application on your device, and debug and test again. Pay careful attention to memory and resource use, as an iPhone's memory is limited. Also ensure your application runs quickly and is responsive. Carefully debugging and testing your application can often be the difference between "yet another widget app" and the "best widget app" on the App Store. Chances are your application is not going to be the first of anything anymore, so try making it the best.

Chapter 6

UIApplication and
UIApplicationDelegate

Key Skills & Concepts

● Understanding the UIApplication class

● Understanding the UIApplicationDelegate protocol

● Handling application startup and termination

● Handling application interruptions

Every iPhone application has one UIApplication. UIApplication is an iPhone application's starting point and is responsible for initializing and displaying your application's UIWindow. It is also responsible for loading your application's first UIView into the UIWindow. Another responsibility UIApplication has is managing your application's life cycle. UIApplication fulfils this management responsibility using a delegate called UIApplicationDelegate. Although UIApplication receives events, it's the UIApplicationDelegate that handles how an application responds to those events. Events the UIApplicationDelegate might handle include application life cycle events, such as startup and shutdown, and system events like incoming phone calls and calendar alerts. In this chapter, after learning how to load an application's root view into the UIWindow, you explore handling system events using the UIApplicationDelegate protocol.

Try This   Adding a UIView and UIViewController to a UIApplicationDelegate

Before continuing, create this chapter's project; this chapter uses the same project throughout. In this project, you start with the simplest iPhone template, a Window-based application and you create an application from scratch. You first create a xib and corresponding view controller. You then modify the application's delegate so it loads the view.

1. Create a new Window-based Application from the New Project dialog. Name the project AddViewProject.

2. In Groups & Files, expand the Classes folder. This folder contains the AddViewProject AppDelegate.h and AddViewProjectAppDelegate.m files. These two files implement the project's custom class that adopts the UIApplicationDelegate protocol.

3. Highlight the Resources folder. CTRL-Click and Select Add | New File from the popup menu. Select User Interfaces from the New File dialog, and select Empty XIB (Figure 6-1).

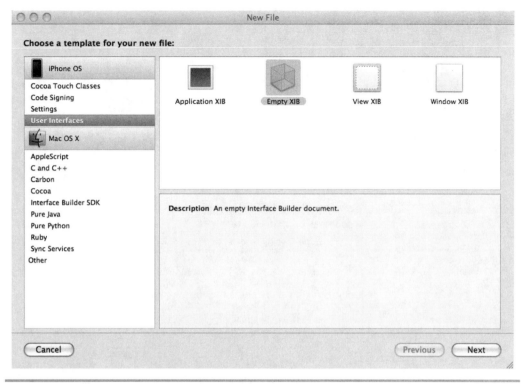

Figure 6-1   Creating an Empty XIB Interface Builder

4. Name the xib FirstViewController and click Finish.

5. Highlight the Classes folder in Groups & Files. Select File | New File from the menu.

6. Select the UIViewController subclass from the Cocoa Touch Classes and click Next (Figure 6-2).

NOTE
You could have created the view controller first and then checked the "With XIB for user interface," check box and Xcode would have generated the xib for you.

7. Name the file FirstViewController.m and ensure the Also Create "FirstViewController.h" check box is selected. Click Finish.

8. Double-click FirstViewController.xib and open it in Interface Builder.

(continued)

Figure 6-2 Creating a UIViewController

9. Select a view from the library, and drag-and-drop it onto the FirstViewController.xib Document window.

10. In the Document window, highlight File's Owner and select FirstViewController as the class in the First View Controller Identity Inspector (Figure 6-3).

11. In the Inspector, set the newly created view as FirstViewController's view outlet (Figure 6-4).

12. Select the view and change its color using the inspector (Figure 6-5).

13. Save FirstViewController.xib and exit Interface Builder.

14. Open AddViewProjectAppDelegate.h, import FirstViewController.h, and create a property referencing the FirstViewController class (Listing 6-1).

Figure 6-3 Select FirstViewController as the file's owner.

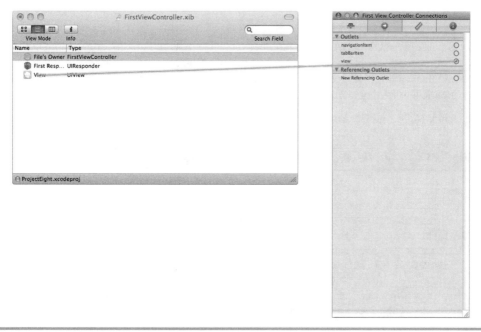

Figure 6-4 Setting the view as the File's Owner view

(continued)

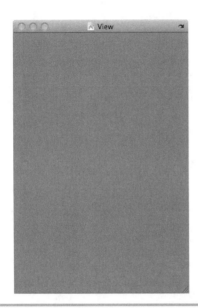
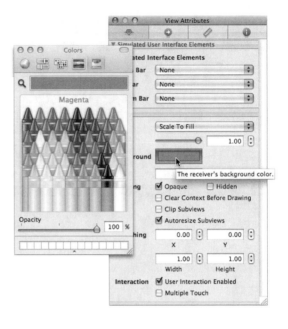

Figure 6-5 Changing the view's color

15. Open AddViewProjectAppDelegate.m, synthesize first, and modify applicationDidFinish
    Launching: so it obtains a reference to FirstViewController from FirstViewController.xib
    and then adds its view as a subview to the window. FirstViewController.m should appear
    identical to Listing 6-2.

16. Click Build And Go. Your colored view should load into the iPhone Simulator (Figure 6-6).

Listing 6-1 AddViewProjectAppDelegate.h interface

```
#import <UIKit/UIKit.h>
#import "FirstViewController.h";
@interface AddViewProjectAppDelegate : NSObject
<UIApplicationDelegate> {
  UIWindow *window;
  FirstViewController *first;
}
@property (nonatomic, retain) IBOutlet UIWindow *window;
@property (nonatomic, retain) FirstViewController *first;
@end
```

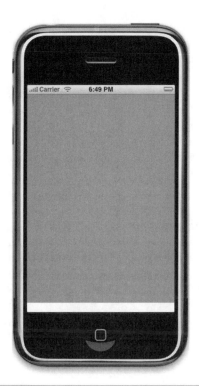

Figure 6-6   The application in iPhone Simulator

Listing 6-2   AddViewProjectAppDelegate.m implementation

```
#import "AddViewProjectAppDelegate.h"
@implementation AddViewProjectAppDelegate
@synthesize window;
@synthesize first;
- (void)applicationDidFinishLaunching:(UIApplication *)application {
  first = [[FirstViewController alloc]
  initWithNibName:@"FirstViewController" bundle:nil];
  [window addSubview: [first view]];
  [window makeKeyAndVisible];
}
- (void)dealloc {
  [window release];
  [first release];
  [super dealloc];
}
@end
```

(continued)

In steps 10 and 11, you manually connected AddViewProjectAppDelegate to its UIView. Moreover, you placed that view in its own nib. Every nib has an owner. Recall that every application has one UIWindow. UIWindow is in a project's MainWindow.xib. That nib's owner is UIApplication. Also notice that Xcode added the AddViewProjectAppDelegate to MainWindow.xib and connected it to the UIWindow and set the UIApplication's delegate.

Nibs you create should have a class adopting the UIViewController protocol as an owner, which is what you did in step 10. In step 9, you tied the UIView created in the nib in Interface Builder to the UIViewController created in Xcode. This is how the two objects "know" about each other. You learn more about UIViewControllers and UIViews—and connecting them—in Chapter 7.

NOTE

Notice that you created FirstViewController's view in its own FirstViewController.xib file. You could have opened MainWindow.xib, dragged a view onto the window, and used this nib for your user interface. But this is not the preferred way of using views in nibs. Apple recommends one nib per view. The reason for this recommendation is that an application must load all views and all controls that reside in the same nib. Using one nib per view reduces your application's memory use because you only load views as needed.

Ask the Expert

Q: **What is that initWithNibName line in Listing 6-2?**

A: This method allows initializing a UIViewController's view from a nib file rather than from code. You use this method when you want to write code that initializes a view controller whose view resides in a nib. You should note that this is just one of several different ways you might load a view from a nib into a class. By book's end, you will be familiar with most of them.

Connecting UIWindow, UIApplication, and UIApplicationDelegate

In the previous section, I only briefly mentioned the connections in MainWindow.xib. But these connections warrant a closer look if you want to understand what the template actually did. Notice the UIWindow in Listing 6-1 is an IBOutlet. Your first experience with IBOutlets was in Chapter 1, you learn more on it in Chapter 7. But realize the window "lives" in the xib, not in the delegate. Although the window is released by the delegate in the dealloc method, it is neither allocated nor initialized by the delegate's code in Listing 6-2. Remember, all the dealloc method in Listing 6-2 is doing is releasing the class's reference to the window, not deallocating the window. Instead, MainWindow.xib handles allocating, initializing, and deallocating the UIWindow.

UIApplication knows to load MainWindow.xib by consulting the NSMainNibFile key in Info.plist file. If you open the AddViewProject project's Info.plist, you will see that the "Main nib file base name" is set to MainWindow. While loading, the nib sets AddViewProjectApp Delegate as UIApplication's delegate and UIWindow as AddViewProjectAppDelegate's window. Both are outlets of their respective class in Interface Builder.

Try This   Exploring MainWindow.xib

1. Open MainWindow.xib and display the document window.

2. Highlight the File's Owner. Notice it is set to UIApplication (Figure 6-7). UIApplication loads MainWindow.xib.

3. Notice that the template added the AddViewProjectAppDelegate object.

4. Notice AddViewProjectAppDelegate's IBOutlet, window, is set to the UIWindow in the nib (Figure 6-8). Also notice that the UIApplication's delegate is set as AddViewProject AppDelegate.

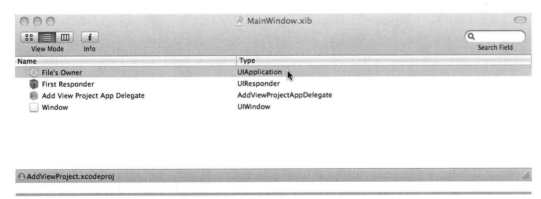

Figure 6-7   UIApplication in the Document window

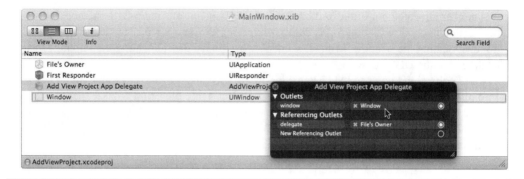

Figure 6-8 AddViewProjectAppDelegate's connections

UIApplication and UIApplicationDelegate

Ignore UIApplication—you almost never modify it. Just know that UIApplication receives system events. It is your job to write code that handles those system events. You write that code in a class adopting the UIApplicationDelegate protocol. This protocol has several life cycle methods that handle application and system events. Table 6-1 lists UIApplicationDelegate's methods. If you begin with a template, Xcode creates the class adopting the UIApplicationDelegate for you, but Xcode does not implement the UIApplicationDelegate's optional event-handling methods. For instance, in this chapter's project, Xcode created the AddViewProjectAppDelegate.h and AddViewProjectAppDelegate.m files. The AddViewProjectAppDelegate class extends NSObject and adopts the UIApplicationDelegate.

```
@interface AddViewProjectAppDelegate : NSObject <UIApplicationDelegate>
```

The application's UIApplication, defined in MainWindow.xib, has a reference to its UIApplicationDelegate as an outlet (Figure 6-8). As UIApplication receives one of the events related to the methods in Table 6-1, it calls the appropriate method in its delegate if implemented.

Ask the Expert

Q: What is a delegate?

A: A delegate is a way to simplify the separation of processing logic from another class. It also avoids inheritance. For instance, subclassing the UIApplication object would be painful. Instead, Apple provides a UIApplicationDelegate. The UIApplication has a reference to the class implementing the UIApplicationDelegate. If implemented, the UIApplication delegates handling an event to the appropriate method in the UIApplicationDelegate. It appears as if UIApplication is handling the event; in reality, its delegate, UIApplicationDelegate, handles the event. Delegates are a common object-oriented design pattern. For more information on delegates and object-oriented programming, refer to the "delegation pattern" on Wikipedia (www.wikipedia.org).

The main.m file

In the AddViewProject project, open main.m in the Other Sources folder in Groups & Files. The file's code is listed in Listing 6-3.

Listing 6-3   File main.m in project

```
#import <UIKit/UIKit.h>
int main(int argc, char *argv[]) {
  NSAutoreleasePool * pool = [[NSAutoreleasePool alloc] init];
  int retVal = UIApplicationMain(argc, argv, nil, nil);
  [pool release];
  return retVal;
}
```

Main creates one UIApplication instance using the UIApplicationMain method. Every project has exactly one UIApplication object. You can obtain a reference to that object by calling UIApplication's sharedApplication class method. This method returns a singleton reference to your application's UIApplication object.

```
UIApplication * myApplication = [UIApplication sharedApplication];
```

You usually will not do much with the UIApplication object other than obtain a reference to its UIApplicationDelegate. You obtain a reference to the UIApplicationDelegate through the following code:

```
UIApplicationDelegate * myDelegate = [[UIApplication
sharedApplication] delegate];
```

Handling Application Life Cycle Events

UIApplication forwards several important events to its UIApplicationDelegate to handle. For instance, applicationSignificantTimeChange: handles a significant time change while your application is running. The method didChangeStatusBarOrientation: handles the event fired when the status bar's orientation is changed from portrait to landscape or landscape to portrait. Table 6-1 lists UIApplicationDelegate's application life cycle event-handling methods.

With the exception of applicationDidFinishLaunching:, the methods in Table 6-1 are not required, but you should implement most of them if you wish developing a robust application.

Two of the more important application life cycle events are your application's startup and shutdown. The applicationDidFinishLaunching: method—a required method—is where you initialize your UIViewControllers, your UIWindow, add a UIView to the window, and then launch your application's user interface. The method is also useful for restoring your application's state, and is where you perform application initialization. The applicationWill Terminate: method is useful for saving your application's state. You might also use this method to perform cleanup.

UIApplicationDelegate Event-Handling Methods	Method Signature
application:didChangeStatusBarFrame:	`-(void) application:(UIApplication *) application didChangeStatusBarFrame: (CGRect) oldStatusBarFrame`
application:didChangeStatusBar Orientation:	`-(void) application: (UIApplication *) application didChangeStatusBarOrie ntation: (UIInterfaceOrientation) oldStatusBarOrientation`
application:handleOpenURL:	`- (BOOL) application: (UIApplication *) application handleOpenURL: (NSURL *) url`
application:willChangeStatusBarFrame:	`- (void) application: (UIApplication *) application willChangeStatusBarFrame: (CGRect) newStatusBarFrame`
application:willChangeStatusBar Orientation:duration:	`-(void) application: (UIApplication *) application willChangeStatusBarOri entation: (UIInterfaceOrientation) newStatusBarOrientation duration: (NSTimeInterval) duration`
applicationDidBecomeActive:	`-(void) applicationDidBecomeActive: (UIApplication *) application`
applicationDidFinishLaunching:	`- (void) applicationDidFinishLaunching: (UIApplication *) application`
applicationDidReceiveMemoryWarning:	`-(void) applicationDidReceiveMemoryWarning: (UIApplication *) application`
applicationSignificantTimeChange:	`-(void) applicationSignificantTimeChange: (UIApplication *) application`
applicationWillResignActive:	`-(void) applicationWillResignActive: (UIApplication *) application`
applicationWillTerminate:	`-(void) applicationWillTerminate: (UIApplication *) application`

Table 6-1   UIApplicationDelegate Event-Handling Methods

TIP

Xcode offers a feature called Code Sense. As you are typing, Xcode will suggest what it thinks you are typing. If correct, press the TAB key and Xcode finishes typing for you. You can ignore the suggestion by continuing to type. If you are not certain the suggestion is correct, press the ESC key and Xcode presents a drop-down list with possible completions (Figure 6-9). If you do not see this feature, ensure Xcode is configured correctly in Xcode Preferences (Figure 6-10).

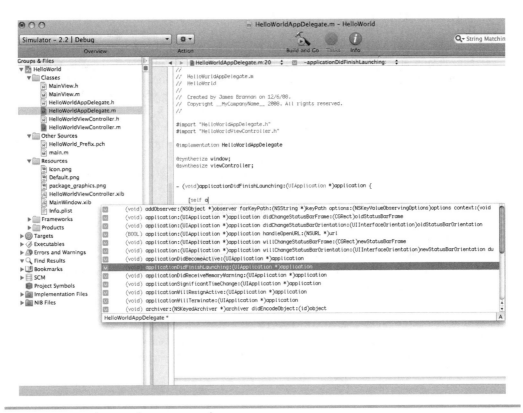

Figure 6-9 Code completion in Xcode

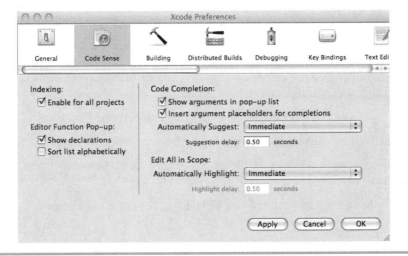

Figure 6-10 Xcode Preferences

Application Interruptions

As your application functions, it is likely to receive interruptions. An incoming phone call causes your application to become inactive. If you decide answering the call, your application terminates. Other events that might cause your application to become inactive include calendar alerts and putting your device to sleep (locking your device). The application WillResignActive: method in UIApplicationDelegate executes just prior to your application becoming inactive. The applicationDidBecomeActive: method executes just after your application becomes active again. For instance, if you are running your application and lock the screen, your application's delegate executes the applicationWillResignActive: method. When you later unlock the screen, your application's delegate executes the applicationDid BecomeActive: method.

Another important method is applicationDidReceiveMemoryWarning: method. The iPhone has limited memory—use too much and the operating system will terminate your application. But the operating system warns your application first. When UIApplication receives this event, it forwards the event to its delegate's applicationDidReceiveMemoryWarning: method. The delegate can then handle the application's response to the warning. For instance, it might release a shared data structure or take other memory reclaiming actions.

CAUTION

Although not required, your application should handle these important events in its UIApplicationDelegate. If it does not, Apple might reject your application when submitted for inclusion in the App Store.

Try This Handling Application Interruptions

In this task, you explore the applicationDidReceiveMemoryWarning:, applicationWillResign Active:, and applicationDidBecomeActive: methods in UIApplicationDelegate.

1. Add the methods applicationDidReceiveMemoryWarning:, applicationDidBecomeActive:, and applicationWillResignActive: to AddViewProjectDelegate's implementation (Add ViewProjectAppDelegate.m). Add a single NSLog statement to each method. The methods should appear similar to Listing 6-4.

2. Click Build And Go, and execute the application in the iPhone Simulator.

3. Select Hardware | Simulate Memory Warning from the iPhone Simulator's menu.

4. Select Hardware | Lock from the iPhone Simulator's menu. Unlock and then quit your application.

5. Review the Debugger Console, which should appear similar to Listing 6-5.

Listing 6-4   AddViewProjectAppDelegate's three additional methods

```
-(void)applicationDidReceiveMemoryWarning:(UIApplication *) application {
    NSLog(@"hey got a memory warning....");
}
-(void)applicationWillResignActive:(UIApplication *) application {
    NSLog(@"hey I'm about to resign active status....");
}
-(void)applicationDidBecomeActive:(UIApplication *) application {
    NSLog(@"hey I'm active....");
}
@end
```

Listing 6-5   Console output from running application

```
[Session started at 2008-12-07 14:56:49 -0500.]
2008-12-07 14:56:50.737 ProjectEight[2465:20b] fired application did
finishLaunching...
2008-12-07 14:56:50.740 ProjectEight[2465:20b] added first view controller
and made it visible...
---snip---
2008-12-07 14:57:03.247 AddViewProject[2465:20b] hey I'm active....
2008-12-07 14:57:08.094 AddViewProject[2465:20b] about to terminate...
```

The application executed the applicationDidBecomeActive: method when you started it and then after you unlocked the Simulator. It called applicationDidReceiveMemoryWarning: when you selected the Simulate Memory Warning menu item. And when the application was about to become inactive after locking, the UIApplicationDelegate executed the application WillResignActive: method.

Summary

The UIApplication is your application's starting point. It is usually the first thing created by the main method in the main.m file. The application is always associated with a delegate. An application's delegate is a class that implements the UIApplicationDelegate protocol. The delegate is where you place code handling your application's life cycle events.

A UIApplication has one UIApplicationDelegate. When using one of Xcode's templates, the connection between the UIWindow, UIApplication, and UIApplicationDelegate is done for you in the MainWindow.xib nib file. Moreover, you almost never have to manually create a UIApplication and UIApplicationDelegate, as every project template creates these objects for you. You also do not need to worry about having main.m create the application, nor do you need worry about implementing the applicationDidFinishLaunching: method, as these methods are almost always generated for you too.

Chapter 7

UIView and UIViewController

Key Skills & Concepts

- Understanding the UIView and UIViewController

- Creating a single view application using the View-based Application Template

- Creating a single view application using the Window-based Application Template

- Understanding an application delegate's root view

- Setting an application's root view in Interface Builder

- Setting an application's root view using code

- Understanding UIView life cycle methods

UIViews are how the iPhone displays information on the screen. The UIView class is responsible for displaying a rectangular area on the screen. The UIViewController manages the UIView and is responsible for handling the view's logic. The UIViewController is the glue between the view—the UIView—and your data classes—the model.

There are many UIView subclasses you might work with while developing an iPhone application. In fact, every graphical component you use on an iPhone graphical user interface (GUI) is a UIView subclass. Technically speaking, everything is a view. But typically, when documentation or some other material refers to a "view," it is referring to a content view. A content view is a view that has a view controller and is responsible for presenting a screen's worth of user interface.

The UIView Class

The UIView's responsibilities are drawing to the screen and handling events associated with a user's interaction with an application. A UIView has an associated UIViewController. The UIViewController manages the view. The view controller loads and unloads its associated views, manages views, and handles application life cycle events for its views.

Every graphical iPhone control you use in Interface Builder is a UIView subclass. Table 7-1 lists the UIView subclasses. Notice that UIScrollView and UIControl both have further subclasses listed in the table's second column.

UIViews function as containers, controls, displays, alerts, action sheets, navigation controls, and as the application's window. In future chapters, you consider most of these UIView types. This chapter limits itself to a simple display view and associated view controller.

UIView Subclasses	Subclasses
UIWindow	
UILabel	
UIPickerView	
UIProgressView	
UIActivityIndicatorView	
UIImageView	
UITabBar	
UIToolBar	
UINavigationBar	
UITableViewCell	
UIActionSheet	
UIAlertView	
UIScrollView	UITableView
	UITextView
UIWebView	
UIControl	UIButton
	UIDatePicker
	UIPageControl
	UISegmentedControl
	UITextField
	UISlider
	UISwitch

Table 7-1   UIView Subclasses in UIKit

The UIViewController Class

The UIViewController manages UIViews. It is responsible for creating, displaying, hiding, and destroying a view. The UIViewControl is also responsible for responding to a view's life cycle events, handling orientation, and serving as a bridge between your application's view and model. The view controller is your application's controller in the model-view-controller design pattern.

View-based Application Template

The easiest route to creating a single view application is using Xcode's View-based Application template. This template creates a single view and view controller for managing the view. While the view-based application is not as useful as Xcode's other project templates, it is useful here, as it generates the most simple iPhone graphical application and provides a simple UIView and UIViewController example. In the next task, you generate an application using this template. But, before continuing, first review IBOutlets and IBActions.

IBOutlet and IBAction

You have already used IBOutlets and IBActions in previous chapters. Without really knowing what they are, you probably already have a good idea of what they accomplish; outlets and actions are how you connect things in a nib with things outside a nib. An outlet connects an instance variable outside a nib to an object in a nib.

IBOutlet is a preprocessor directive, evaluates to void, and is ignored by the compiler, but all you really need to know is that IBOutlet is how Interface Builder knows the variable was created for its use. When adding a class, Interface Builder scans the class for IBOutlets and knows those variables are intended as outlets. You can then easily connect your graphical component to the variable, as Interface Builder adds the outlets to the inspector automatically for you to select. Note, though, Interface Builder doesn't connect the outlets to anything; it just adds them. You are responsible for adding any connections.

Actions are messages sent from objects in the nib to methods outside the nib. You define an action in your code using the IBAction keyword. Like IBOutlet, it's a preprocessor directive and evaluates to void. You define an action in your code using the IBAction keyword. Also, like IBOutlet, when you add a class to Interface Builder, it scans the class for IBActions and adds them to the inspector for you to select. You can then connect user interface events to a specific method in your code. Note that a method designated as an action must not return a value, as the preprocessor replaces IBAction with void, and so all the compiler sees is void. An action also takes a single parameter, sender. The sender is the id of the control calling the action. So if a UIButton instance called changeLabelValue, the sender would be the pointer to the UIButton.

```
- (IBAction) changeLabelValue: (id) sender;
```

IBOutlet and IBAction don't require much explanation, as you use these two directives so frequently they become second nature. Any instance variable external to Interface Builder that must communicate with a control in Interface Builder must be an IBOutlet. Any method that must be called from a control in Interface Builder must be an IBAction.

Try This Using a View-based Application Template

1. Create a new View-based Application using the template. Name the project SimpleView.

2. Expand classes and notice Interface Builder created the SimpleViewViewController class for you. Expand Resources and notice the template generated a separate nib, SimpleViewViewController.xib, for the SimpleViewViewController.

3. Open SimpleViewViewController.h and add a label and method for changing the label's value. Make the label an IBOutlet and the method an IBAction (Listing 7-1).

4. Open SimpleViewViewController.m and add the IBOutlet and IBAction definitions (Listing 7-2).

5. Open SimpleViewViewController.xib in Interface Builder and change the view's color. Add a UILabel and a UIButton to the UIView.

6. Notice that SimpleViewViewController is the File's Owner. Connect SimpleViewView Controller's theLabel outlet to the label.

7. Connect SimpleViewViewController's changeTheLabel action to the button. Select Touch Up Inside.

8. Save and exit Interface Builder.

9. Click Build And Go to run the application.

Listing 7-1   SimpleViewViewController.h

```
#import <UIKit/UIKit.h>
@interface SimpleViewViewController : UIViewController {
 IBOutlet UILabel * theLabel;
}
@property (nonatomic, retain) UILabel * theLabel;
- (IBAction) changeLabelValue: (id) sender;
@end
```

Listing 7-2   SimpleViewViewController.m

```
#import "SimpleViewViewController.h"
@implementation SimpleViewViewController
@synthesize theLabel;
- (IBAction) changeLabelValue : (id) sender {
  [theLabel setText:@"Hello World."];
  UIButton *theBut = sender;
```

(continued)

```
    NSLog(theBut.currentTitle);
    theBut.enabled = NO;
    [theBut setTitle:@"Pressed Already" forState: UIControlStateDisabled];
}
- (void)dealloc {
    [theLabel release];
    [super dealloc];
}
@end
```

Take a moment to examine what the View-based Application template did for you. It created the SimpleViewViewController.xib and it also created a UIViewController subclass, SimpleView ViewController, by creating the SimpleViewViewController.h and SimpleViewViewController.m files. Moreover, it added the controller to the delegate (Listing 7-3).

In the delegate, the template created the application's window and view controller as outlets (Listings 7-3 and 7-4). In the delegate's applicationDidFinishLaunching: method, the template added the view controller's view to the window and then displayed the window. Notice that nowhere does the code allocate or initialize its window or view controller. Instead, the Info.plist specifies that MainWindow.xib is the application's main nib, so it knows to load the MainWindow.xib and the nib handles window and view controller initialization.

In the MainWindow nib, the template set the nib's file's owner to UIApplication. The template set SimpleViewAppDelegate as the application's delegate and set the delegate's window to the window in MainWindow.xib.

The template also added a view controller to MainWindow.xib and set it as the delegate's root view controller. Every delegate must have a root view controller. The root view controller in MainWindow.xib comes from the SimpleViewViewController.xib, also created by the template.

The template created the UIView in its own xib, SimpleViewViewController.xib. It set SimpleViewViewController.xib's file's owner to SimpleViewViewController. It also set the controller's view to the view in the xib.

Listing 7-3   SimpleViewAppDelegate.h

```
#import <UIKit/UIKit.h>
@class SimpleViewViewController;
@interface SimpleViewAppDelegate : NSObject <UIApplicationDelegate> {
    UIWindow *window;
    SimpleViewViewController *viewController;
}
@property (nonatomic, retain) IBOutlet UIWindow *window;
@property (nonatomic, retain) IBOutlet SimpleViewViewController
*viewController;
@end
```

Listing 7-4   SimpleViewAppDelegate.m

```
#import "SimpleViewAppDelegate.h"
#import "SimpleViewViewController.h"
@implementation SimpleViewAppDelegate
@synthesize window;
@synthesize viewController;
- (void)applicationDidFinishLaunching:(UIApplication *)application {
  [window addSubview:viewController.view];
  [window makeKeyAndVisible];
}
- (void)dealloc {
  [viewController release];
  [window release];
  [super dealloc];
}
@end
```

Try This Using a Window-based Application Template

The View-based Application template hides many development details. If new to iPhone programming, chances are the View-based Application template does not help clarify a UIView, UIViewController, and their relationship. To help make their relationship clearer, you should understand what the View-based Application template accomplishes automatically.

Unlike a View-based Application template, a Window-based Application template requires understanding UIViews and UIViewControllers. When using the Window-based Application template, you must manually create a view and view controller and wire them together. In this project, you create a single view application starting with a Window-based Application template. Creating a Window-based Application should solidify your understanding of the steps behind its creation.

1. Create a new Window-based Application and name it SimpleWindow.

2. Highlight Resources and create an empty xib. Name the xib FirstViewController.xib.

3. Highlight Classes and add a UIViewController named FirstViewController. Xcode should have created FirstViewController.h and FirstViewController.m. Be certain the checkbox to create a xib is not checked.

4. Open SimpleWindowAppDelegate.h and import the FirstViewController. Add a UIViewController property to SimpleWindowAppDelegate.h so it appears the same as Listing 7-5.

(continued)

5. Modify SimpleWindowAppDelegate.m so it appears like Listing 7-6. Notice you must synthesize rootViewController and add its view to the window as a subview in the delegate's applicationDidFinishLaunching: method.

6. Build the application. This step is important, if you do not build or save the changes, any added actions or outlets will not appear in Interface Builder.

7. Open FirstViewController.xib in Interface Builder. Open the document window and notice that the File's Owner isn't set. Also notice there is no UIView.

8. Drag a view from the library to the document window. Change the view's color.

9. Select File's Owner and change its class to FirstViewController in the Object Identity Inspector pane.

10. Click the Connections Inspector and connect the view outlet to the view you added to the document window.

11. Save and close the FirstViewController's document window. Open MainWindow.xib in Interface Builder.

12. Notice that there is no UIViewController or view set in the document window.

13. Drag a view controller from the library to the document window (Figure 7-1).

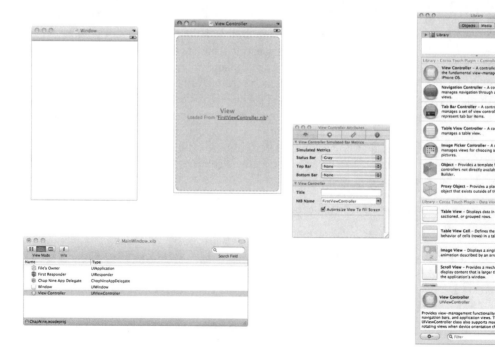

Figure 7-1 Adding FirstViewController to Mainwindow.xib

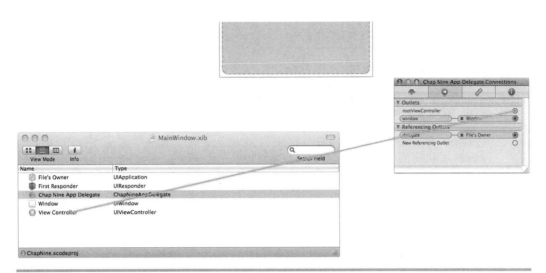

Figure 7-2 Setting Mainwindow.xib's root view controller

14. In the view controller's inspector, change its NIB Name to FirstViewController and its type to FirstViewController.

15. Select Simple Window App Delegate in the document window. In its connections inspector, notice the rootViewController outlet. Connect this to the view controller just added (Figure 7-2).

16. Save and quit Interface Builder.

17. Click Build And Go to run the application. The view in FirstViewController.xib is loaded into the window and displayed.

Listing 7-5 SimpleWindowAppDelegate.h

```
#import <UIKit/UIKit.h>
@class FirstViewController;
@interface SimpleWindowAppDelegate : NSObject <UIApplicationDelegate> {
  UIWindow *window;
  FirstViewController *rootViewController;
}
@property (nonatomic, retain) IBOutlet FirstViewController
*rootViewController;
@property (nonatomic, retain) IBOutlet UIWindow *window;
@end
```

(continued)

Listing 7-6   SimpleWindowAppDelegate.m

```
#import "SimpleWindowAppDelegate.h"
#import "FirstViewController.h"
@implementation SimpleWindowAppDelegate
@synthesize window;
@synthesize rootViewController;
- (void)applicationDidFinishLaunching:(UIApplication *)application {
  [window addSubview:rootViewController.view];
  [window makeKeyAndVisible];
}
- (void)dealloc {
  [window release];
  [rootViewController release];
  [super dealloc];
}
@end
```

In step 15, you connected the FirstViewController to the application's delegate. This was an important step; it allowed the nib to set the delegate's root view controller for you. The root view controller is the UIViewController that is first loaded by an application delegate. Remember, the application knew to load MainWindow.xib because it was in the application's Info.plist. The application loaded MainWindow.xib, saw the FirstViewController object that was added to the document window and saw that the delegate's root view controller was set to FirstViewController. The application also knew the controller came from FirstViewController .xib. Because of the object, variable, and nib setting, the application knew to allocate and initialize a FirstViewController instance from FirstViewController.xib when loading MainWindow.xib. Because these relationships were established in Interface Builder, no manual code was necessary. This is how the View-based Application template builds a simple application, which you just duplicated manually using the Window-based application template.

NOTE

In this example, you manually created a xib and linked it to its associated view controller. Step 3 specifically instructed you to not check the checkbox that also created a xib; had you checked the checkbox, Xcode would have created a xib, and automatically made all the necessary connections for you.

Ask the Expert

Q: Hey, wait a minute. What does @class precompiler directive mean in Listing 7-3, and why are you not importing the class's header?

A: The @class is a compiler directive that informs the compiler that a class of that type will exist. It is what's called a forward declaration, so named because it is informing the compiler before the class is actually declared.

UIViewController and Application Life Cycle Events

UIViewController handles important life cycle events for its associated UIViews. Table 7-2 lists the UIViewController's view life cycle instance methods.

Note that several methods in Table 7-2 are similar to an application delegate's life cycle methods—for instance, the didReceiveMemoryWarning: method. Do not let this similarity confuse you; remember, life cycle methods in the view controller are for the controller's associated view and not the application as a whole. Conversely, life cycle methods in the delegate are designed to handle events for the application as a whole.

Instance Method for View Life Cycle Management	When Called
didReceiveMemoryWarning:	Called when a controller receives a memory warning
didRotateFromInterfaceOrientation:	Called after a view controller's view rotates
viewDidAppear:	Called after a controller's view appears
viewDidDisappear:	Called after a controller's view disappears
viewDidLoad:	Called after a controller's view loads into memory
viewWillAppear:	Called just before a controller's view appears
viewWillDisappear:	Called just before a controller's view disappears
willRotateToInterfaceOrientation:duration:	Called when a controller begins rotating
willAnimateFirstHalfOfRotationToInterfaceOrientation:duration:	Called just before the first half of a view's rotation
willAnimateSecondHalfOfRotationFromInterface Orientation:duration:	Called just before the second half of a view's rotation

Table 7-2   UIViewController's Instance Methods for View Life Cycle Management

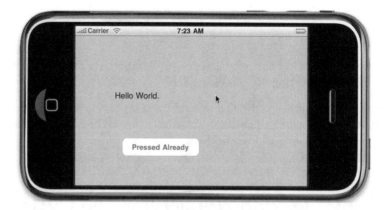

Figure 7-3 Running the application in landscape mode

Try This Exploring Several Life Cycle Methods

1. Open the SimpleView project in Xcode.

2. Create a new UIViewController class named Dummy. Open Dummy.m and note that Xcode generates most of the needed life cycle methods for you and then comments them. It even provides short descriptions of what each method does for you.

3. Delete the Dummy.m and the Dummy.h files.

4. Add the life cycle methods in Listing 7-7 to the FirstViewController.m file. Because FirstViewController's parent class, UIViewController, declares all these methods, you are not required adding a declaration for the methods in FirstViewController's header file.

5. Click Build And Go to run the application.

6. When the application is running, turn the simulator sideways by selecting Hardware | Rotate right from the simulator's menu (Figure 7-3).

7. Simulate a memory warning by selecting Hardware | Simulate Memory Warning.

8. Quit the application. The console's output should appear similar to Listing 7-8.

Listing 7-7 Life Cycle Methods added to FirstViewController.m

```
-(BOOL)shouldAutorotateToInterfaceOrientation:(UIInterfaceOrientation)
interfaceOrientation {
  return YES;
}
```

```
- (void)didReceiveMemoryWarning {
  NSLog(@"received memory warning....");
  [super didReceiveMemoryWarning];
}
- (void)viewDidLoad {
  NSLog(@"view did load...");
  [super viewDidLoad];
}
- (void)viewWillAppear:(BOOL)animated {
  NSLog(@"view will appear...");
}
- (void)viewDidUnload {
  NSLog(@"view did unload...");
}
- (void)didRotateFromInterfaceOrientation:(UIInterfaceOrientation)
fromInterfaceOrientation {
  NSLog(@"view rotated....");
}
```

Listing 7-8 Console's logging

```
[Session started at 2009-06-18 07:19:59 -0400.]
2009-06-18 07:20:07.503 SimpleView[267:20b] view did load...
2009-06-18 07:20:10.815 SimpleView[267:20b] Click Me
2009-06-18 07:20:15.293 SimpleView[267:20b] Received simulated memory
warning.
2009-06-18 07:20:15.294 SimpleView[267:20b] received memory
warning....
2009-06-18 07:20:33.478 SimpleView[267:20b] view rotated....
```

Ask the Expert

Q: Hey, wait a minute. What does shouldAutoRotateToInterfaceOrientation: mean in Listing 7-7?

A: This method is for allowing or disallowing a view to rotate. To allow a view to rotate, return YES. To disallow, return NO.

Summary

This chapter discussed the UIView and UIViewController classes. When developing an iPhone application, every content view should have its own nib. Remember, placing views in their own nib conserves memory by only loading the components needed to render the current view. The development pattern for creating a view is straightforward: Subclass a UIViewController in Xcode. Create the UIView in its own nib. Then, in the nib, connect the view to the view controller. To make your code easier to test and debug, keep the name consistent between the view, view controller, and nib. Implement any view-related life cycle methods you wish to handle in the view's view controller. Keep your custom code to a minimum, though—remember, the controller's job is to serve as glue code between your view and model. Consider placing more advanced code in helper classes, and then have your controller use these helpers.

Now that you understand how to build each screen's content, you can learn how to develop views that aggregate your individual views into a multiple-screen application. In the next chapter, you begin exploring multiview applications with the UITabBar and UITabBarController. After learning about tab bars, you move to the navigation controllers and then tables. These views let you aggregate content views into richer multiscreen applications.

Chapter 8

UITabBar and UITabBarController

Key Skills & Concepts

- Understanding tab bars

- Using the tab bar Application template

- Creating an Application that uses a tab bar

- Adding tabs to a tab bar

- Customizing a tab bar

A tab bar consists of two or more tabs along a window's bottom. Each tab contains a view controller. As a user selects a tab, the tab loads its view controller, which in turn loads and displays its associated view. In this chapter, you explore creating tabbed applications. In the first task, you create a tabbed application using Xcode's Tab Bar Application template. After examining this template's results, you manually add a third tab to the tab bar. In the next task, you start with a Window-based Application template and create a two-tab application. In this task, you solidify your understanding by manually duplicating the steps taken by the Tab Bar Application template. The chapter's final task illustrates allowing users to customize a tab bar's tabs when it contains five or more tabs.

UITabBar, UITabBarController, UITabBarItem, and UITabBarControllerDelegate

The tab bar is useful for presenting different application subtasks or different views of the same data. If you own an iPhone or iPod touch, you are certainly familiar with a tab bar controller, as several applications use tab bars. The Clock application, for instance, has a tab bar containing tabs with different subtasks (Figure 8-1). Each tab is a different subtask: World Clock, Alarm, Stopwatch, and Timer. The iPod application illustrates a tab bar containing different views of the same data (Figure 8-2). The Artists tab organizes your multimedia by artist; the Album tab organizes your media by album. Each tab is a different view of the same data, your iTunes multimedia. The iPod application illustrates another tab bar feature. When a tab bar has more than four tabs, it displays a More tab. Upon pressing More, the tab bar presents the remaining tabs in a selectable list (Figure 8-3). You can also modify the iPod application's tab bar using the Edit button. Clicking the Edit button displays the tabs in a view that allows you to modify which tabs are displayed in the tab bar (see Figure 8-3). When presented with an application that contains a task with multiple subtasks or an application that requires different views of the same data, use a tab bar.

Figure 8-1   The Clock application has a tab for each subtask.

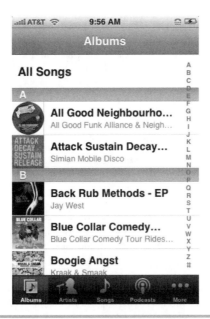

Figure 8-2   The iPod application has a tab for each data view.

Figure 8-3 The iPod application uses a More tab to display tabs.

NOTE

Do not use a tab bar for sequential navigation or data drill-down. The navigation control and tables are more appropriate choices for navigating sequential lists and data drill-down.

You create a tab bar using the UITabBar class. A UITabBar displays two or more tabs along a window's bottom edge. Individual tabs are UITabBarItem class instances. You tie these classes together using the UITabBarController and UITabBarControllerDelegate. Each UITabBarItem contains its own view controller. Click a tab, and the UITabBarItem loads its view controller. The view controller displays its view.

NOTE

A tab's view controller might be an advanced view, like a table or a navigation controller. Chapter 9 illustrates placing a navigation controller in a tab. Chapter 10 illustrates placing a navigation controller in a tab and then a table in the navigation controller.

A UITabBar has an associated UITabBarController and UITabBarDelegate. The UITabBarController manages the UIViewController objects in each tab. For instance, if a user wishes to add, remove, or rearrange tab bar items, the UITabBarController is responsible for implementing the behavior. You will see how to accomplish a rearrangeable tab bar later in this chapter. But first, consider the easiest tab bar implementation: the Tab Bar Application template.

Try This Using the Tab Bar Application Template

The Tab Bar Application template is the easiest route to creating a tabbed application, and unlike last chapter's Single View Application template, this template is a more useful starting point for real-world projects. In this task, you create a simple tab bar application using the Tab Bar Application template. After examining the template's results, you manually add a third tab to the tab bar.

1. Create a new Tab Bar Application by selecting the template in the New Project dialog. Name the project TabBarExOne.

2. In Groups & Files, expand Classes And Resources. At first glance, it appears the template created the same classes as it would for a View-based Application. However, the template added several tab bar related classes for you, making this a slightly more complex application.

3. Open TabBarExOneAppDelegate.h and notice the application's delegate adopts the UIT abBarControllerDelegate protocol. It also declares a UITabBarController property as an IBOutlet (Listing 8-1).

4. Open MainWindow.xib and review the document window. The template added a Tab Bar Controller.

5. The template also added TabBarExOneAppDelegate as a proxy object to MainView .xib. Review TabBarExOneAppDelegate's connections in the Inspector. Notice Xcode added a tabBarController property as an IBOutlet. Interface Builder subsequently knew the application delegate had a tabBarController outlet and connected it to the Tab Bar Controller in the document window.

6. In the document window, in List View, expand Selected First View Controller (First) and notice the Tab Bar Item (First). The second view controller also has a tab bar item associated with it.

7. Highlight the second view controller in the document window. Notice in the controller's inspector that the UIViewController is from an external nib, the template specified the view controller's Nib name (Figure 8-4). Also notice the template took a shortcut. Rather than creating a UIViewController for the second SecondView.xib, it used a generic UIViewController. If you wished, you could easily remedy this by adding a new UIViewController class to the Xcode project and changing SecondView.xib's view controller's class to the class created.

8. Build and run the application. A simple two-tab application runs in the simulator.

(continued)

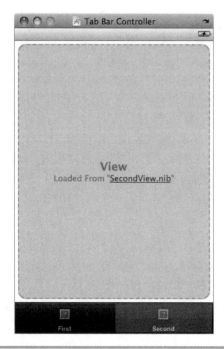

Figure 8-4 The second tab bar item's view controller is from another nib.

Listing 8-1 The TabBarExOneAppDelegate adopts the UITabBarControllerDelegate protocol.

```
#import <UIKit/UIKit.h>
@interface TabBarExOneAppDelegate : NSObject <UIApplicationDelegate,
UITabBarControllerDelegate> {
  UIWindow *window;
  UITabBarController *tabBarController;
}
@property (nonatomic, retain) IBOutlet UIWindow *window;
@property (nonatomic, retain) IBOutlet UITabBarController
*tabBarController;
@end
```

9. Open MainWindow.xib in Interface Builder.

10. On the tab bar controller's canvas, click the tab bar item labeled First. Be careful—only click once. Clicking the item once selects the tab bar item's view controller. You know you clicked once if the Inspector tabs have "View Controller" in their title.

11. Click the tab bar item twice, and you select the actual tab bar item. The Inspector tabs should have "Tab Bar Item" in their title.

12. Save and close Interface Builder.

13. Click Build And Go and run the application in the simulator.

The Tab Bar Application template generates a two-tabbed application. You will most certainly find situations where you need more tabs. Adding another tab to a tab bar is not difficult. In the next task, you add a third tab to the application.

Try This Adding a Tab Bar Item to a Tab Bar Application

1. If closed, open the last task's application in Xcode. Create another UIViewController and name the controller ThirdViewController. Ensure the checkbox that creates an accompanying xib is also selected. Xcode should generate the ThirdViewController.h, ThirdViewController.m, and ThirdViewController.xib files.

2. Open ThirdViewController.xib in Interface Builder. Change the view's color to something other than white. Save and exit Interface Builder.

3. Open MainWindow.xib in Interface Builder. Drag a UIViewController from the library to the document window. Change the UIViewController's class to ThirdViewController.

4. Highlight the tab bar controller and open its Tab Bar Attributes Inspector.

5. Add a tab bar item to the View Controllers list. Name the item Search, and notice a third tab appears on the tab bar controller canvas.

6. Click the third tab bar item once. In the Inspector, change the class from UIViewController to ThirdViewController. Also change the nib name to ThirdViewController.

7. Click the third tab bar item two times. Change the tab's identifier to Search in the Tab Bar Item Attributes Inspector. A magnifying glass and Search appears in the tab (Figure 8-5).

8. Save and exit Interface Builder.

9. Build and run the application. The application now has a third tab bar item (Figure 8-6).

(continued)

Figure 8-5 Changing a tab bar item's image to Search

Figure 8-6 Running the three-tab application in iPhone Simulator

Try This Creating a Tab Bar Application from Scratch

Using a template is well and good, but doesn't teach you how to actually build a tabbed application (unless you are using the template). So in this task, you duplicate the Tab Bar Application template's steps, but start with a Window-based Application template and manually add the tab bar items to your project. It is no more difficult than using the template—just slightly more tedious.

1. Create a new Window-based Application and name it TabBarExTwo.

2. Open TabBarExTwoAppDelegate.h and change it so it adopts the UITabBarController Delegate protocol (Listing 8-2). Add a UITabBarController property as an IBOutlet. The UITabBarControllerDelegate.h should appear like Listing 8-2. Don't forget to synthesize the controller in UITabBarControllerDelegate.m. Save and build.

3. Create a new UIViewController class and name it FirstViewController. Be certain it also creates an associated xib. Xcode should generate the FirstViewController.h, FirstViewController.m, and FirstViewController.xib files.

4. Create another UIViewController and associated xib named SecondViewController.

5. Open FirstViewController.xib and change the view's color. Open SecondViewController .xib and change the view's color.

6. Save and exit Interface Builder.

7. Open MainWindow.xib and add a UITabBarController to the document window. Interface Builder should show the tab bar controller's canvas.

8. Select the TabBarExTwoAppDelegate's Connections Inspector and connect its tabBarController outlet to the tab bar controller in the document window.

9. In the document window, ensure the view mode displays the items as a list. Expand the tab bar controller, select the Selected View Controller (Item 1), and change its class to FirstViewController in the First View Controller Identity Inspector. Change its Nib Name to FirstViewController.

10. Change View Controller (Item 2) to the SecondViewController, using the same steps as the previous step. Do not forget to set the NIB Name to SecondViewController in the Second View Controller Attributes Inspector.

11. Change the first tab's identifier to Recents and the second tab's identifier to Downloads (Figure 8-7).

12. Save and close Interface Builder.

13. Open TabBarExTwoAppDelegate.m. Add the tab bar controller to the applicationDidFinish Launching method (Listing 8-3).

(continued)

Figure 8-7 The first and second tab identifiers

Listing 8-2 TabBarExTwoAppDelegate.h modified to use a UITabBarController

```
#import <UIKit/UIKit.h>
@interface TabBarExTwoAppDelegate : NSObject <UIApplicationDelegate,
UITabBarControllerDelegate> {
  UIWindow *window;
  UITabBarController *tabBarController;
}
@property (nonatomic, retain) IBOutlet UIWindow *window;
@property (nonatomic, retain) IBOutlet UITabBarController
*tabBarController;
@end
```

Listing 8-3 TabBarExTwoAppDelegate.m modified to use a UITabBarController

```
#import "TabBarExTwoAppDelegate.h"
@implementation TabBarExTwoAppDelegate
@synthesize window;
@synthesize tabBarController;
```

```
- (void)applicationDidFinishLaunching:(UIApplication *)application {
  [window addSubview:tabBarController.view];
  [window makeKeyAndVisible];
}
- (void)dealloc {
  [window release];
  [tabBarController release];
  [super dealloc];
}
@end
```

14. Click Build And Go, and a two-tab application runs in the iPhone Simulator (Figure 8-8).

Figure 8-8   Two-tabbed application running in iPhone Simulator

Try This Allowing Users to Customize a Tab Bar

Sometimes you might wish to add more than four tabs to your application. However, the iPhone tab bar can only display four tabs and a More tab. When a user presses More, the excess tabs appear in a selectable list. By default, a navigation bar with an Edit button is displayed across the window's top. A user can then tap Edit and modify which tabs he or she wishes to see displayed on the tab bar.

The default behavior is to allow all tab bar items to be editable. If you wish to modify this default and limit which tabs are editable, you must modify the toolbar. In this task, you add more than four tabs to the first task's tab bar. You then make the tab bar non-editable, followed by making only some tabs editable.

1. Open TabBarExOne and add a new view controller. Name the class FourthViewController. Ensure it also creates an associated xib. Xcode should create the FourthViewController.h, FourthViewController.m, and FourthViewController.xib files.

2. Open FourthViewController.xib in Interface Builder. Change the view's color.

3. Close FourthViewController.xib and open MainWindow.xib in Interface Builder.

4. Add three more tabs by adding One, Two, and Three to the View Controllers in the Tab Bar Controller Attributes Inspector (Figure 8-9).

Figure 8-9 Adding three view controllers to the project

5. Change each view controller's class to FourthViewController. Also change each view controller's NIB name to FourthViewController.

NOTE

You would never use the same view controller for three different tabs in a real project.

6. Save and quit Interface Builder.

7. Build and run in the iPhone Simulator. Notice it added the fourth tab and a More tab (Figure 8-10). When you click the More tab, it displays a UITableView with the other two tabs (Figure 8-11). When you click either tab, the tab's associated view controller's view is displayed.

8. Click the Edit button, and a screen where you can configure the tab bar items is displayed (Figure 8-12).

Figure 8-10 Application displaying four tabs and a More button

(continued)

Figure 8-11 Clicking the More tab displays the remaining two tabs in a list.

Figure 8-12 Clicking the Edit button displays a view for configuring the tab bar's tabs.

Figure 8-13 Replacing a couple tabs with Two and Three

9. Try dragging Two and Three to the tab bar and replacing a couple of the other tabs (Figure 8-13). Click Done and exit the program.

10. Open TabBarExOneAppDelegate.m and add the following line to the applicationDidFinish Launching method.

    ```
    tabBarController.customizableViewControllers = nil;
    ```

11. Click Build And Go. Notice the Edit button appears but clicking it results in no tabs displayed.

12. Now modify applicationDidFinishLaunching again. Change the code so it matches Listing 8-4.

13. Click Build And Go. Notice you can only edit First and Second (Figure 8-14).

(continued)

Figure 8-14 Only First and Second are editable.

Listing 8-4 Setting the customizableViewControllers

```
- (void)applicationDidFinishLaunching:(UIApplication *)application {
  NSMutableArray * conts = [[[NSMutableArray alloc] init]
autorelease];
  [conts addObject:[tabBarController.viewControllers
objectAtIndex:0]];
  [conts addObject:[tabBarController.viewControllers
objectAtIndex:1]];
  tabBarController.customizableViewControllers = conts;
  [window addSubview:tabBarController.view];
}
```

A tab bar's default behavior is to allow users to rearrange, delete, and add tabs when a tab bar contains more than four tabs. To disable editing all tabs, set the tab bar controller's customizableViewControllers to nil. To disable only some tags, add the tabs that should be editable to the customizableViewControllers. Tabs not added to customizableViewControllers are automatically made non-editable.

Summary

As this chapter illustrated, creating a tabbed application is easy. First, ensure your application has a UITabBarControllerDelegate. Although you can create your own class to adopt the UITabBarControllerDelegate protocol, using the application's delegate is easier. But note, more complex applications that use tab bars should have a custom delegate associated with the tab bar and should not have the application's main delegate adopt the UITabBarController Delegate. After changing your application's delegate to adopt the UITabBarController Delegate, add a UITabBarController property to the delegate. Then add a UITabBarController to MainWindow.xib and connect the controller to the application delegate's tabBarController property. After connecting the delegate and tab bar controller, connect the individual UITabBarItem objects to view controllers. Creating tabbed applications is that easy.

In this chapter, you learned how to create a tab bar, its associated controller, and delegate. This chapter didn't have much in the way of explanation, as tab bars are easiest learned by doing. You created a tabbed application using both a template and manually. If you still do not understand tab bars, you should definitely reread this chapter, as tab bars are a navigation component you will use frequently for developing iPhone applications. Think of all the situations you use tabs in a desktop application—tabs are as ubiquitous on iPhone applications. But remember conventional user interface (UI) wisdom: Use tab bars for subtasks and for different views on the same data set. Do not use tab bars for tasks involving sequential steps. A navigation bar and its associated controller are much more useful for this navigation. In the next chapter, you learn how to create and use a navigation bar and its associated controller. Moreover, you will place a navigation bar in a view controller as a tab bar item. After learning about the navigation bar, you then explore tables. After learning about a table's fundamentals, you will place a navigation item and a table in the same view controller in an individual tab. After learning about tables, you will then have the fundamentals for creating the navigation for virtually all iPhone applications.

Chapter 9

UINavigationBar and
UINavigationController

Key Skills & Concepts

● Understanding a UINavigationBar, UINavigationController, and a UINavigationItem

● Understanding how to use a navigation bar in a simple application

● Understanding how to programmatically manipulate a navigation bar's items

● Adding a navigation bar to a tab in a tabbed application

A navigation bar is displayed along a window's top, just below the status bar. The navigation bar optionally contains a title for each view displayed and one or more buttons. Typically, the button on the bar's right, when clicked, takes the user to the next step in another view, although sometimes applications use the right button as a "done" button. The button on the bar's left is a Back button, returning to the previous view. Navigation bars are often used with tables, where a table is displayed with a navigation bar above it. When a user clicks a table's rows, the navigation bar's associated navigation controller takes the user to more detailed information about the selected item. For instance, the App Store application allows a user to refine his or her categories until the application of interest is found (Figure 9-1). For instance, if a user clicked Games, the navigation controller would take the user to a Games subcategory. If the user then clicked All Games, the navigation controller would take the user to a table of all games in the App Store. If a user wished to go back a step, he or she would press the button on the navigation bar's upper-left area. This button is the Back button. Note the navigation controller labeled the button's title with the previous view's title.

The navigation bar and navigation controller are useful for applications requiring hierarchical navigation, such as data drill-down. In the App Store application, you drill down to increasingly specific categories until reaching a list of items rather than further subcategories. When you select an item, it takes you to a more detailed view of your selection. Navigation bars are also useful for applications with multiple steps in a single task. In this chapter, you learn how to use a navigation bar and its associated classes. In the first task, you start with a Window-based application and manually create an application consisting of three views managed by a navigation controller. In the second task, you duplicate the Utility Application template. Although this template uses a navigation bar, the template is odd, compared to other Apple-provided templates. Rather than using Interface Builder, this template does almost everything using code. Moreover, this template uses a navigation bar without using an associated navigation controller. After finishing duplicating the Utility Application template, the chapter presents a navigation controller embedded in a tab bar's tab. This is perhaps this chapter's most useful task and should not be skipped. You will find embedding a navigation controller in a tab a ubiquitous requirement when developing iPhone applications.

Figure 9-1   Using the App Store application

UINavigationBar, UINavigationController, and UINavigationItem

Below the status bar but above the application window's content, many applications have a navigation bar. Navigation bars display the current view's title and contain one or more buttons for navigating to other screens. In this chapter's introduction, you viewed the App Store application, a typical use for a navigation bar. The Notes application also uses a navigation bar (Figure 9-2). The navigation bar appears above the yellow notepad. Upon clicking the + key, the navigation bar displays a new note page. The navigation bar's title is New Note and contains a back button labeled "Notes" and a right button labeled "Done." Upon tapping either button, the application returns the user to the application's primary page.

You add navigation bars to an application using the UINavigationBar class. You almost never use a UINavigationBar class directly, instead using UINavigationBar's controller, UINavigationController. You control a UINavigationBar using a UINavigationController. A UINavigationController uses a stack data structure to manage one or more view controllers. The first view controller, or the root view controller, is the first item on the stack. To navigate to other views, you push the view's view controller onto the stack. To return to the previous view, you pop the current view from the stack.

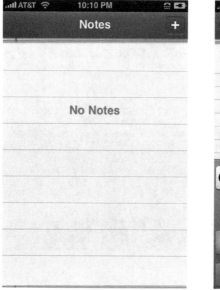

Figure 9-2   The Notes App uses a navigation bar.

Ask the Expert

Q: What is a stack?

A: A stack is a data structure used to hold a collection of objects. You can only add or remove objects from the stack's top. Envision a stack of plates: You add plates to the top and remove plates from the top. Removing from the bottom would cause the plates to topple and break. The stack data structure has the same FIFO (first in first out) requirements. Placing a new item on the stack is called "pushing," while removing an item from the stack is called "popping."

Try This Building a Three-View Application Using a Navigation Bar

It is easiest to learn the UINavigationController by example. In this task, you create a simple application containing three views. You navigate between the three views using a navigation bar. The first view has a button on the navigation bar's right, which says "Next." Upon clicking the button, the application takes you to the next view. This view has a Back button and a button in the view rather than on the navigation bar. Upon clicking the button in the view, the application takes you to a third view. The third view has a navigation bar and a title.

1. Create a new Window-based Application. Name the application ThreeViewNavCont.

2. Create three UIViewController classes, naming them FirstViewController, SecondViewController, and ThirdViewController. Be certain to also generate xib files for each class.

3. Open each of the xibs and change the view's color to a unique color.

4. Save and exit Interface Builder.

5. Open MainWindow.xib and drag a navigation controller from the library to the Document window (Figure 9-3). Notice Interface Builder shows the navigation controller's canvas with a navigation bar and a view.

6. Select the navigation controller's view controller. You can do this through the document window, by clicking the disclosure arrow next to navigation controller and then selecting the view controller. Alternatively, you can select the view directly in the navigation controller's canvas. Change the controller's class to FirstViewController in the Inspector. Also change its NIB name to FirstViewController in the Inspector (Figure 9-4).

(continued)

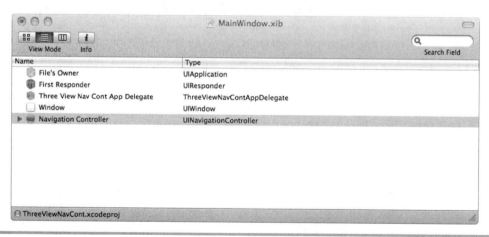

Figure 9-3 Adding a navigation controller to MainWindow.xib

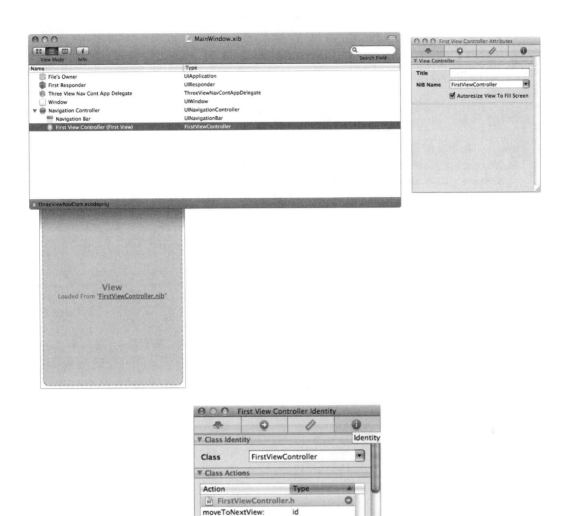

Figure 9-4 Changing the view controller to FirstViewController

(continued)

7. Save and exit Interface Builder.

8. Open ThreeViewNavContAppDelegate.h in Xcode. Add a UINavigationControllerIBOutlet declaration to the header file (Listing 9-1).

Listing 9-1   ThreeViewNavContAppDelegate.h

```
#import<UIKit/UIKit.h>
@interface ThreeViewNavContAppDelegate : NSObject<UIApplicationDelegate> {
  IBOutlet UIWindow *window;
  IBOutlet UINavigationController * navController;
}
@property (nonatomic, retain) IBOutlet UIWindow *window;
@property (nonatomic, retain) IBOutlet UINavigationController *
navController;
@end
```

9. Add the UINavigationController to ThreeViewNavContAppDelegate.m and add the UINavigationController's view to the window (Listing 9-2). Save and build.

Listing 9-2   ThreeViewNavContAppDelegate.m

```
#import "ThreeViewNavContAppDelegate.h"
@implementation ThreeViewNavContAppDelegate
@synthesize window;
@synthesize navController;
- (void)applicationDidFinishLaunching:(UIApplication *)application {
  [window addSubview: navController.view];
  [window makeKeyAndVisible];
}
- (void)dealloc {
  [window release];
  [navController release];
  [super dealloc];
}
@end
```

10. Open MainWindow.xib in Interface Builder. Right-click ThreeViewNavContApp Delegate in the document window and connect the navController outlet to the UINavigationController in the document window (Figure 9-5).

11. Save and exit Interface Builder.

12. Click Build And Go to run the application, and FirstViewController's view should appear (Figure 9-6).

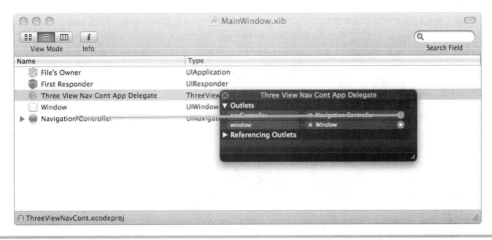

Figure 9-5 Connecting the navigation controller

Figure 9-6 The application running in iPhone Simulator

(continued)

The first step to using a navigation bar is to add a navigation controller to a document window. Upon adding the navigation controller, Interface Builder also adds a root view controller and you changed this view controller to your view controller. Making this connection in Interface Builder allows the nib to manage the property's life cycle. When you build and run the application, the application knows MainWindow.xib is the application's main nib and loads it. Upon loading, the nib initializes the objects it manages, which includes the navigation controller property, navController. The navigation controller loads its root view controller. Because the root view controller has an associated navigation item, the navigation controller adds a navigation bar above the view with the navigation item's title. Because MainWindow.xib handles all the application's initialization, all you do in the applicationDidFinishLaunching method is add the view to the window. After adding the navigation controller, you must provide navigation controls so a user can move from view to view. You can either add a button to the navigation bar itself or add a control to a view's canvas. The next few steps do both.

13. Open MainWindow.xib and select the navigation item in the document window (Figure 9-7). Change the navigation item's title to First View.

14. Drag a bar button item from the library to the navigation bar (Figure 9-8). Rename the button "Next."

15. Save and exit Interface Builder.

16. Open FirstViewController.h and add a new action called moveToNextView (Listing 9-3). Import SecondViewController and add SecondViewController as a property.

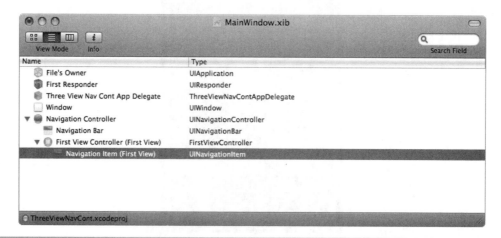

Figure 9-7   Selecting the navigation item in the Document window

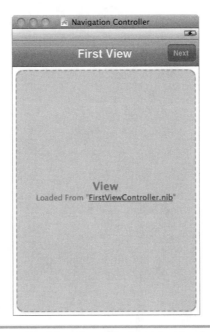

Figure 9-8   Adding a button to FirstViewController's navigation bar

Listing 9-3   FirstViewController.h

```
#import<UIKit/UIKit.h>
#import "SecondViewController.h"
@interface FirstViewController : UIViewController {
  SecondViewController * second;
}
@property (nonatomic, retain) SecondViewController * second;
- (IBAction) moveToNextView: (id) sender;
@end
```

17. Open FirstViewController.m and implement moveToNextView, as in Listing 9-4.

Listing 9-4   FirstViewController.m

```
#import "FirstViewController.h"
@implementation FirstViewController
@synthesize second;
- (IBAction) moveToNextView: (id) sender{
  self.second = [[[SecondViewController alloc]
```
(continued)

```
    initWithNibName:@"SecondViewController" bundle:nil] autorelease];
    [self.navigationController pushViewController:self.second animated:
YES];
}
- (void)dealloc {
[second release];
[super dealloc];
}
@end
```

18. Build the application.

19. Open MainWindow.xib in Interface Builder, select the FirstViewController, and connect its moveToNextView action to the Next button (Figure 9-9).

20. Save and exit Interface Builder.

21. Click Build And Go to run the application. Tapping the Next button results in the second view being displayed (Figure 9-10). Tap First View, and the application returns to the first view.

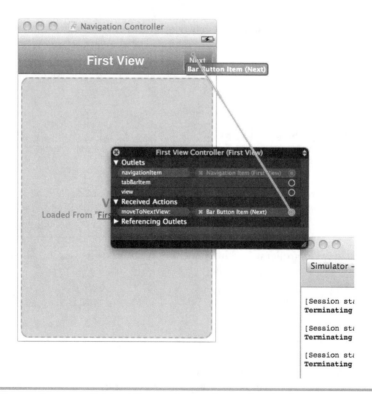

Figure 9-9   Connecting moveToNextView action to the navigation button

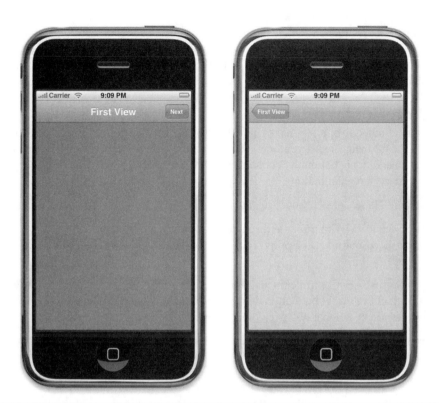

Figure 9-10   The application running in iPhone Simulator

In step 13, you changed the default title to your view's title. Actually, to be specific, you changed the default title to your view controller's navigation item's title. In step 14, you added a bar button item to the navigation bar and set it as the navigation bar item's rightBarButtonItem. Establishing this connection ensures the application displays the button on the bar's right. You then created an action that, when clicked, pushes the second view controller onto the navigation controller's stack. The navigation controller displays this view and a navigation bar containing the new view's navigation bar element. Notice you must push view controllers onto the stack manually through code, as in Listing 9-4.

```
[self.navigationController pushViewController:self.second animated: YES];
```

If a view controller is in a navigation controller's stack, then the navigationController property automatically refers to the navigation controller managing the stack. So, the navigation controller in ThreeViewNavContAppDelegate pushes FirstViewController's SecondViewController onto the stack. Note that setting the animated parameter to YES causes the view to slide in from the left.

(continued)

As the task illustrates, creating an application using a navigation controller and associated navigation bar is not difficult. The Back button, and popping a view controller from the navigation controller, is implemented for you. You provide the control and action to push view controllers onto the navigation controller's stack.

Adding Another View

You are not limited to bar buttons if you wish to push views onto a navigation controller's stack. In the following steps, you first add a bar button item to SecondViewController. You then add an additional button to SecondViewController's view, but instead of it being a bar button, you use a regular button.

1. Open the ThreeViewNavCont project in Xcode.

2. Open SecondViewController and add an IBOutlet for a UIBarButtonItem to SecondViewController as a property. Name the property navBut; don't forget to synthesize the property.

3. Open SecondViewController.m and implement the viewDidLoad method to set the navigationItem's right bar button item to navBut. Note that every UIViewController has a navigationItem and that it is a read-only property.

4. Open SecondViewController.xib in Interface Builder and add a new bar button item to the document window (Figure 9-11). Connect the newly added bar button item to the navBut outlet.

5. Save and exit Interface Builder.

6. Build and run the application, and the second view now displays its title in the navigation bar (Figure 9-12). But notice, clicking the Next button in the navigation bar has no effect because you haven't connected it to a method yet.

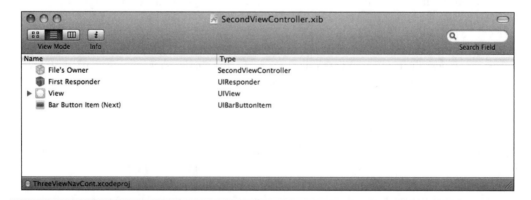

Figure 9-11 Adding a UIBarButtonItem

Figure 9-12 The application displaying the second view controller's navigation item's title

7. Open SecondViewController.h and add a new action called moveToNextView (Listing 9-5). Import ThirdViewController and ThreeViewNavContAppDelegate. Add a ThirdViewController as a property.

8. Open SecondViewController.m and implement moveToNextView, as in Listing 9-6. Save and build.

9. Open SecondViewController.xib in Interface Builder. Connect the bar button's selector to the File's Owner moveToNextView action (Figure 9-13).

10. Save and exit Interface Builder.

11. Build and run the application. The second view now has a Next button and tapping it moves to the next view (Figure 9-14). Now consider pushing a view onto the stack using a regular button.

(continued)

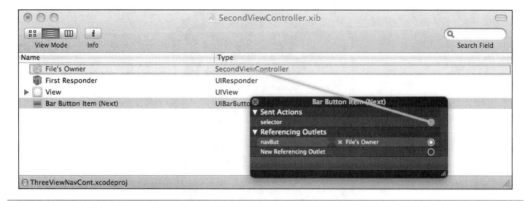

Figure 9-13 Connecting the bar button to the moveToNextView action

Figure 9-14 The second view with a Next button

Figure 9-15   Connecting button to moveToNextView method

12. Open SecondViewController.xib and add a button to the view. Connect the button to moveToNextView (Figure 9-15). Connect to the button's Touch Up Inside action.

13. Save and exit Interface Builder.

14. Build and run the application. Click the button on the second view, and it, too, navigates to the third view.

Using a button rather than a bar button item is that easy. Typically, though, in most iPhone applications, you will see a table in the view rather than a button (see Figure 9-1). For instance, SecondViewController might have an embedded table listing categories. Upon clicking a table row, you would invoke the moveToNextView method, passing the specific table row's identifier as a parameter. The App Store application is an example of this type of navigation (see Figure 9-1).

Listing 9-5   SecondViewController.h

```
#import<UIKit/UIKit.h>
#import "ThirdViewController.h"
@interface SecondViewController : UIViewController {
```

(continued)

```
    ThirdViewController * third;
    IBOutlet UIBarButtonItem * navBut;
}
@property (nonatomic, retain) IBOutlet UIBarButtonItem * navBut;
@property (nonatomic, retain) ThirdViewController * third;
-(IBAction) moveToNextView: (id) sender;
@end
```

Listing 9-6   SecondViewController.m

```
#import "SecondViewController.h"
@implementation SecondViewController
@synthesize third;
@synthesize navBut;
- (void) viewDidLoad{
  self.navigationItem.title = @"SecondView";
  self.navigationItem.rightBarButtonItem = navBut;
}
- (IBAction) moveToNextView: (id) sender{
  self.third = [[[ThirdViewController alloc]
  initWithNibName:@"ThirdViewController" bundle:nil] autorelease];
  [self.navigationController pushViewController: self.third animated:
YES];
}
- (void)dealloc {
  [third release];
  [super dealloc];
}
@end
```

Try This Duplicating the Utility Application

If you create a Utility Application using the Utility Application template, and then review the code, you will notice it uses a UINavigationBar a little differently than you might expect. But you can duplicate the template's result using more standard code, which is what you do in this task.

1. Create a new Window-based Application. Name it UtilityProjectTwo.

2. Add two UIViewController classes named FirstViewController and SecondViewController; be certain to have Xcode create nibs for both.

3. Open both nibs in Interface Builder and change the background color of both views.

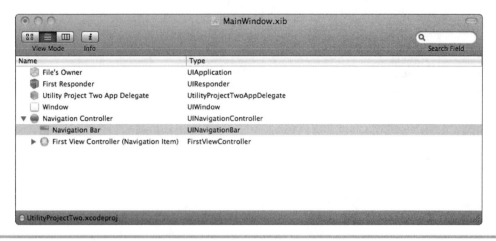

Figure 9-16 Adding a navigation controller

4. Following the same steps as the last exercise, add a navigation controller to MainWindow .xib and set the FirstViewController as the root view controller (Figure 9-16). Do not forget to create a navController IBOutlet in UtiltityProjectTwoAppDelegate and set the navController outlet in MainWindow.xib.

5. Change the window's background color to black.

6. Open FirstViewController.xib in Interface Builder. Drag a button onto the view's canvas. Change the button's type to Info Light in the Button Attributes Inspector (Figure 9-17).

7. Save and exit Interface Builder.

8. Open FirstViewController.h and FirstViewController.m and modify both files to match Listings 9-7 and 9-8.

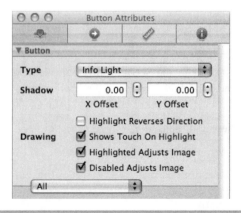

Figure 9-17 Changing the button's type

(continued)

Listing 9-7   FirstViewController.h

```
#import<UIKit/UIKit.h>
#import "SecondViewController.h"
@interface FirstViewController : UIViewController {
  SecondViewController * second;
}
@property (nonatomic, retain) SecondViewController * second;
- (IBAction)showDetails:(id)sender;
@end
```

Listing 9-8   FirstViewController.m

```
#import "FirstViewController.h"
@implementation FirstViewController
@synthesize second;
- (void) viewWillAppear: (BOOL) animated{
  [self.navigationController setNavigationBarHidden:YES
animated: NO];
}
- (IBAction)showDetails:(id)sender {
  self.second = [[[SecondViewController alloc]
  initWithNibName:@"SecondViewController" bundle:nil] autorelease];
  self.second.modalTransitionStyle =
UIModalTransitionStyleFlipHorizontal;
  [self presentModalViewController:self.second animated:YES];
}
- (void)dealloc {
  [second release];
  [super dealloc];
}
@end
```

9. Open SecondViewController.h and SecondViewController.m and modify both files to match Listings 9-9 and 9-10. Save and Build the application.

Listing 9-9   SecondViewController.h

```
#import<UIKit/UIKit.h>
@interface SecondViewController : UIViewController {
}
- (IBAction) popSecondView;
@end
```

Listing 9-10   SecondViewController.m

```
#import "SecondViewController.h"
@implementation SecondViewController
- (IBAction) popSecondView{
  [self dismissModalViewControllerAnimated:YES];
}
- (void)dealloc {
  [super dealloc];
}
@end
```

10. Open FirstViewController.xib and connect the button to the showDetails action.

11. Open SecondViewController.xib and add a navigation bar to the view's canvas just below the view's status bar. Also add a bar button item to the newly added navigation bar.

12. Change the navigation bar's style to Black Translucent (Figure 9-18). Save and close the nib.

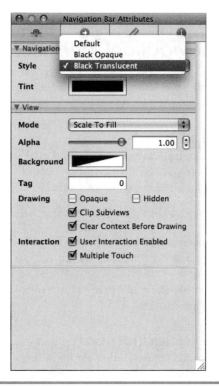

Figure 9-18   Changing to Black Translucent

(continued)

13. Connect the newly added bar button item to the File's Owner popSecondView Action.

14. Save and exit Interface Builder.

15. Build and run the application.

Refer to FirstViewController in Listing 9-8. The first problem with trying to duplicate the Utility Application template's results is how to make the navigation bar invisible on the first view but visible on the second view. Adding the following line to the viewWillAppear: method in FirstViewController accomplishes the invisible/visible requirement and ensures the navigation bar is hidden on the first view.

```
[self.navigationController setNavigationBarHidden:YES animated: NO];
```

The showDetails: method is the action connected to the First View's info button. When you click the info button, it invokes showDetails:. Note that when the navigation controller pops the second view from the stack, the first view's viewWillAppear: is invoked, ensuring the navigation bar is again hidden.

More on the UINavigationController

You are not limited to pushing items onto a stack. You can also pop items off the stack. You can also modify the navigation bar, hiding elements, adding new ones, and making other modifications.

Pushing and Popping

You pop view controllers from a stack using the method popViewControllerAnimated:. This method pops the top view controller off the navigation controller's stack and updates the displayed view to the stack's next view controller's view.

```
(UIViewController *) popViewControllerAnimated: (BOOL) animated
```

The method takes one parameter, which indicates if the transition should be animated. The method also returns the popped view controller, should you wish to retain it for future use.

Other methods you might use include popToRootViewControllerAnimated: and popToViewController:animated:. Refer to Apple's online reference, "UINavigationController Class Reference," for more information.

Configuring the Navigation Bar

In the previous example, you hid the navigation bar by calling the navigation controller's setNavigationBarHidden: method.

```
- (void) setNavigationBarHidden: (BOOL) hidden animated: (BOOL) animated
```

This method hides or displays the navigation bar, depending upon if you passed YES or NO as the initial parameter. You also specify if the navigation bar should slide in from the top by specifying YES for the animated parameter.

You might also change a navigation bar's style by changing its style property. You can use code to change the navigation bar's style, but the easiest way to do this is through Interface Builder. You can also change a navigation bar's color. You change the color using the tintColor property.

Try This Using a Navigation Controller in a Tab

Applications usually use a navigation bar with other navigation views, such as a tab bar or table view. You haven't learned about table views yet—you won't learn about using a table view with a navigation bar until Chapter 10. However, you learned about the tab bar in Chapter 8. A navigation bar might be placed within a tab bar. For instance, returning to the App Store application, notice the navigation screens are steps within the Categories tab (see Figure 9-1). The Featured, Categories, Top 25, and Updates tabs are different views on the same data. The Search tab is a subtask. Within the Categories tab, there is a navigation bar combined with a table view. This combination provides a way to drill down hierarchically to a specific application.

Although you don't learn about tables until Chapter 10, consider a navigation bar in a tab.

1. Create a new Window-based Application. Name the application NavInTab.

2. Create two new UIViewController classes. Name the first FirstTabViewController and the second StepTwoViewController; be certain to create nibs for both.

3. Open both newly created nibs and change the background color for each view.

4. Open MainWindow.xib and add a UITabBarController to the document.

5. Delete the first tab bar view controller. Drag a navigation controller to the document and drop it so it is the first item below the tab bar (Figure 9-19).

6. Change the navigation controller's root view controller to FirstTabViewController by changing its class and nib name in the Inspector. The canvas should indicate the view is from FirstTabViewController.nib (Figure 9-20).

7. Change the navigation item's title from "Root View Controller" to "step one."

8. Drag a bar button item from the library to the navigation item in the Document window (Figure 9-21). Change the button's title to "Next." The button should automatically be set as the navigation item's rightBarButtonItem. If not, connect the navigation item's rightBarButton outlet to the newly added bar button item.

9. Save and exit Interface Builder.

(continued)

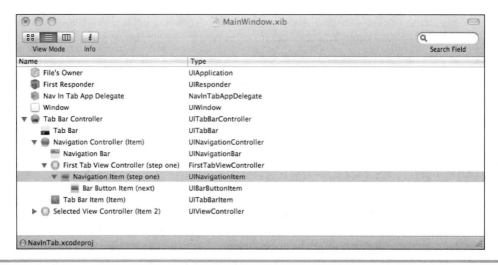

Figure 9-19 Adding a navigation controller

Figure 9-20 Canvas indicates view is from a different nib

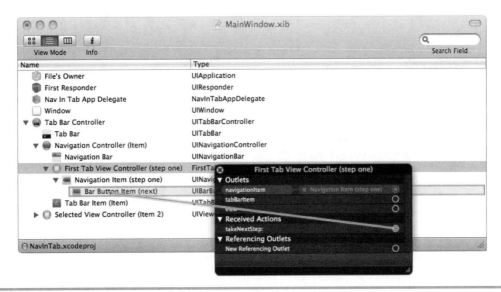

Figure 9-21 Bar button added to document window

10. Open NavInTabAppDelegate.h and NavInTabAppDelate.m and adopt the UITabBarController Delegate protocol. Also add a UITabBarController property and a UINavigationController property. Modify applicationDidFinishLaunching so it loads the tabBarController property's root view. The files should match Listings 9-11 and 9-12. Save and build.

Listing 9-11   NavInTabAppDelegate.h

```
#import<UIKit/UIKit.h>

@interface NavInTabAppDelegate : NSObject<UIApplicationDelegate,
UITabBarControllerDelegate> {
UIWindow *window;
UITabBarController *tabBarController;
UINavigationController *navBarController;
}
@property (nonatomic, retain) IBOutlet UIWindow *window;
@property (nonatomic, retain) IBOutlet UITabBarController
*tabBarController;
@property (nonatomic, retain) IBOutlet UINavigationController *
navBarController;
@end
```

(continued)

Listing 9-12 NavInTabAppDelegate.m

```objc
#import "NavInTabAppDelegate.h"
@implementation NavInTabAppDelegate
@synthesize window;
@synthesize tabBarController;
@synthesize navBarController;
- (void)applicationDidFinishLaunching:(UIApplication *)application {
  [window addSubview:tabBarController.view];
  [window makeKeyAndVisible];
}
- (void)dealloc {
  [window release];
  [tabBarController release];
  [navBarController release];
[super dealloc];
}
@end
```

11. Open MainWindow.xib in Interface Builder and connect the NavInTabAppDelegate's navBarController to the newly added navigation controller (Figure 9-22). Connect the tabBarController to the newly added tab bar controller.

12. Save and exit Interface Builder.

13. Open StepTwoViewController.h and implement the viewDidLoad method so that it sets the navigationItem's title to "step two" (Listing 9-13).

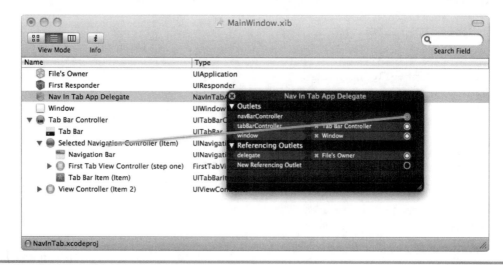

Figure 9-22 Connecting the navBarController

Listing 9-13   SecondViewController'sviewDidLoad method

```
- (void)viewDidLoad {
  [super viewDidLoad];
  self.navigationItem.title = @"step two";
}
```

14. Open FirstTabViewController.h and import StepTwoViewController.h and
    NavInTabAppDelegate.h. Also add the method signature, takeNextStep (Listing 9-14).

Listing 9-14   FirstTabViewController.h

```
#import<UIKit/UIKit.h>
#import "StepTwoViewController.h"
#import "NavInTabAppDelegate.h"
@interface FirstTabViewController : UIViewController {
}
- (IBAction) takeNextStep: (id) sender;
@end
```

15. Open FirstTabViewController.m and implement the newly added action. The file should
    match Listing 9-15.

Listing 9-15   FirstTabViewController.m

```
#import "FirstTabViewController.h"
@implementation FirstTabViewController
- (IBAction) takeNextStep : (id) sender{
  StepTwoViewController *varSecondViewController = [[StepTwoViewController
alloc] initWithNibName:@"StepTwoViewController" bundle:nil];
  [self.navigationController pushViewController:varSecondViewController
animated: YES];
}
- (void)dealloc {
  [super dealloc];
}
@end
```

16. Open MainWindow.xib and connect the bar button item to the FirstViewController's
    takeNextStep method.

17. Save and exit Interface Builder.

18. Build and run the application in the iPhone Simulator. You should have a two-tab
    application, where the first tab has an embedded navigation control (Figure 9-23).

(continued)

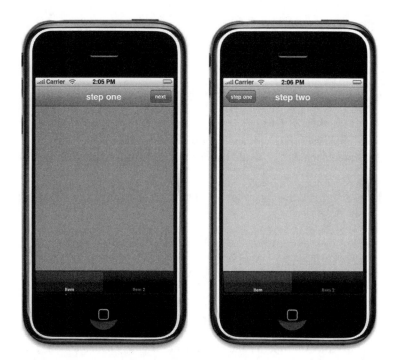

Figure 9-23 The finished application in iPhone Simulator

Summary

Creating an application with a navigation bar is straightforward. In the application's MainWindow.xib, add a UINavigationController. Set the navigation controller's root view controller, and create one or more other view controllers. Then add code that pushes the view controllers onto the navigation controller's stack. When a view controller is pushed onto the stack, it becomes the topmost view controller, and so the application displays the view controller's view. Popping a view controller off the stack is provided by default if you do not make the navigation bar's Back button invisible. If you do make the Back button invisible, or somehow disable the button, you must use one of the navigation controller's methods for popping view controllers.

In this chapter, you learned how to create an application containing a navigation controller with three views. You then used a navigation controller to duplicate the Utility Application template's results. Finally, you embedded a navigation controller within a tab in a tab bar. But this chapter did omit the most common navigation controller use: a table combined with a navigation controller. In the next chapter, after learning about tables, I correct this omission by presenting a navigation controller combined with a table controller. After learning about this combination, you will have a good enough knowledge of view controllers that you should be able to tackle most iPhone application navigation strategies.

Chapter 10

Tables Using UITableView and UITableViewController

Key Skills & Concepts

- Understanding table views

- Understanding table view delegates

- Understanding table view data sources

- Grouping and indexing table rows

- Selecting table rows

- Modifying a table's appearance

- Using a table in a navigation controller

- Editing a table's rows

Table views display content in a list. Tables have a single column and multiple rows. They can scroll vertically and display large data sets. For example, the Notes application is a good example of an application containing a table.

Note's first screen is a list comprised of zero or more notes. In Figure 10-1, the list contains three notes. Each row presents the note's text, transcription time, and a disclosure arrow.

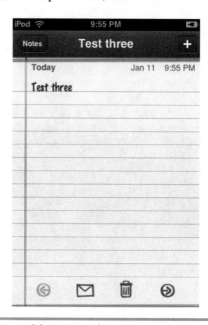

Figure 10-1 The Notes application consists of a UITableView and UINavigationBar.

Figure 10-2 Creating a new note using the Notes application

The disclosure arrow indicates that details are on the next screen. Upon tapping a row, the application takes the user to the detail view for that particular row's note (Figure 10-2).

Tables can be grouped and indexed. For instance, the Music application on an iPod touch uses an index (Figure 10-3). The Settings application's rows are grouped (Figure 10-4).

Table rows might also contain a picture and other customizations, as the YouTube and App Store applications illustrate (Figure 10-5).

As the applications in the first five figures illustrate, the table view is a powerful control for listing items. You can modify rows, add images, select rows, and edit them. In this chapter, you learn how to use tables. You learn how to build a table, change its style to grouped, add an index to it, and accessorize it. You also learn how to place a table in a navigation controller and how to edit a table's rows. It is a long chapter, but the table view is a powerful control.

UITableView

The UITableView class represents a table view. This class is for displaying and editing information lists. It consists of a single column of multiple rows. Users can scroll vertically to navigate through a table's rows. Each row contains a cell. You can customize that cell's appearance considerably.

You can index tables and create tables with zero or more sections. When you create a table, you have a choice of two styles: UITableViewStylePlain or UITableViewStyleGrouped. A plain table style presents a table like that in Figure 10-3. A grouped table presents a table like that in Figure 10-4. You see examples implementing both styles later in this chapter.

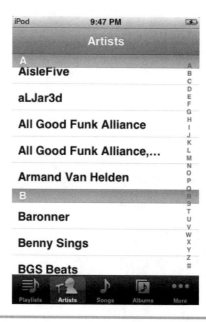

Figure 10-3 The Music application on an iPod touch uses a UITableView with an index.

Figure 10-4 The Settings application uses a grouped UITableView.

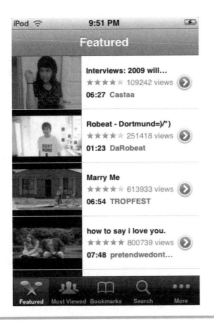 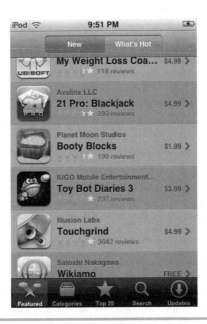

Figure 10-5 The YouTube and App Store applications use images and custom cells.

UITableView classes have an associated UITableViewController, a UITableViewDelegate, and a UITableViewDataSource. The UITableViewController is the controller class for a table view. You create an instance of this class to manage the UITableView. The UITableViewDelegate is a protocol you adopt in a custom class you write. This protocol allows you to manage selections, configure headers and footers, and manage cells. The UITableViewDataSource is also a protocol you adopt in a custom class. This protocol allows you to manage a table's data source.

UITableViewDelegate and UITableViewDataSource

The UITableViewDelegate and UITableViewDataSource are protocols at least one class in your application must adopt if your application contains a UITableView. You can create your own custom classes to adopt these protocols, or create a UITableViewController that automatically adopts these protocols. If you choose to use a UITableViewController rather than custom classes, you simply connect the table view's dataSource and delegate outlets to the UITableViewController. You can then implement both protocols' methods in the UITableViewController.

UITableViewDelegate

A UITable's delegate adopts the UITableViewDelegate protocol. This protocol manages selections, headers, footers, and other tasks. Table 10-1 lists the methods covered in this chapter.

Method	Description
tableView:heightForRowAtIndexPath:	Provides height to use in displaying a row.
tableView:accessoryButtonTappedForRowWithIndexPath:	Handles a row's detail disclosure button after it is tapped.
tableView:willSelectRowAtIndexPath:	Handles a row about to be selected.
tableView:didSelectRowAtIndexPath:	Handles a row once it is selected.
tableView:editingStyleForRowAtIndexPath:	Returns the editing style of a row. This determines if a cell displays an insertion accessory, deletion accessory, or no accessory.

Table 10-1 UITableViewDelegate Methods in this Chapter

UITableViewDataSource

A UITable's data source adopts the UITableViewDataSource protocol. A table's data source provides the table with its data. Table 10-2 lists the UITableViewDataSource protocol methods covered in this chapter.

tableView:numberOfRowsInSection: and tableView:cellForRowAtIndexPath:

Required methods that every table's data source must implement are the tableView: numberOfRowsInSection and tableView:cellForRowAtIndexPath methods.

Method	Description
tableView:numberOfRowsInSection:	Provides the number of rows in a section.
tableView:cellForRowAtIndexPath:	Obtains cell from a data source to place at a particular row.
numberOfSectionsInTableView:	Obtains the number of sections in a table view from a data source.
sectionIndexTitlesForTableView:	Obtains titles for a table view from a data source.
tableView:commitEditingStyle: forRowAtIndexPath:	Commits a cell's editing.
tableView:canEditRowAtIndexPath:	Returns a Boolean value, informing a table view if a row can be edited.
tableView:canMoveRowAtIndexPath:	Returns a Boolean value, informing a table view if a row can be moved.
tableView:moveRowAtIndexPath:toIndexPath:	Allows a table cell to be moved.

Table 10-2 UITableViewDataSource Methods in this Chapter

```
- (NSInteger)tableView:(UITableView *) tableView
numberOfRowsInSection: (NSInteger) section
- (UITableViewCell *)tableView:(UITableView *) tableView
cellForRowAtIndexPath: (NSIndexPath *) indexPath
```

The tableView:numberOfRowsInSection: method informs the data source how many rows a section contains. The tableView:cellForRowAtIndexPath: method provides a table view with its cells.

Try This | Adopting the UITableViewDelegate and UITableViewDataSource

In this first task, you create a UIViewController and have it manage the table view. You also implement a custom class that adopts the UITableViewDelegate and UITableViewDataSource.

Creating an Empty Table

1. Create a new Window-based application. Name the application TableProjectOne.

2. Create a new UIViewController subclass. Name the class MyViewController.

3. Create a new empty xib named MyViewController.

4. Open MyViewController.xib.

5. Add a view to the document window and add a table view to the view (Figure 10-6). Be certain to resize the table view to completely fill the view.

6. Change the File's Owner to MyViewController. Connect the File's Owner view to the view in the document window.

7. Save and exit Interface Builder.

8. Add a MyViewController as an IBOutlet to TableProjectOneAppDelegate (Listings 10-1 and 10-2).

9. Modify applicationDidFinishLaunching so it adds the viewController property's view. Build the application.

10. Open MainWindow.xib and drag a View Controller to the document window. Change its class and Nib Name to MyViewController.

11. Connect the TableProjectOneAppDelegate's viewController outlet to the MyViewController added to the document window.

12. Save and exit Interface Builder.

13. Build and run the application. The application loads an empty table into the iPhone Simulator (Figure 10-7).

(continued)

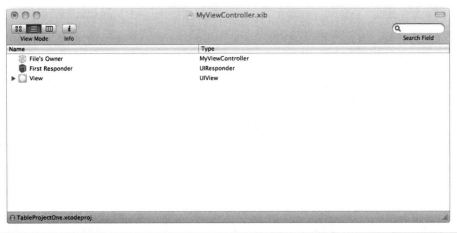

Figure 10-6 Adding a UITableView to an Interface Builder project

NOTE

In steps 1–13, you added the table view as a subview to the view in the MyViewController Nib. If you preferred, you could omit the extra view and just add the table view directly as the nib's view. But note, you would also change MyViewController from a UIViewController, to a UITableViewController. Point is, you don't have to put the UITableView inside a UIView in order to use it. A UITableView can be added directly to the XIB and connected to a table view controller's view outlet, and it will work the same way. The next Try This example illustrates.

Figure 10-7   An application with an empty UITableView

Listing 10-1   TableProjectOneAppDelegate.h

```
#import <UIKit/UIKit.h>
#import "MyViewController.h"
@interface TableProjectOneAppDelegate : NSObject
<UIApplicationDelegate> {
 UIWindow *window;
 IBOutlet MyViewController * viewController;
}
@property (nonatomic, retain) IBOutlet MyViewController *
viewController;
@property (nonatomic, retain) IBOutlet UIWindow *window;
@end
```

(continued)

Listing 10-2 TableProjectOneAppDelegate.m

```
#import "TableProjectOneAppDelegate.h"
@implementation TableProjectOneAppDelegate
@synthesize window;
@synthesize viewController;
- (void)applicationDidFinishLaunching:(UIApplication *)application {
  [window addSubview:self.viewController.view];
  [window makeKeyAndVisible];
}
- (void)dealloc {
  [window release];
  [viewController release];
  [super dealloc];
}
@end
```

In this task's first step, you created a UITableView as a subview of a UIView. When the UIViewController loads and displays its view, the view automatically displays its subview, the table view. But all it loads is an empty table. To actually load data into the table, you must implement a delegate and a data source. Moreover, the data source must actually provide data for the table. In the next few steps, you create a delegate and data source for the table.

Adding a Delegate and Data Source

1. Create a new NSObject named TableHandler. Change TableHandler so it adopts the UITableViewDelegate and UITableViewDataSource protocols (Listings 10-3 and 10-4).

2. Add an NSArray property and a method named fillList for filling the array.

3. Implement the fillArray method so the application has data to load into the table's cells.

4. Implement the tableView:numberOfRowsInSection: and tableView:cellForRowAtIndexPath: methods.

5. Modify MyViewController to have a TableHandler property (Listings 10-5 and 10-6). Ensure the property is an IBOutlet.

6. Implement the viewDidLoad method in MyViewController so that it calls its TableHandler's fillList method.

7. Save and compile.

8. Open MyViewController.xib and drag an object to the document window. Change the object's class to TableHandler (Figure 10-8).

9. Connect the File's Owner myHandler outlet to the newly added TableHandler (Figure 10-9).

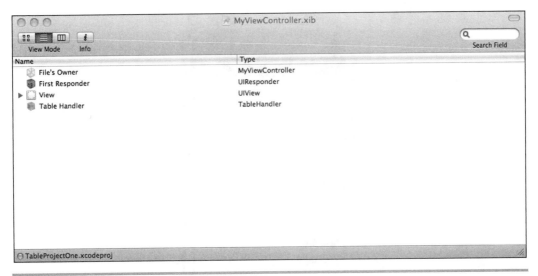

Figure 10-8 Adding a TableHandler reference to Interface Builder

10. Connect the table view's dataSource and delegate outlets to the newly added TableHandler.

11. Save and exit Interface Builder.

12. Click Build And Go. The application displays 20 rows (Figure 10-10).

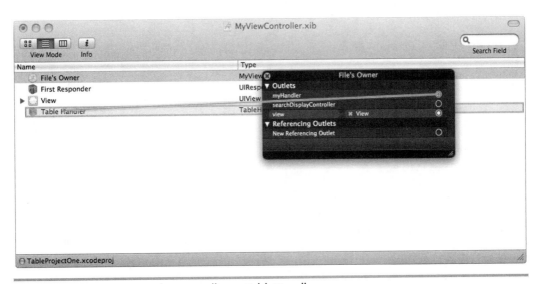

Figure 10-9 Connecting the controller to TableHandler

(continued)

Figure 10-10 The project running in iPhone Simulator

Listing 10-3 TableHandler.h

```
#import <Foundation/Foundation.h>
@interface TableHandler : NSObject <UITableViewDelegate,
UITableViewDataSource> {
 NSArray * tableDataList;
}
@property (nonatomic, retain) NSArray * tableDataList;
- (void) fillList;
@end
```

Listing 10-4 TableHandler.m

```
#import "TableHandler.h"
@implementation TableHandler
@synthesize tableDataList;
- (void) fillList {
```

```
NSArray * tempArray = [[[NSArray alloc] initWithObjects:@"Item One",
@"Item Two", @"Item Three", @"Item Four", @"Item Five", @"Item Six",
@"Item Seven", @"Item Eight", @"Item Nine", @"Item Ten", @"Item Eleven",
@"Item Twelve", @"Item Thirteen", @"Item Fourteen", @"Item Fifteen",
@"Item Sixteen", @"Item Seventeen", @"Item Eighteen", @"Item Nineteen",
@"Item Twenty", nil] autorelease];
self.tableDataList = tempArray;
}
-(NSInteger) tableView : (UITableView *) tableView numberOfRowsInSection:
(NSInteger) section {
return [self.tableDataList count];
}
-(UITableViewCell *) tableView : (UITableView *) tableView
cellForRowAtIndexPath: (NSIndexPath *) indexPath {
UITableViewCell *cell = [tableView
dequeueReusableCellWithIdentifier:@"acell"];
if(cell == nil) {
cell = [[[UITableViewCell alloc] initWithStyle:UITableViewCellStyle
Default reuseIdentifier:@"acell"] autorelease];
}
cell.textLabel.text = [self.tableDataList objectAtIndex:[indexPath row]];
return cell;
}
- (void)dealloc {
[tableDataList release];
[super dealloc];
}
@end
```

Listing 10-5   MyViewController.h

```
#import <UIKit/UIKit.h>
#import "TableHandler.h"
@interface MyViewController : UIViewController {
IBOutlet TableHandler * myHandler;
}
@property (nonatomic, retain) IBOutlet TableHandler * myHandler;
@end
```

Listing 10-6   TableProjectOneAppDelegate.m

```
#import "MyViewController.h"
@implementation MyViewController
@synthesize myHandler;
```

(continued)

```
- (void) viewDidLoad {
 [self.myHandler fillList];
}
- (void)dealloc {
 [self.myHandler release];
 [super dealloc];
}
@end
```

UITableViewController

The UITableViewController manages a table view. The UITableView can use objects defined in a table's nib to define a table's delegate and data source, or it can use itself as the delegate and data source. For instance, in the previous example, you set the table's delegate and data source properties to the TableHandler class. You could have added a UITableViewController, set it as the table's File's Owner, and then set its outlets to TableHandler.

If you do not provide a delegate and data source in a table's nib, a UITableViewController sets its data source and delegate to itself. By doing this, the UITableViewController saves you the work of having to create your own classes so they adopt the delegate and data source. You still must implement any data source and delegate methods desired. However, rather than implementing these methods in separate custom classes, you implement them in a UITableViewController subclass. The UITableViewController then functions as the table's controller, delegate, and data source.

Try This Using a UITableViewController

In the last Try This task, you did things the hard way. However, the task's purpose was to illustrate adding a table view as a subview, with no controller. In this Try This task, you use a UITableViewController. Moreover, rather than adding a table view as a subview, you add it directly to the xib as the primary view.

1. Create a new Window-based application. Name the application TableProjectTwo.

2. Create a new UITableViewController subclass. Name the class MyTableViewController (Listings 10-9 and 10-10).

3. Create a new empty xib named MyTableViewController.

4. Open MyTableViewController.xib.

5. Add a table view to the document window (Figure 10-11).

6. Change the File's Owner to MyTableViewController if it is not already. Connect the File's Owner view to the table view in the document window.

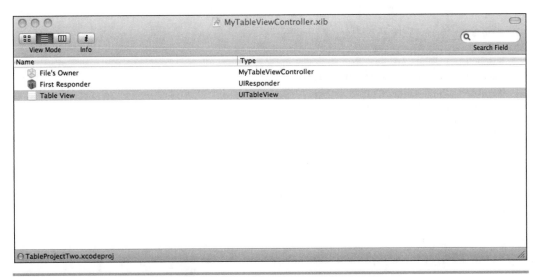

Figure 10-11   Adding a UITableView to an Interface Builder project

7. Connect the newly added table view's dataSource and delegate outlets to the File's Owner.

8. Save and exit Interface Builder.

9. Add a MyTableViewController as an IBOutlet to TableProjectTwoAppDelegate (Listings 10-7 and 10-8). Do not forget to import MyTableViewController.

10. Modify applicationDidFinishLaunching so it adds the viewController property's view. Build the application.

11. Open MainWindow.xib and drag a Table View Controller to the document window. Change its class and Nib Name to MyTableViewController.

12. Connect the TableProjectTwoAppDelegate's viewController outlet to the MyTableViewController added to the document window.

13. Save and exit Interface Builder.

14. Implement the table delegate and datasource methods the same as you did in TableHandler in this chapter's first Try This task.

15. Modify MyTableViewController so that it has an NSArray called tableDataList and have it populated in the viewDidLoad method.

16. Build and run the application. The application loads an empty table into the iPhone Simulator. The results should match the previous task's results (Figure 10-10).

(continued)

Listing 10-7 TableProjectTwoAppDelegate.

```
#import <UIKit/UIKit.h>
#import "MyTableViewController.h"
@interface TableProjectTwoAppDelegate : NSObject
<UIApplicationDelegate> {
 UIWindow *window;
 IBOutlet MyTableViewController * viewController;
}
@property (nonatomic, retain) IBOutlet MyTableViewController *
viewController;
@property (nonatomic, retain) IBOutlet UIWindow *window;
@end
```

Listing 10-8 TableProjectTwoAppDelegate.m

```
#import "TableProjectTwoAppDelegate.h"
@implementation TableProjectTwoAppDelegate
@synthesize window;
@synthesize viewController;
- (void)applicationDidFinishLaunching:(UIApplication *)application {
 [window addSubview:self.viewController.view];
 [window makeKeyAndVisible];
}
- (void)dealloc {
 [window release];
 [viewController release];
 [super dealloc];
}
#import <Foundation/Foundation.h>
@interface MyTableViewController : UITableViewController {
 NSArray * tableDataList;
}
@property (nonatomic, retain) NSArray * tableDataList;
@end
```

Listing 10-9 MyTableViewController.m

```
#import "MyTableViewController.h"
@implementation MyTableViewController
@synthesize tableDataList;
- (void) viewDidLoad {
 NSArray * tempArray = [[[NSArray alloc] initWithObjects:@"Item One",
```

```
@"Item Two", @"Item Three", @"Item Four", @"Item Five", @"Item Six",
@"Item Seven", @"Item Eight", @"Item Nine", @"Item Ten", @"Item Eleven",
@"Item Twelve", @"Item Thirteen", @"Item Fourteen", @"Item Fifteen",
@"Item Sixteen", @"Item Seventeen", @"Item Eighteen", @"Item Nineteen",
@"Item Twenty", nil] autorelease];
 self.tableDataList = tempArray;
}
- (NSInteger) tableView : (UITableView *) tableView
numberOfRowsInSection: (NSInteger) section {
 return [self.tableDataList count];
}
- (UITableViewCell *) tableView : (UITableView *) tableView
cellForRowAtIndexPath: (NSIndexPath *) indexPath {
 UITableViewCell *cell = [tableView
dequeueReusableCellWithIdentifier:@"acell"];
 if(cell == nil) {
 cell = [[[UITableViewCell alloc] initWithStyle:UITableViewCellStyle
Default reuseIdentifier:@"acell"] autorelease];
 }
 cell.textLabel.text = [self.tableDataList objectAtIndex:[indexPath
row]];
 return cell;
}
- (void)dealloc {
 [tableDataList release];
 [super dealloc];
}
@end
```

Grouping and Indexing

Tables have two main styles: grouped and plain. Figure 10-3 illustrates a table with a plain style, while Figure 10-4 illustrates a table with a grouped style. Plain tables might also be indexed. An index sorts the rows and makes navigation quicker by letting a user jump to different locations in the index.

Grouped Table Style

Grouping is accomplished by changing a UITableView's style to grouped. You then tell a UITableView's data source how many sections belong in the table and how many rows belong in each section. The class adopting the UITableViewDataSource protocol informs the table how many sections via the numberOfSectionsInTableView method. It informs the table how many rows are in each section via the tableView:numberOfRowsInSection: method.

```
- (NSInteger)numberOfSectionsInTableView:(UITableView *)tableView
- (NSInteger)tableView:(UITableView *) tableView
numberOfRowsInSection: (NSInteger)section
```

Each grouping might have a title. You add titles by having your UITableViewDataSource protocol adoption implement the tableView:titleForHeaderInSection method. This method provides a table view with a title for a section's header. You might also wish adding a footer to each grouping by implementing the tableView:titleForFooterInSection: method.

```
- (NSString *)tableView:(UITableView *)tableView titleForHeaderIn
Section:(NSInteger)section
- (NSString *)tableView:(UITableView *)tableView titleForFooterIn
Section:(NSInteger)section
```

Try This Grouping

1. Copy TableProjectOne from the first task to a new location. Open the newly copied TableProjectOne in Xcode.

2. Modify the array in TableHandler so tableDataList consists of an array of five arrays (Listing 10-10).

3. Add the numberOfSectionsInTableView and titleForHeaderInSection methods to TableHandler.m (Listing 10-11).

4. Modify numberOfRowsInSection to return 2.

5. Modify cellForRowAtIndexPath so it uses the section and the row (Listing 10-12).

6. Open MyViewController.xib in Interface Builder.

7. Change the table view's Style from Plain to Grouped (Figure 10-12).

8. Save and exit Interface Builder. Click Build And Go. The table's rows are grouped (Figure 10-13).

The fillList method initializes an NSArray of five NSArrays. The numberOfSectionsInTable View method simply returns five. Although not realistic, this number matches the number of data arrays (tempArrayA through tempArrayB). The tableView:titleForHeaderInSection is hard-coded to return A, B, C, D, or E, depending upon the current section. When the table loads, five sections are created, each with a title from the titleForHeaderInSection method. Each row's content is determined from the cellForRowAtIndexPath method.

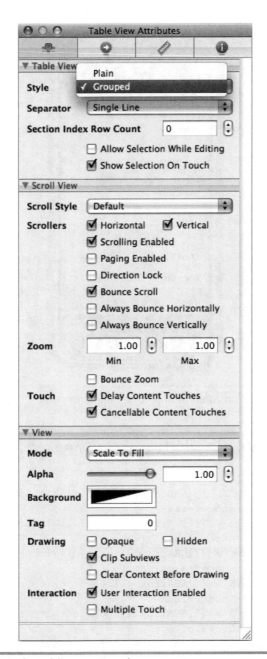

Figure 10-12   Changing the table to grouped

(continued)

Figure 10-13 The application running in iPhone Simulator

Listing 10-10 Table's list modified to an array of arrays

```
- (void) fillList {
 NSArray * tempArrayA = [[[NSArray alloc] initWithObjects:@"AItem One",
@"AItem Two", nil] autorelease];
 NSArray * tempArrayB = [[[NSArray alloc] initWithObjects:@"BItem Three",
@"BItem Four", nil] autorelease];
 NSArray * tempArrayC = [[[NSArray alloc] initWithObjects:@"CItem Five",
@"CItem Six", nil] autorelease];
 NSArray * tempArrayD = [[[NSArray alloc] initWithObjects:@"DItem Seven",
@"DItem Eight", nil] autorelease];
 NSArray * tempArrayE = [[[NSArray alloc] initWithObjects:@"EItem Nine",
@"EItem Ten", nil] autorelease];
 NSArray * tempArray = [[[NSArray alloc] initWithObjects:tempArrayA,
tempArrayB, tempArrayC, tempArrayD, tempArrayE, nil] autorelease];
 self.tableDataList = tempArray;
 }
```

Listing 10-11   Modifications to TableHandler.m to support grouping

```
- (NSInteger) numberOfSectionsInTableView: (UITableView *) tableView {
 return 5;
}
- (NSString *) tableView: (UITableView *) tableView
titleForHeaderInSection: (NSInteger) section {
 switch (section) {
 case 0: return @"A"; break;
 case 1: return @"B"; break;
 case 2: return @"C"; break;
 case 3: return @"D"; break;
 case 4: return @"E"; break;
 }
 return nil;
}
- (NSInteger) tableView : (UITableView *) tableView
numberOfRowsInSection: (NSInteger) section {
 return 2;
}
```

Listing 10-12   The cellForRowAtIndexPath modified to use row and section

```
- (UITableViewCell *) tableView : (UITableView *) tableView
cellForRowAtIndexPath: (NSIndexPath *) indexPath {
 UITableViewCell *cell = [tableView dequeueReusableCellWithIdentifier:
@"acell"];
 if(cell == nil) {
 cell = [[[UITableViewCell alloc] initWithStyle:UITableViewCellStyle
Default reuseIdentifier: @"acell"] autorelease];
 }
 cell.textLabel.text = [[self.tableDataList objectAtIndex:indexPath.
section]
objectAtIndex:indexPath.row];
 return cell;
}
```

Indexing

Tables can be indexed. To index a table, a table's style should be plain. As with grouping, you implement the numberOfSectionsInTableView: and tableView:numberOfRowsInSection:

methods, but you also implement a third method: sectionIndexTitlesForTableView:. This method, implemented in your UITableViewDataSource adoptee, creates the titles that appear along a table's right side. Upon clicking one of these values, a user is taken directly to the group with the corresponding title.

```
- (NSArray *) sectionIndexTitlesForTableView:(UITableView *) tableView
```

Try This Indexing

1. Open the TableProjectOne from the grouping Try This task.

2. Open MyViewController.xib and change the table view's style to Plain.

3. Save and exit Interface Builder. Click Build And Go. Notice the application is still grouped, but the table's appearance is changed (Figure 10-14).

Figure 10-14 A plain table with groupings

4. Implement the sectionIndexTitlesForTableView method, as in Listing 10-13, in TableHandler.m.

5. Click Build And Go. The application has an index (Figure 10-15).

Listing 10-13 The sectionIndexTitlesForTableView method

```
- (NSArray *) sectionIndexTitlesForTableView: (UITableView *)
tableView {
 NSArray * keys = [[[NSArray alloc] initWithObjects: @"A", @"B", @"C",
@"D", @"E",nil] autorelease];
 return keys;
}
```

Figure 10-15 The indexed table running in iPhone Simulator

(continued)

NOTE

Don't let this chapter's reliance on simple NSArrays fool you into thinking you must use this collection class to hold a table's data. You can use any collection class, or any other method you deem appropriate, provided you implement methods to obtain the data correctly.

Images in Tables

Adding an image to a table, provided you are happy with the image appearing in the row's upper-left corner, is not difficult. Simply add an image to the cell in the tableView: cellForRowAtIndexPath: method. Remember, this method loads a UITableViewCell into a row. You can use this method to initialize a table cell with an image using the UITableViewCell's imageView.image property. The image is then displayed in the table's row.

Try This Adding an Image

1. Open the last task's project. From the book's Resources folder, add the images power.png, icon.png, package.png, web.png, and colorize.png to the project's Resources folder.

2. Modify the tableView:cellForRowAtIndexPath: method to match Listing 10-14.

3. Click Build And Go. Notice the images overrun the table cell bounds (Figure 10-16).

Listing 10-14   The tableView:cellForRowAtIndexPath: method added to TableHandler.m

```
- (UITableViewCell *) tableView : (UITableView *) tableView
cellForRowAtIndexPath: (NSIndexPath *) indexPath {
 UITableViewCell *cell = [tableView
 dequeueReusableCellWithIdentifier:@"acell"];
 if(cell == nil) {
 cell = [[[UITableViewCell alloc] initWithStyle:
UITableViewCellStyleDefault reuseIdentifier:@"acell"] autorelease];
 }
 cell.textLabel.text = [[self.tableDataList objectAtIndex: indexPath.
section] objectAtIndex: indexPath.row];
 UIImage * image;
 switch (indexPath.section) {
 case 0: image = [UIImage imageNamed:@"power.png"]; break;
 case 1: image = [UIImage imageNamed:@"Icon.png"]; break;
```

```
case 2: image = [UIImage imageNamed:@"package_graphics.png"]; break;
case 3: image = [UIImage imageNamed:@"colorize.png"]; break;
case 4: image = [UIImage imageNamed:@"web.png"]; break;
}
cell.imageView.image = image;
return cell;
}
```

4. Scale the images in Preview. Make the images 32 × 32 pixels.

5. Re-import the images into the project.

6. Click Build And Go. The images display correctly (Figure 10-17).

Figure 10-16   Images are too large to display in the application's table rows.

(continued)

Figure 10-17 Resized images displayed correctly

Selecting Rows

The UITableView allows you to select a row. Typically, a table presents rows to a user, where each row is an item in a hierarchical list. Upon selecting a row, the user is generally taken to another view presenting the item's details. You implement the tableView: willSelectRowAtIndex: and tableView:didSelectRowAtIndexPath: methods if you wish to allow a user to select a row.

```
- (NSIndexPath *) tableView:(UITableView *) tableView
willSelectRowAtIndexPath: (NSIndexPath *) indexPath
```

```
- (void) tableView:(UITableView *) tableView didSelectRowAtIndexPath:
(NSIndexPath *) indexPath
```

The tableView:willSelectRowAtIndexPath: method allows the delegate to react to a row about to be selected. The tableView:didSelectRowAtIndexPath: method allows a reaction to a row's selection. These methods are useful because they allow you to implement custom behavior in a table's delegate when a row is selected.

Try This   Row Selection

1. Open the last task's project in Xcode.

2. Add the tableView:willSelectRowAtIndexPath: and the tableView: didSelectRowAtIndexPath: methods in Listing 10-15 to TableHandler.m.

3. Click Build And Go. The application looks the same as the previous task's results. Clicking the items should result in logging similar to Listing 10-16.

Listing 10-15   The tableView:willSelectRowAtIndexPath: and tableView: didSelectRowAtIndexPath: methods

```
-(NSIndexPath *) tableView: (UITableView *) tableView willSelectRowAt
IndexPath: (NSIndexPath *) indexPath {
 NSLog(@"I selected the item at the %d array and %d item, the value is: %@",
indexPath.section, indexPath.row,
 [[self.tableDataList objectAtIndex: indexPath.section] objectAtIndex:
 indexPath.row]);
 return indexPath;
}
-(void)tableView:(UITableView *) tableView didSelectRowAtIndexPath:
(NSIndexPath *) index {
 NSLog(@"Yes I did....");
}
```

Listing 10-16   Debugger Console logging

```
[Session started at 2009-01-09 13:25:41 -0500.]
2009-01-09 13:25:45.453 TableProjectOne[2089:20b] I selected the item
at the 0 array and 0 item, the value is: AItem One
2009-01-09 13:25:45.454 TableProjectOne[2089:20b] Yes I did....
2009-01-09 13:25:48.372 TableProjectOne[2089:20b] I selected the item
at the 1 array and 0 item, the value is: BItem Three
2009-01-09 13:25:48.373 TableProjectOne[2089:20b] Yes I did....
```

Changing Row Height

A couple of sections ago, you added images that were too large to display in a table's row. The correct way to fix this is usually to resize the images. However, sometimes you want to display a larger image, text with a large font, or a custom cell. One way you can add space in a table's row is by increasing the row's height. You increase a row's height using the heightForRowAtIndexPath method.

Try This Changing Row Height

1. Open the previous task project in Xcode.

2. Add the heightForRowAtIndexPath: method in Listing 10-17 to TableHandler.m.

3. Click Build And Go, and the rows are 90 pixels tall (Figure 10-18).

Figure 10-18 The application running with 90-pixel-high rows in iPhone Simulator

Listing 10-17   The heightForRowAtIndexPath method added to TableView

```
-(CGFloat) tableView : (UITableView *) tableView
heightForRowAtIndexPath: (NSIndexPath *) indexPath {
  return 90;
}
```

Accessorizing Table Cells

You can tell a cell to place a check mark, disclosure arrow, or detailed disclosure button in the cell by setting the cell's accessoryView or accessoryType properties. Accessories are visual user interface clues for users. For instance, the check mark might inform a user that he or she has already selected a row. A disclosure arrow or a detailed disclosure button might hint to a user that he or she can select the row to view the row's details in another view. The check mark and disclosure button are visual clues for a user and do not provide events that respond to a user tapping them. However, the detailed disclosure button can respond to a user tapping it.

Try This Accessorizing a Table Cell

1. Open the previous project in Xcode and comment the sectionIndexTitlesForTableView method in TableHandler.m.

2. Add the tableView:accessoryButtonTappedForRowWithIndexPath: method to TableHandler.m (Listing 10-18). Also modify the tableView:cellForRowAtIndexPath: method to add the accessories to the table cells.

3. Click Build And Go. The rows contain accessories (Figure 10-19). When you tap the detailed disclosure button, the table calls the tableView:accessoryButtonTappedForRow WithIndexPath: method.

Listing 10-18   The tableView:cellForRowAtIndexPath: and tableView:accessoryButton TappedForRowWithIndexPath: methods

```
- (UITableViewCell *) tableView : (UITableView *) tableView
cellForRowAtIndexPath: (NSIndexPath *) indexPath {
  NSUInteger section = [indexPath section];
  UITableViewCell *cell = [tableView dequeueReusableCellWithIdentifier:
@"acell"];
```

(continued)

Figure 10-19 Accessorized table rows

```
if(cell == nil) {
cell = [[[UITableViewCell alloc] initWithStyle:
UITableViewCellStyleDefault reuseIdentifier:@"acell"] autorelease];
}
cell.textLabel.text = [[self.tableDataList objectAtIndex:section]
objectAtIndex:[indexPath row]];
UIImage * image;
switch (indexPath.section) {
case 0: image = [UIImage imageNamed:@"power.png"]; break;
case 1: image = [UIImage imageNamed:@"Icon_resize.png"]; break;
case 2: image = [UIImage imageNamed:@"package_graphics_resize.png"];
break;
case 3: image = [UIImage imageNamed:@"colorize.png"]; break;
case 4: image = [UIImage imageNamed:@"web.png"]; break;
}
```

```
cell.imageView.image = image;
if(indexPath.section == 0) {
cell.accessoryType = UITableViewCellAccessoryDisclosureIndicator;
} else if(indexPath.section == 1) {
cell.accessoryType = UITableViewCellAccessoryDetailDisclosureButton;
} else {
cell.accessoryType = UITableViewCellAccessoryCheckmark;
}
return cell;
}
-(void) tableView:(UITableView *) tableView
accessoryButtonTappedForRowWithIndexPath: (NSIndexPath *) indexPath {
NSLog(@"hey now....");
}
```

Customizing a Table Cell

Tables can be customized. Sometimes you might wish to format data differently than provided by the default UITableViewCell. The most direct way to accomplish formatting a table cell is by adding a view to the UITableViewCell. You do this in code, by adding a subview to a cell when initializing it in the tableView:cellForRowAtIndexPath method. Another technique is to create a subclass of a UITableViewCell and then create its graphical layout using Interface Builder.

Try This Customizing a Cell Using Interface Builder

1. Create a new Navigation-based Application. Name the application CustomizedCell.

2. Create a new subclass of UITableViewCell. Note that Xcode provides a template for this class. Name the class MyCellView. Be certain to deselect the Use Core Data for storage checkbox if selected.

3. In MyCellView, create a new UILabel outlet named theTextLabel (Listings 10-19 and 10-20).

4. Click Save And Build.

5. Drag the image money.png from this book's Resources folder to the Resources folder in the project. Save.

6. Create a new Empty XIB. Name the file MyCellView.xib and open it in Interface Builder.

7. Add a Table View Cell from the library to the document window.

(continued)

8. Change the cell's class from UITableViewCell to MyCellView.

9. Double-click My Cell View in the document window to open the cell's canvas.

10. In the Inspector, select money.png as the cell's image. Change the cell's background to yellow. Also, be certain to set the Identifier to MyCell (Figure 10-20).

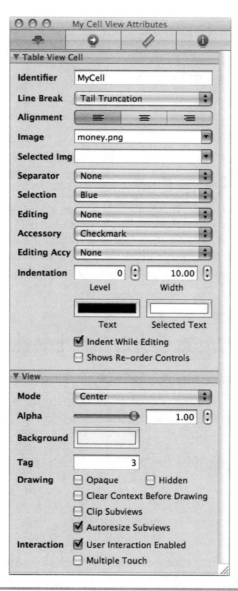

Figure 10-20 Setting the identifier to MyCell

Figure 10-21   Adding UIImageView and UILabels to a view canvas

CAUTION

If you do not set a cell's identifier, the cell can never be reused. This means every call to tableView:cellForRowAtIndexPath: results in a new table cell.

11. Drag a UIImageView and two UILabels to the canvas (Figure 10-21). Type some text in one label; delete the other label's text. Set the image view's image to money.png.

12. Connect the MyCellView's theTextLabel outlet to the newly added label.

13. Save and exit Interface Builder.

14. Open RootViewController.xib in Interface Builder and change the table view's background to yellow. Save and exit Interface Builder.

15. Modify RootViewController to implement the UITableViewController methods needed so they match Listings 10-21 and 10-22.

16. Modify the tableView:cellForRowAtIndexPath: method to set the cell's accessory, background color, and image.

17. Click Build And Go. The table cells have the customized appearance (Figure 10-22).

Listing 10-19   MyCellView.h

```
#import <UIKit/UIKit.h>
@interface MyCellView : UITableViewCell {
 IBOutlet UILabel * theTextLabel;
}
@property (nonatomic, retain) IBOutlet UILabel * theTextLabel;
@end
```

Listing 10-20   MyCellView.m

```
#import "MyCellView.h"
@implementation MyCellView
@synthesize theTextLabel;
```

(continued)

```
- (void)dealloc {
 [theTextLabel release];
 [super dealloc];
}
@end
```

Listing 10-21   RootViewController.h

```
#import <UIKit/UIKit.h>
#import "MyCellView.h"
@interface RootViewController : UITableViewController {
}
@end
```

Figure 10-22   Application with background color

Listing 10-22 RootViewController.m

```objc
#import "RootViewController.h"
#import "CustomizedCellAppDelegate.h"
@implementation RootViewController
- (NSInteger)numberOfSectionsInTableView:(UITableView *)tableView {
 return 1;
}
- (NSInteger)tableView: (UITableView *) tableView
numberOfRowsInSection: (NSInteger) section {
 return 5;
}
- (CGFloat) tableView : (UITableView *) tableView
heightForRowAtIndexPath: (NSIndexPath *) indexPath {
 return 110;
}
- (UITableViewCell *)tableView:(UITableView *) tableView
cellForRowAtIndexPath: (NSIndexPath *) indexPath {
 MyCellView *cell = (MyCellView *) [tableView
dequeueReusableCellWithIdentifier: @"MyCell"];
 if(cell == nil) {
 cell = [[[NSBundle mainBundle] loadNibNamed:@"MyCellView" owner:self
options:nil] objectAtIndex:0];
 }
 [cell.theTextLabel setText:@"Just some static text."];
 NSString *imagePath = [[NSBundle mainBundle] pathForResource:@"money"
ofType:@"png"];
 cell.imageView.image = [UIImage imageWithContentsOfFile:imagePath];
 [cell setAccessoryType:UITableViewCellAccessoryCheckmark];
 cell.contentView.backgroundColor = [UIColor yellowColor];
 cell.backgroundView.backgroundColor = [UIColor yellowColor];
 return cell;
}
- (void)dealloc {
 [super dealloc];
}
@end
```

Notice in the previous example that you initialize the cell every time it's called in the tableView:CellForRowAtIndexPath: method. This initialization is per Apple's documentation, Table View Programming Guide for iPhone OS. The "tableView:cellForRowAtIndexPath: should always reset all content when reusing a cell." That is why in the tableView: cellForRowAtIndexPath: you set the cell's background color, image, and label text. In a more realistic example, you would probably vary a cell's content depending upon the row.

(continued)

Implementing a UITableViewCell in its own nib does not require implementing a UITableViewCell class, as you did in the example. However, if you wish to override a UITableViewCell's method, such as setSelected, you must implement your own custom class. You then set the UITableViewCell's type in Interface Builder to be your custom subclass. In this example, that class is MyCellView. Implementing a custom UITableViewCell subclass is also a convenient location to place IBOutlets and IBActions for the controls on your custom UITableViewCell control.

NOTE

For more information on table-view cells, refer to the "A Closer Look at Table-View Cells" in Apple's "Table View Programming Guide" for iPhone OS.

Using Tables with Navigation Bars and Tabs

Almost every application using a table associates that table with a navigation bar. Moreover, in applications of any complexity, the application also usually organizes its tasks into different tabs. For instance, the iPod application has different tabs for different views of its data. The Artists tab, for instance, shows a user's multimedia sorted by artist. At the iPod application's top is a navigation bar. When a user selects an artist row, the navigation controller pushes another view onto the navigation controller and displays it.

In the following Try This, I try to instill some real-world credibility to this chapter by having you implement a table in a navigation controller that is in a tab-bar tab. Although initially confusing, this is such a common user interface pattern that you should definitely understand the next task.

Try This   Using a Table in a Navigation Controller in a Tab

This is a long, but useful task. Much of it is repetition from previous chapters, but the combination of a table in a navigation controller in a tab is such a common application pattern that it is worth presenting here in detail, even if much of the task is repetitive.

Creating and Connecting the Views

1. Create a new Window-based Application. Name the application TabNavTable.

2. Add a UITabBarController as an IBOutlet to TabNavTableAppDelegate. Name the outlet myCont (Listings 10-23 and 10-24).

3. Change TabNavTableAppDelegate's applicationDidFinishLaunching method in TabNavTableAppDelegate to load the newly added tab bar controller's root view.

4. Save and open MainWindow.xib in Interface Builder.

5. Add a Tab Bar Controller from the library to the document window.

6. Delete the tab bar controller's root view controller, Selected View Controller (Item 1).

7. Add a Navigation Controller in the previously deleted root view controller's place (Figure 10-23).

8. Change the navigation controller's view controller, View Controller (Root View Controller), from a UIViewController to a UITableViewController. Leave its type as UITableViewController; in a few steps, you change it to your own class, MyTableViewController.

9. Connect TabNavTableAppDelegate's myCont property to the tab bar controller (Figure 10-24).

10. Save and exit Interface Builder.

11. Create a new subclass of UITableViewController. Name the class MyTableViewController and add the table view controller methods in Listings 10-25 and 10-26.

12. Add an NSMutableArray named tableDataList and populate it in MyTableViewController's viewDidLoad method.

13. Create a new empty nib named MyTableViewController. Open the nib in Interface Builder.

14. Add a Table View from the library to the document window.

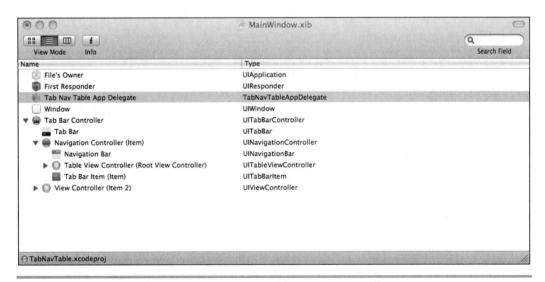

Figure 10-23   Navigation controller in place of tab's view controller

(continued)

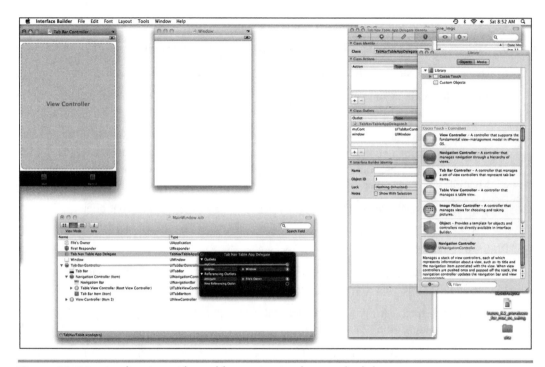

Figure 10-24 Application with a table, navigation bar, and tab bar

NOTE

In step 14 you are adding the table directly to the nib as the main view. Contrast this with how you added the table view in this chapter's first Try This example. Both techniques work.

15. In the document window, change MyTableViewController.xib's File's Owner to MyTableViewController.

16. Connect the File's Owner view outlet to the newly added table view that you added to the document window.

17. Connect the table view's dataSource and delegate outlets to File's Owner.

18. Save and close MyTableViewController.xib. Open MainWindow.xib in Interface Builder.

19. In the document window, expand Tab Bar Controller, and then expand Navigation Controller (Item). Change the Table View Controller (Navigation Item) from a UITableViewController to MyTableViewController. Don't forget to change its NIB Name in the Inspector to MyTableViewController to show the table is loaded from another nib.

Figure 10-25 Table in a tab bar

20. Save and exit Interface Builder.

21. Click Build And Go. The first tab contains a navigation bar and a table view (Figure 10-25).

Listing 10-23   TabNavTableAppDelegate.h

```
#import <UIKit/UIKit.h>
@interface TabNavTableAppDelegate : NSObject <UIApplicationDelegate> {
 UIWindow *window;
 IBOutlet UITabBarController * myCont;
}
@property (nonatomic, retain) IBOutlet UIWindow *window;
@property (nonatomic, retain) IBOutlet UITabBarController * myCont;
@end
```

(continued)

Listing 10-24 TabNavTableAppDelegate.m

```
#import "TabNavTableAppDelegate.h"
@implementation TabNavTableAppDelegate
@synthesize window;
@synthesize myCont;
- (void)applicationDidFinishLaunching:(UIApplication *)application {
 [window addSubview: myCont.view];
 [window makeKeyAndVisible];
}
- (void)dealloc {
 [myCont release];
 [window release];
 [super dealloc];
}
@end
```

Listing 10-25 MyTableViewController.h

```
#import <UIKit/UIKit.h>
@interface MyTableViewController : UITableViewController {
 NSMutableArray * tableDataList;
}
@property (nonatomic, retain) NSMutableArray * tableDataList;
@end
```

Listing 10-26 MyTableViewController.m

```
#import "MyTableViewController.h"
@implementation MyTableViewController
@synthesize tableDataList;
- (void) viewDidLoad {
 NSMutableArray * tempArray = [[[NSMutableArray alloc]
initWithObjects:@"Item One",
@"Item Two", @"Item Three", @"Item Four", @"Item Five", @"Item Six",
@"Item Seven",
@"Item Eight", @"Item Nine", @"Item Ten", @"Item Eleven", @"Item Twelve",
@"Item Thirteen", @"Item Fourteen", @"Item Fifteen", @"Item Sixteen",
@"Item Seventeen",
@"Item Eighteen", @"Item Nineteen", @"Item Twenty", nil] autorelease];
 self.tableDataList = tempArray;
}
```

```
- (NSInteger) tableView : (UITableView *) tableView
numberOfRowsInSection: (NSInteger) section {
 return [self.tableDataList count];
}
- (UITableViewCell *) tableView : (UITableView *) tableView
cellForRowAtIndexPath:(NSIndexPath *) indexPath {
 UITableViewCell *cell = [tableView
 dequeueReusableCellWithIdentifier:@"acell"];
 if(cell == nil) {
 cell = [[[UITableViewCell alloc] initWithStyle:
UITableViewCellStyleDefault reuseIdentifier:@"acell"] autorelease];
 }
 cell.textLabel.text = [self.tableDataList objectAtIndex:[indexPath
row]];
 return cell;
}
- (void)dealloc {
 [tableDataList release];
 [super dealloc];
}
@end
```

Handling Row Selections

1. Add an IBOutlet to MyTableViewController that references a UINavigationController. Name the outlet navCont. Don't forget to synthesize it and to release it. Save and compile.

2. Open MainWindow.xib in Interface Builder.

3. In the document window, expand Tab Bar Controller and then Navigation Controller (Item). Connect MyTableViewController's navCont outlet to the Navigation Controller (Item).

4. Save and exit Interface Builder.

5. Click Build And Go. If you completed the steps correctly, there is no change in the application's appearance.

6. Create a new UIViewController subclass and name it TableViewDetailsViewController (Listings 10-27 and 10-28). Although you leave this class empty in this task, in a real-world project, this class would contain logic. If you wish, select the checkbox to also create an accompanying xib for the class.

(continued)

7. If you didn't already, create a new View xib and name it TableViewDetailsViewController .xib. Open it in Interface Builder.

8. Change the view's background color.

9. Ensure the File's Owner class is set to TableViewDetailsViewController. Also ensure the File's Owner view outlet is connected to the view in the document window.

10. Save and exit Interface Builder.

11. Open MyTableViewController and import TableViewDetailsViewController.h.

12. Implement the tableView:didSelectRowAtIndexPath method in MyTableViewController (Listing 10-29).

13. Build and run in iPhone Simulator. Upon clicking a row, you are taken to the details page (Figure 10-26).

Figure 10-26 Clicking the row takes the user to details view.

Listing 10-27 TableViewDetailsViewController.h

```
#import <Foundation/Foundation.h>
@interface TableViewDetailsViewController : UIViewController {
}
@end
```

Listing 10-28 TableViewDetailsViewController.m

```
#import "TableViewDetailsViewController.h"
@implementation TableViewDetailsViewController
@end
```

Listing 10-29 The tableView:didSelectRowAtIndexPath: method added to MyTableViewController

```
- (void)tableView:(UITableView *)tableView didSelectRowAtIndexPath:
(NSIndexPath *) indexPath {
 NSLog(@"pushing...");
 TableViewDetailsViewController * temp = [[
[TableViewDetailsViewController alloc] initWithNibName:
@"TableViewDetailsViewController" bundle:nil] autorelease];
 [self.navCont pushViewController:temp animated:YES];
}
```

Editing Table Cells

Table cells can be edited. You can add new rows, delete existing rows, and reorder rows. The way it works is like this: A user clicks a button that puts the table into edit mode. Edit mode displays insert or delete accessories used for adding and deleting rows. These accessories are displayed on a cell's left side. Editing mode displays reorder accessories on a table cell's right side.

Getting to Edit Mode

This chapter ends by discussing how to edit a table. Tables not only display data, they also allow adding rows, deleting rows, and changing the order of rows. A table has two modes: its normal display mode and edit mode. When a table is in edit mode, it can display accessories for inserting, deleting, and rearranging table cells. An application places a table in edit mode by sending a message to the table view's setEditing:animated: method. For instance, you might call a table's setEditing:animated: method by implementing an IBAction called by a button on a form.

```
(IBAction) edit {
[self.myTableView setEditing:YES animated:YES];
}
```

However, a self-created button is not how tables are usually placed into edit mode. Rather than specifically creating an action and manually calling a method, you usually use a navigation item and let it automatically activate a table view's edit mode. Remember, 90 percent of the time you will implement a table view in a navigation controller. That navigation controller's navigation bar can contain a right button. One choice you have when creating a navigation bar button is creating an Edit button.

```
self.navigationItem.rightBarButtonItem = myTableController.
editButtonItem;
```

When you set that button to a table controller's editButtonItem, the controller automatically knows to enter edit mode.

Edit Mode Methods

tableView:canEditRowAtIndexPath:, tableView:canMoveRowAtIndexPath:, tableView: commitEditingStyle:forRowAtIndexPath:, and tableView:commitEditingStyle: forRowAtIndexPath: are four methods you should implement in your UITableViewDataSource protocol adoptee.

```
- (BOOL)tableView:(UITableView *)tableView canEditRowAtIndexPath:
(NSIndexPath *)indexPath

- (BOOL)tableView:(UITableView *)tableView canMoveRowAtIndexPath:
(NSIndexPath *)indexPath

- (void)tableView:(UITableView *)tableView commitEditingStyle:
(UITableViewCellEditingStyle) editingStyle forRowAtIndexPath:
(NSIndexPath *) indexPath

- (UITableViewCellEditingStyle)tableView:(UITableView *) tableView
editingStyleForRowAtIndexPath:(NSIndexPath *) indexPath
```

A table knows a row is editable by the tableView:canEditRowAtIndexPath: method. If you wish all rows to be editable, simply have the method return YES; otherwise, implement code to determine if a particular row is editable. If you omit this method, no rows are editable.

The tableView:editingStyleForRowAtIndexPath: method informs the table what style editing accessory the row should have. If this method returns a UITableViewCellEditingStyleNone,

Figure 10-27 A table where the first and last rows have no editing style

no accessory is displayed. If this method returns UITableViewCellEditingStyleDelete, the delete accessory is displayed. And if the method returns UITableViewCellEditingStyleInsert, the insert accessory is displayed. The following example code in Listing 10-30 and Figure 10-27 illustrates.

Listing 10-30   The tableView:editingStyleForRowAtIndexPath method

```
- (UITableViewCellEditingStyle)tableView:(UITableView *)tableView
editingStyleForRowAtIndexPath:(NSIndexPath *)indexPath {
 if(indexPath.row == 0 || indexPath.row == [self.workoutArray count]-
1) {
 return UITableViewCellEditingStyleNone;
 }
 return UITableViewCellEditingStyleDelete;
}
```

A table knows a table row is movable by the tableView:canMoveRowAtIndexPath: method. Like the tableView:canEditRowAtIndexPath: method, simply have the method return YES if all rows are moveable; otherwise, write your own custom code. If you omit this method, no rows are movable.

The tableView:canMoveRowAtIndexPath: method only prevents particular rows from being directly moved by a user. A user can still move another row to the position held by the unmovable row, thus moving the unmovable row indirectly. To prevent this behavior, you can implement the tableView:targetIndexPathForMoveFromRowAtIndexPath: toProposedIndexPath: method in your table view's delegate. If a proposed move is acceptable, return the proposedDestinationIndexPath; otherwise, return the sourceIndexPath. The method's signature follows.

```
- (NSIndexPath *)tableView:(UITableView *)tableView
targetIndexPathForMoveFromRowAtIndexPath:(NSIndexPath
*)sourceIndexPath
toProposedIndexPath:(NSIndexPath *)proposedDestinationIndexPath
```

The tableView:commitEditingStyle:forRowAtIndexPath: commits a row insertion or deletion. Notice the editingStyle parameter. If a row is deleted, the table view sends a UITable ViewCellEditingStyleDelete style as the editingStyle parameter. If a row is inserted, the table view sends a UITableViewCellEditingStyleInsert style. It uses the editingStyle parameter to tell it which action resulted in the method being called.

This method is for implementing code that handles a row insertion or deletion. For instance, in this chapter, data comes from an NSArray or NSMutableArray. When using an NSMutableArray as a data source for a table, deleting a row means you must delete the corresponding item from the array. If inserting, you must add an item at the index where the row was inserted and remove the item from its old location in the array.

Try This Editing Rows

1. Copy the TabNavTable project to a new location and open it in Xcode.

2. Create a new view controller class called AddItemViewController (Listings 10-31 and 10-32). If you wish, select the "With XIB for user interface" checkbox and create an associated xib.

3. Add a reference to MyTableViewController in AddItemViewController; however, instead of importing MyTableViewController, use the @class macro (Listings 10-33 and 10-34). Name the property parentTable.

4. Add an IBOutlet for a UITextField. Name the text field addedName. Add an IBOutlet for a bar button item. Name the button doneButton. Do not forget to synthesize the outlets/properties.

5. Add an IBAction called exitAndSave.

6. Open MyTableViewController and import AddItemViewController. Add a property referencing the AddItemViewController. Name the reference addItemController. Also, add a method named exitAndSave and an IBAction named enterAddMode. Note that exitAndSave takes an NSString as a parameter and is not an IBAction.

7. Add an IBOutlet for a bar button item named addButton.

8. Change the viewDidLoad method so that it sets its navigation item's rightBarButtonItem to its editButtonItem and its navigation item's leftBarButtonItem to addButton.

9. Implement the UITableViewDataSource protocol methods: tableView: canEditRowAtIndexpath:, tableView:commitEditingStyle:forRowAtIndex:, tableView: moveRowAtIndexPath:toIndexPath:, tableView: editingStyleForRowAtIndexPath:, and tableView:canMoveRowAtIndexPath:.

10. If you didn't already when creating the view controller, create a new View XIB named AddItemViewController.xib. Open the nib in Interface Builder.

11. Ensure the File's Owner is an AddItemViewController, if it is not set it to this class. Ensure its view is connected to the view in the document window.

12. Add a bar button item to the document window. Change the newly added bar button's identifier to Done.

13. Connect the File's Owner doneButton outlet to the newly created Done button.

14. Add a UITextField to the canvas. Attach it to the File's Owner addedName outlet.

15. Connect the File's Owner exitAndSave action to the newly added Done bar button item.

16. Save and exit Interface Builder.

17. Open AddItemViewController and implement the viewDidLoadMethod so that it initializes its navigationItem's title to "Add Item" and its rightBarButtonItem to its doneButton.

18. Open MyTableViewController.xib in Interface Builder and add a bar button item to the document window. Change the button's identifier to Add.

19. Connect the File's Owner enterAddMode property to the newly added bar button item. Also connect the File's Owner addButton to the newly added bar button item.

20. Return to MyTableViewController and implement the exitAndSave and the enterAddMode methods like Listing 10-32.

21. Return to AddItemViewController and implement the exitAndSave method like Listing 10-34.

22. Ensure all your properties are being properly released in each class dealloc method.

23. Save and exit Interface Builder.

24. Click Build And Go.

(continued)

Figure 10-28 The table view in edit mode

When the application starts, it presents the user with the table view. Upon tapping the Edit button, the application presents the table in edit mode (Figure 10-28). If the user clicks one of the table's delete accessories, the accessory rotates 90 degrees and presents a Delete button (Figure 10-29). Upon clicking Delete, the row is deleted. When a user clicks and drags the move accessory on the right, he or she can move the row to the new location desired (Figure 10-30).

If a user decides to add a row, he or she taps the Add button, which presents the user with a view to enter the new object's details (Figure 10-31). If the user decides to cancel this action, he or she simply taps the Back button. If the user decides to save the record, he or she taps the Done button, which saves the record and returns the user to the table with the newly added table row (Figure 10-32).

To support moving rows, you implemented the tableView:moveRowAtIndexPath: toIndexPath: method. In that method, you obtained the object from its old position in the tableDataList, removed it, and then added it to its new location. You also implemented the tableView:canMoveRowAtIndexPath: and tableView:canEditRowAtIndexPath: methods. If you needed to only allow certain rows to be editable, you would add that code to the tableView:canEditRowAtIndexPath: method. If you needed to only allow certain rows to be movable, you would add code to the tableView:canMoveRowAtIndexPath: method. Here, both methods simply return YES.

Figure 10-29   Deleting a row

Figure 10-30   Moving a row

(continued)

Figure 10-31 Adding an item

Figure 10-32 The table view with the newly added item

Supporting delete functionality requires a little more code than moving rows, but not much. You implemented the tableView:commitEditingStyle:forRowAtIndexPath: method. In the example, this method removes an object from the index and deletes the row from the table.

Notice you disallowed inserting rows by implementing the tableView:editingStyleForRow AtIndexPath: and having it return UITableViewCellEditingStyleDelete. This method informs a table what accessory, if any, it should display in a row when the table enters edit mode. Here, it displays the delete accessory.

You did not implement insert functionality at all. Inserting uses similar logic to deleting a row, only the style is UITableViewCellEditingStyleInsert. You would also implement code to initialize an object and then insert it in the data source at the proper location. For instance, in the previous example, you could change it to support inserting rows if you changed tableView: editingStyleForRowAtIndexPath: to return UITableViewCellEditingStyleInsert and added the following lines to the tableView:commitEditingStyle:forRowAtIndex: method:

```
else if (editingStyle == UITableViewCellEditingStyleInsert) {
 self.tableDataList insertObject:@"Uninitialized" atIndex:indexPath.
row];
 [tableView insertRowsAtIndexPaths:[NSArray arrayWithObject:indexPath]
withRowAnimation:YES];
}
```

In this example, however, adding a row does not use a table's edit mode. Although it is possible to insert a row using a table's edit mode, it is often not practical. Usually, a table lists items, where each row represents an individual item. Because each item has details associated with it, adding is often accomplished using a separate view controller. Here, you added a left bar button with an addition symbol. When a user clicks the button, it calls MyTableViewController's enterAddMode method. This method presents the AddItemViewController's view. Note that AddItemViewController and MyTableViewController both have references to each other. Upon finishing entering the new item, a user clicks Done, and the Done button fires AddItemViewController's exitAndSave method. This method calls MyTableViewController's exitAndSave method. and the row is added as the table's last row.

Listing 10-31   MyTableViewController.h

```
#import <UIKit/UIKit.h>
#import "TableViewDetailsViewController.h"
#import "AddItemViewController.h"
@interface MyTableViewController : UITableViewController {
 NSMutableArray * tableDataList;
 IBOutlet UINavigationController * navCont;
 AddItemViewController * addItemController;
 IBOutlet UIBarButtonItem * addButton;
}
```

(continued)

```
@property (nonatomic, retain) UINavigationController * navCont;
@property (nonatomic, retain) NSMutableArray * tableDataList;
@property (nonatomic, retain) AddItemViewController *
addItemController;
@property (nonatomic, retain) UIBarButtonItem * addButton;
- (IBAction) exitAndSave: (NSString *) newValue;
- (IBAction) enterAddMode: (id) sender;
@end
```

Listing 10-32   MyTableViewController.m

```
#import "MyTableViewController.h"
@implementation MyTableViewController
@synthesize tableDataList;
@synthesize navCont;
@synthesize addItemController;
@synthesize addButton;
- (IBAction) enterAddMode: (id) sender {
self.addItemController = [[[AddItemViewController alloc]
initWithNibName:
@"AddItemViewController" bundle:nil] autorelease];
 [self.navCont pushViewController:self.addItemController animated:YES];
 self.addItemController.parentTable = self;
}
- (void) exitAndSave : (NSString *) newValue {
 [self.tableDataList addObject: newValue];
 [self.navCont popToRootViewControllerAnimated:YES];
 [self.tableView reloadData];
}
- (void) viewDidLoad {
 NSMutableArray * tempArray = [[[NSMutableArray alloc] initWithObjects:
@"Item One", @"Item Two", @"Item Three", @"Item Four", @"Item Five",
@"Item Six",
@"Item Seven", @"Item Eight", @"Item Nine", @"Item Ten", @"Item Eleven",
@"Item Twelve", @"Item Thirteen", @"Item Fourteen", @"Item Fifteen",
@"Item Sixteen", @"Item Seventeen", @"Item Eighteen", @"Item Nineteen",
@"Item Twenty", nil] autorelease];
 self.tableDataList = tempArray;
 self.navigationItem.rightBarButtonItem = self.editButtonItem;
 self.navigationItem.leftBarButtonItem = self.addButton;
}
- (NSInteger) tableView : (UITableView *) tableView
numberOfRowsInSection: (NSInteger) section {
 return [self.tableDataList count];
}
```

```
- (UITableViewCell *) tableView : (UITableView *) tableView
cellForRowAtIndexPath: (NSIndexPath *) indexPath {
 UITableViewCell *cell = [tableView dequeueReusableCellWithIdentifier:
@"acell"];
 if(cell == nil) {
 cell = [[[UITableViewCell alloc] initWithStyle:
UITableViewCellStyleDefault reuseIdentifier:@"acell"] autorelease];
 }
 cell.textLabel.text = [self.tableDataList objectAtIndex:[indexPath
row]];
 return cell;
}
- (void)tableView:(UITableView *)tableView didSelectRowAtIndexPath:
(NSIndexPath *) indexPath {
 TableViewDetailsViewController * temp = [[
[TableViewDetailsViewController alloc] initWithNibName:
@"TableViewDetailsViewController" bundle:nil] autorelease];
 [self.navCont pushViewController:temp animated:YES];
}

- (void)tableView:(UITableView *)tableView commitEditingStyle:
(UITableViewCellEditingStyle)editingStyle forRowAtIndexPath:
(NSIndexPath *) indexPath {
 if (editingStyle == UITableViewCellEditingStyleDelete) {
 [self.tableDataList removeObjectAtIndex:indexPath.row];
 [tableView deleteRowsAtIndexPaths:[NSArray arrayWithObject:indexPath]
withRowAnimation:YES];
 }
 else if (editingStyle == UITableViewCellEditingStyleInsert) {
 [self.tableDataList insertObject:@"Uninitialized" atIndex:indexPath.
row];
 [tableView insertRowsAtIndexPaths:[NSArray arrayWithObject:indexPath]
withRowAnimation:YES];
 }
}
- (void)tableView:(UITableView *)tableView moveRowAtIndexPath:
(NSIndexPath *) fromIndexPath toIndexPath:(NSIndexPath *) toIndexPath {
 id object = [[self.tableDataList objectAtIndex:fromIndexPath.row]
retain];
 [self.tableDataList removeObjectAtIndex:fromIndexPath.row];
 [self.tableDataList insertObject:object atIndex: toIndexPath.row];
 [object release];
}
```

(continued)

```
-(UITableViewCellEditingStyle) tableView: (UITableView *) tableView
editingStyleForRowAtIndexPath: (NSIndexPath *) indexPath {
 return UITableViewCellEditingStyleDelete;
}
- (BOOL)tableView:(UITableView *)tableView canMoveRowAtIndexPath:
(NSIndexPath *) indexPath {
 return YES;
}
- (BOOL)tableView:(UITableView *)tableView canEditRowAtIndexPath:
(NSIndexPath *) indexPath {
 return YES;
}
- (void)dealloc {
 [tableDataList release];
 [navCont release];
 [addItemController release];
 [addButton release];
 [super dealloc];
}
@end
```

Listing 10-33   AddItemViewController.h

```
#import <UIKit/UIKit.h>
@class MyTableViewController;
@interface AddItemViewController : UIViewController {
 MyTableViewController * parentTable;
 IBOutlet UITextField * addedName;
 IBOutlet UIBarButtonItem * doneButton;
}
@property (nonatomic, retain) UITextField * addedName;
@property (nonatomic, retain) MyTableViewController * parentTable;
@property (nonatomic, retain) IBOutlet UIBarButtonItem * doneButton;
- (IBAction) exitAndSave: (id) sender;
@end
```

Listing 10-34   AddItemViewController.m

```
#import "AddItemViewController.h"
@implementation AddItemViewController@synthesize addedName;
@synthesize parentTable;
@synthesize doneButton;
@synthesize addedName;
```

```
- (void) viewDidLoad {
 self.navigationItem.title = @"Add Item";
 self.navigationItem.rightBarButtonItem = self.doneButton;
}
- (void)dealloc {
 [parentTable release];
 [doneButton release];
 [addedName release];
 [super dealloc];
}
- (IBAction) exitAndSave: (id) sender {
 [self.parentTable exitAndSave:self.addedName.text];
}
@end
```

Summary

This was a long and difficult chapter. But the UITableView is arguably the iPhone's most difficult, yet most important, view. If you do not understand the UITableView and its associated classes, you do not understand iPhone programming. In this chapter, you learned how to use a UITableView and its associated classes. You learned how to implement a table view's delegate and data source in a custom class. You also learned how to group a table and how to index it. And you learned how to customize a table cell's appearance.

After learning how to implement a table and customize it, you then learned a technique for adding a table to a navigation controller contained in a tab. This was a long task, but as it is such a ubiquitous layout pattern, it is a necessary task. After learning this technique, you then learned how to add, move, and delete rows from a table.

NOTE

There are many more methods and properties you can use to customize a table cell's behavior and appearance than presented in this chapter. For more, refer to the online class references for each of the classes covered in this chapter and also reference Apple's "Table View Programming Guide" for iPhone OS.

Chapter 11

Activity Progress and Alerting Users

Key Skills & Concepts

● Using a UIActivityIndicatorView to indicate processing

● Using a UIProgressView to indicate processing

● Using a UIAlertView to warn users

● Using a UIActionSheet to inform users

● Using application badges to remind users of items needing their attention

While processing, many times an application must inform users that they must wait. A poorly constructed application provides no graphical clue that the application is busy processing; a well-constructed application does provide a graphical clue. The iPhone SDK provides the UIActivityIndicatorView and UIProgressView classes to tell a user to "please wait, I'm processing." The UIActivityIndicatorView uses a spinning "gear" to tell a user an application is processing and that it will eventually complete. The UIProgressView control also tells a user to "please wait," but it provides a visual clue as to how much processing remains. The two controls' names highlight their difference: The activity indicator shows activity, while the progress view shows progress.

A user-friendly application also informs a user when something unexpected occurs, and it informs a user when his or her decision might be potentially damaging. Moreover, the application informs the user in a way that highlights the importance of the problem. Sometimes unexpected events occur or a user makes a potentially destructive decision. For these situations an application presents an alert dialog. Alerts provide information in a box separate from the underlying interface. This separation reinforces the alert's message that the situation is important and unusual, separate from an application's typical functionality. Alerts are also modal, meaning a user can do nothing else until clicking one of the alert's buttons to release it. Action sheets are similar to alerts, but provide alternatives to actions and slide in from an application's top (desktop OS X applications) or from an application's bottom (iPhone applications). You use action sheets for similar situations to an alert, but action sheets are more appropriate for actions more integrated with an application.

Showing Activity—the UIActivityIndicatorView

A UIActivityIndicatorView class creates an animated indeterminate progress indicator. This control tells the user to "please wait, I'm processing." The control does not tell the user how long he or she must wait. Apple's reference for this class, which refers to the visual element

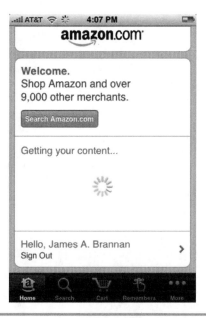

Figure 11-1   An activity indicator on Amazon.com's application

as an animated "gear," illustrates an activity indicator in use (Figure 11-1). When I start the Amazon.com application, it fetches my content from its web server. Fetching this content takes time—how much time, the application doesn't know—and so the application uses a UIActivityIndicatorView.

Using a UIActivityIndicatorView in an application is easy. Begin the indicator's animation by calling its startAnimating method, and stop the indicator's animation by calling the stopAnimating method. If you wish to hide the indicator when not animated, set the property hidesWhenStopped to YES. You can also specify the activity indicator's size and style using its activityIndicatorViewStyle property. The indicator types are large white (UIActivityIndicatorV iewStyleWhiteLarge), white (UIActivityIndicatorViewStyleWhite), and gray (UIActivityView StyleGray). Figure 11-2 illustrates setting this property in Interface Builder. Figure 11-3 shows the three styles in iPhone Simulator.

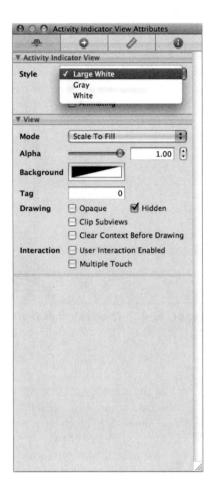

Figure 11-2 Setting a UIActivityIndicatorView's style

Figure 11-3   Three different UIActivityIndicatorView styles

Try This   Using a UIActivityIndicatorView

1. Create a new View-based Application. Name the application ActivityAndProgress.

2. Open ActivityAndProgressViewController, add an IBOutlet for a UIActivityIndicatorView, and add an IBAction called doIt (Listings 11-1 and 11-2). Save and build.

3. Open ActivityAndProgressViewController.xib in Interface Builder.

4. Drag a button and activity indicator view from the library to the view's canvas (Figure 11-4).

5. Connect the File's Owner doIt action to the button's Touch Up Inside event. Connect the myActivityView outlet to the activity indicator view added to the canvas (Figure 11-5).

(continued)

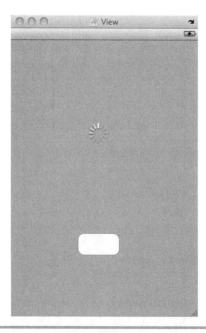

Figure 11-4 Adding a button and activity indicator to a view's canvas

6. Select the activity indicator view, and open its view attributes in the Inspector. Ensure the indicator's Hide When Stopped and Hidden check boxes are checked (Figure 11-6).

7. Click Build And Go to run the application in the iPhone Simulator.

8. Click the button two times (Figure 11-7).

Listing 11-1 ActivityAndProgressViewController.h

```
#import <UIKit/UIKit.h>
@interface ActivityAndProgressViewController : UIViewController {
  IBOutlet UIActivityIndicatorView * myActivityView;
}
@property (nonatomic, retain) IBOutlet UIActivityIndicatorView *
myActivityView;
- (IBAction) doIt: (id) sender;
@end
```

Listing 11-2 ActivityAndProgressViewController.m

```
#import "ActivityAndProgressViewController.h"
@implementation ActivityAndProgressViewController
@synthesize myActivityView;
```

```
- (IBAction) doIt: (id) sender {
  if( [myActivityView isAnimating])
    [myActivityView stopAnimating];
  else
    [myActivityView startAnimating];
}
- (void)dealloc {
  [myActivityView release];
  [super dealloc];
}
@end
```

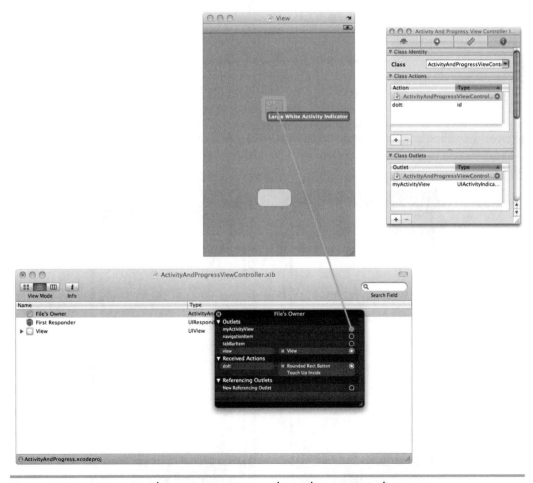

Figure 11-5 Connecting the myActivityView outlet to the activity indicator

(continued)

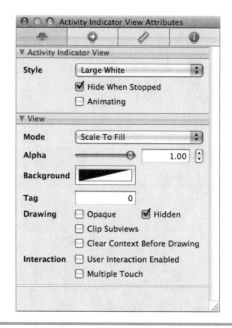

Figure 11-6 Ensuring the indicator's Hide When Stopped and Hidden check boxes are checked

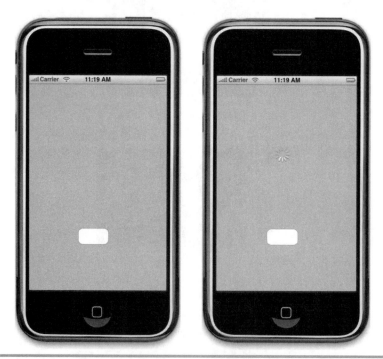

Figure 11-7 The application running in iPhone Simulator

When the application loads, it hides the activity indicator, as it is not animating. When you first click the button, the application displays the activity indicator and begins animating it. The next time you click the button, the application stops animating the indicator and hides it.

Showing Progress—the UIProgressView

A progress bar shows a task's progress. It is intended as a "please wait, I'm processing and I have this much processing remaining" for tasks with a known duration. For instance, an application might process a file's content, and as the file is processing, the application calculates the percentage remaining and displays it using a progress bar. As the file's content is processed, the progress bar updates its display to reflect the new percentage remaining until completion.

Creating a progress bar is more involved than an activity indicator. However, it is still not difficult. Before beginning the task, note that a common technique in many books and online tutorials is to set a progress view in an alert. Although easy, as of this book's writing, Apple neither supports nor recommends this technique. The recommended way of displaying a UIProgressView is by creating a new view with a transparent background and showing the progress bar in the new view. Because the view overlays the content view, the progress bar is modal. That is the strategy taken here.

Try This Using a UIProgressView

1. Open the ActivityAndProgress project from the previous task.

2. Create a new UIViewController named PleaseWaitViewController. Ensure that it also creates an associated xib named PleaseWaitViewController.

3. Add an IBOutlet for a UIProgressView to PleaseWaitViewController (Listings 11-3 and 11-4).

4. Drag starcopy.png from the book's Resources folder to the Resources folder in Xcode.

5. Build and then open PleaseWaitViewController.xib in Interface Builder.

6. Add an image view from the library to the view's canvas. Select starcopy.png as the image and set the mode to Scale To Fill.

(continued)

Figure 11-8 PleaseWaitViewController's view in Interface Builder

7. Add a label and a progress view from the library to the view's canvas (Figure 11-8).

8. Connect the UIProgressView on the canvas to the myProgress outlet in PleaseWaitView Controller.

9. Save and exit Interface Builder.

10. Open ActivityAndProgressController.h, and import the PleaseWaitViewController and the application's delegate.

11. Add an IBOutlet for a PleaseWaitViewController. Add a method called moveBar. Listing 11-5 contains the completed ActivityAndProgressController.h.

12. Open ActivityAndProgressController.m and implement the methods to match Listing 11-6. Note that doIt has changed from the previous task.

13. Open ActivityAndProgressController.xib in Interface Builder and add several controls (Figure 11-9). The selection is not important, as they are not used.

14. Add a view controller from the library to the document window. Change the controller's class to PleaseWaitViewController. Also, change the controller's NIB name to PleaseWait ViewController.

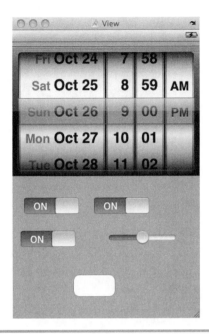

Figure 11-9   ActivityAndProgressViewController's canvas

15. Connect the File's Owner myActivityView outlet to the newly added controller.

16. Save and exit Interface Builder.

17. Click Build And Go. After the application loads in iPhone Simulator (Figure 11-10), click the button. The PleaseWaitViewController's view is displayed and the progress view updates (Figure 11-11). Upon completion, the application removes the view and displays the original view once again.

Listing 11-3   PleaseWaitViewController.h

```
#import <UIKit/UIKit.h>
@interface PleaseWaitViewController : UIViewController {
 IBOutlet UIProgressView * myProgress;
}
@property (nonatomic, retain) IBOutlet UIProgressView * myProgress;
@end
```

(continued)

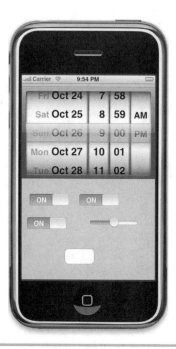

Figure 11-10 The application running in iPhone Simulator

Figure 11-11 The application displaying the UIProgressView you added to the project

Listing 11-4   PleaseWaitViewController.m

```
#import "PleaseWaitViewController.h"
@implementation PleaseWaitViewController
@synthesize myProgress;
- (void)dealloc {
  [myProgress release];
  [super dealloc];
}
@end
```

Listing 11-5   ActivityAndProgressViewController.h modified for this task

```
#import <UIKit/UIKit.h>
#import "PleaseWaitViewController.h"
#import "ActivityAndProgressAppDelegate.h"
@interface ActivityAndProgressViewController : UIViewController {
 IBOutlet PleaseWaitViewController * myActivityView;
}
@property (nonatomic, retain) IBOutlet PleaseWaitViewController *
myActivityView;
- (void) moveBar: (id) object;
- (IBAction) doIt: (id) sender;
@end
```

Listing 11-6   ActivityAndProgressViewController.m modified for this task

```
#import "ActivityAndProgressViewController.h"
@implementation ActivityAndProgressViewController
@synthesize myActivityView;
int completed = 0;
- (void) moveBar: (id) object {
  completed ++;
  myActivityView.myProgress.progress = completed/20.0f;
  if(completed > 20) {
    [object invalidate];
    [self.myActivityView.view removeFromSuperview];
    [self.view setAlpha:1.0f];
    completed = 0;
    self.myActivityView.myProgress.progress = 0;
  }
}
```

(continued)

```
- (IBAction) doIt: (id) sender {
  myActivityView.view.backgroundColor = [UIColor clearColor];
  [self.view setAlpha:0.7f];
  [((ActivityAndProgressAppDelegate *)[UIApplication
sharedApplication].delegate).window insertSubview:myActivityView.view
aboveSubview: self.view];
  [NSTimer scheduledTimerWithTimeInterval: 0.5 target: self selector:
@selector(moveBar:) userInfo: nil repeats: YES];
}
- (void)dealloc {
  [myActivityView release];
  [super dealloc];
}
@end
```

This task is pretty cool. You first created a separate view controller and view to contain the UIProgressView. Not happy with just a normal view, you added an image and placed the controls over the image. Later, when setting the view's background color to clear, this created the impression of a non-rectangular view (see Figure 11-8).

Ask the Expert

Q: So you create a non-rectangular view by using a UIImageView on a clear view?

A: Yes, this is one technique. A more robust technique is drawing the user interface yourself, but drawing a user interface from scratch is hard. Using a UIImageView on a view with a clear background is easy. Make your application's window clear, the views clear, and then place any controls so that they overlay the image. For instance, Figure 11-12 illustrates a simple non-rectangular view.

You also added a UIProgressView to the PleaseWaitViewController (Listing 11-3) as an outlet. You then added a PleaseWaitViewController (Listing 11-5) as an outlet. This allows you to reference both the PleaseWaitViewController and its UIProgressView from code in Activity AndProgressViewController.

In ActivityAndProgressViewController, you created a method called moveBar and modified the doIt method. The doIt method is called when a user clicks the button on the ActivityAndProgressViewController. The method first sets its myActivity view's background color to clear, making the view transparent.

```
myActivityView.view.backgroundColor = [UIColor clearColor];
```

Figure 11-12   A simple non-rectangular view

The method then sets the view's alpha level, giving it a faded, semi-transparent appearance.

```
[self.view setAlpha:0.7f];
```

The doIt method also then gets a reference to the application's window and adds myActivity's view above the ActivityAndProgressViewController's view.

```
[((ActivityAndProgressAppDelegate *)[UIApplication sharedApplication]
.delegate).window insertSubview:
myActivityView.view aboveSubview: self.view];
```

To simulate a long-standing task, you use an NSTimer, which every half a second calls ActivityAndProgressViewController's moveBar method.

```
[NSTimer scheduledTimerWithTimeInterval: 0.5 target:  self selector:
@selector(moveBar:) userInfo: nil repeats: YES];
```

The moveBar method updates the progress bar until it reaches 20. It then invalidates the timer, removes PleaseWaitViewController's view, and sets the original view's alpha back to full strength. It also reinitializes the UIProgressView's progress value to zero.

```
[NSTimer scheduledTimerWithTimeInterval: 0.5 target: self selector:
@selector(moveBar:) userInfo: nil repeats: YES];
```

Ask the Expert

Q: What is an NSTimer?

A: The NSTimer is a timer. Timers fire events at a specified interval. For instance, you set the interval to 0.5 seconds. You specified the target, self, and the message, moveBar. Every 0.5 seconds, the timer fires, executing the moveBar method in ActivityAndProgress ViewController. To make a timer repeat, you specify YES for the repeats parameter. To remove a time, you invalidate the timer. For more information, refer to the NSTimer Class Reference.

Alerting Users

Use alerts to inform users of impending actions that might be destructive, "are you sure" types of messages. Usually these are a result of some unexpected action. Alerts should have two buttons: an "okay" button and a "cancel" button. Use alerts sparingly to avoid annoying users.

Use action sheets to inform users of alternatives to an action. As Apple points out in their documentation, the Photos application contains a good example of using an action sheet (Figure 11-13). The user has a choice: use the photo as wallpaper, e-mail the photo, assign it to a contact, or do nothing (cancel). Action sheets are also appropriate when informing a user he or she is performing a potentially destructive task.

Figure 11-13 An action sheet in the Photo application

UIAlertView and UIAlertViewDelegate

A UIAlertView presents a modal alert to users. The alert appears and floats above the underlying view. Displaying a UIAlertView is easy: Create the class and display it. As the alert is modal, a user can do nothing else until clicking one of the alert's buttons. The UIAlertViewDelegate handles the alert's button actions. If you add buttons to an alert, implement the clickedButtonAtIndex: method in your delegate. Other methods you might implement include the alertViewCancel: or didPresentAlertView: methods. For a complete listing, refer to Apple's UIAlertViewDelegate Protocol Reference.

Alerts should not be misused. Present too many alerts, and you have an annoying application, where users take alerts, if at all. Also, place buttons according to Apple's recommendation. When alerting a user to a potentially destructive outcome, place the Cancel button on the right (Figure 11-14). When alerting a user to a harmless action, place the Cancel button on the left (Figure 11-15).

Figure 11-14 Alert warning of a potentially destructive action

Figure 11-15 Alert warning of a benign action

Try This Creating a Simple UIAlertView

1. Create a new View-based Application. Name the application AlertsProgress.

2. Change AlertsProgressViewController to adopt the UIAlertViewDelegate protocol (Listing 11-7).

3. Open AlertsProgressViewController.m and add an alert to the viewDidLoad method (Listing 11-8). Also, implement the didDismissWithButtonIndex: delegate method.

4. Click Build And Go to run the application (Figure 11-16). Tap the button, and the button's index is logged to the Debugger Console.

Figure 11-16 A simple alert

Listing 11-7   AlertsProgressViewController.h

```
#import <UIKit/UIKit.h>
@interface AlertsProgressViewController : UIViewController
<UIAlertViewDelegate> {
}
@end
```

Listing 11-8   AlertsProgressViewController.m

```
#import "AlertsProgressViewController.h"
@implementation AlertsProgressViewController
- (void)viewDidLoad {
   [super viewDidLoad];
```

(continued)

```
    UIAlertView * myAlert = [[[UIAlertView alloc] initWithTitle:@"View
Loaded" message:@"View loaded successfully." delegate:nil
cancelButtonTitle:@"OK" otherButtonTitles:nil] autorelease];
    [myAlert show];
}
- (void)alertView:(UIAlertView *)alertView didDismissWithButtonIndex:
(NSInteger) buttonIndex {
    NSLog(@"buttonIndex: %i", buttonIndex);
}
- (void)dealloc {
    [super dealloc];
}
@end
```

In this simple application, the view's controller implements a UIAlertViewDelegate.
Upon clicking the button, the delegate's clickedButtonAtIndex method executes. This method
determines which button a user clicked and routes the user accordingly. The clickedButtonAtIndex
method is an instance method declared in UIAlertViewDelegateProtocol and has the following
signature:

```
- (void)alertView:(UIAlertView *) alertView clickedButtonAtIndex:
(NSInteger) buttonIndex
```

The method takes the clicked button's index as an NSInteger via the buttonIndex
parameter. After processing, this method dismisses the alert.

You created a UIAlertView instance through the following code:

```
UIAlertView * myAlert = [[[UIAlertView alloc] initWithTitle:@"View
Loaded" message:@"View loaded successfully." delegate:self
cancelButtonTitle:nil otherButtonTitles:@"OK", nil] autorelease];
```

This method is convenient for initializing the alert view. If you wish, you can add more
buttons to an alert using the otherButtonTitles parameter in the initWithTitle method. The next
task illustrates an alert with two buttons.

Try This Using an Alert with Multiple Buttons

1. Open AlertsProgress in Xcode.

2. Modify AlertsProgressViewController's viewDidLoad method so it matches Listing 11-9.

3. Click Build And Go to run the application. The alert shows two buttons (Figure 11-17). Click either button, and the button's index is logged to the debugger console. You use this index to determine which button is clicked and route processing accordingly.

Listing 11-9   Code to display an alert with two buttons

```
-(void)viewDidLoad {
  [super viewDidLoad];
  UIAlertView * myAlert = [[[UIAlertView alloc] initWithTitle:
@"View Loaded" message:@"View loaded successfully." delegate:self
cancelButtonTitle:@"OK" otherButtonTitles:@"Cancel",nil] autorelease];
  [myAlert show];
}
```

Figure 11-17   An alert with two buttons

UIActionSheet and UIActionSheetDelegate

While an alert displays as a pop-up box, the UIActionSheet slides in from a view's bottom, a view's toolbar, or a view's tab bar. You set where a toolbar slides in from when you display the action sheet. For instance, the following code slides the action sheet from the view's bottom.

```
[myActionSheet showInView:self.view];
```

The action sheet's bottom is aligned with the view's bottom. Note that if you use this setting when using a tab bar or toolbar, the action sheet's bottom is hidden by the bar. To prevent this, you display the action sheet using the showFromTabBar: or showFromToolBar: method. For instance, the following code slides the action sheet from the tab bar's top and aligns the action sheet's bottom with the bottom of the tab bar.

```
[myActionSheet showFromTabBar:self.view];
```

UIActionSheets are otherwise very similar to UIAlertViews. You specify an action sheet's delegate by creating a class adopting the UIActionSheetDelegate. You use this delegate to implement button actions. Methods are similar to UIAlertViewDelegate's. For instance, the following code handles a button click.

```
- (void)actionSheet:(UIActionSheet *)actionSheet clickedButtonAtIndex:
(NSInteger) buttonIndex
```

Try This Using a UIActionSheet

1. Open AlertsProgress in Xcode.

2. Open AlertsProgressViewController.h and change the class so it adopts the UIActionSheetDelegate protocol (Listing 11-10).

3. Add an IBAction called removeAll. In the method's implementation, add a UIActionSheet that asks the user for confirmation (Listing 11-11). Remove the viewDidLoad method.

4. Open AlertsProgressViewController.xib in Interface Builder, add a button to the view, and connect the removeAll action in the File's Owner to the button's Touch Up Inside event (Figure 11-18). Save and exit Interface Builder.

5. Open AlertsProgressViewController.m and implement the didDismissWithButtonIndex: method (Listing 11-11).

6. Click Build And Go to run the application (Figure 11-19). Click each button in the action sheet, and the debugger console should produce logging results similar to Listing 11-12.

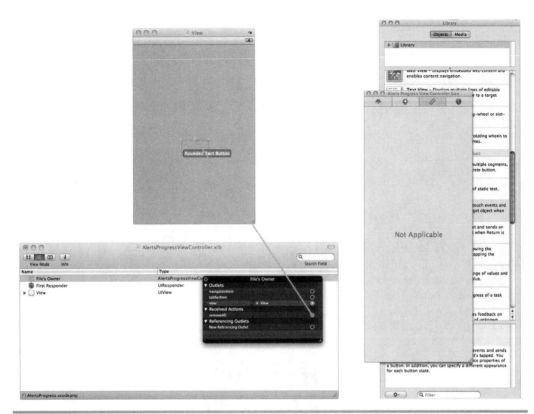

Figure 11-18 Connecting File's Owner removeAll action to a button

---

Listing 11-10   AlertsProgressViewController.h

```
#import <UIKit/UIKit.h>
@interface AlertsProgressViewController : UIViewController
<UIActionSheetDelegate> {
}
- (IBAction) removeAll: (id) sender;
@end
```

Listing 11-11   AlertsProgressViewController.m

```
#import "AlertsProgressViewController.h"
@implementation AlertsProgressViewController
- (IBAction) removeAll: (id) sender {
  UIActionSheet * myActionSheet = [[[UIActionSheet alloc] initWithTitle:
@"Remove all?" delegate:self cancelButtonTitle:@"No" destructiveButtonTitle:
@"Yes" otherButtonTitles:@"Not Sure",nil] autorelease];
```

(continued)

```
     [myActionSheet showInView:self.view];
}
- (void) actionSheet: (UIActionSheet *) actionSheet didDismissWithButton
Index: (NSInteger) buttonIndex {
  NSLog(@"buttons index: %i", buttonIndex);
  if(buttonIndex == [actionSheet cancelButtonIndex]) {
    NSLog(@"cancelled...");
  }
}
-(void)dealloc {
  [super dealloc];
}
@end
```

Listing 11-12   Debugger console output

```
[Session started at 2009-01-17 10:00:55 -0500.]
2009-01-17 10:00:59.432 AlertsProgress[861:20b] buttons index: 0
2009-01-17 10:01:01.936 AlertsProgress[861:20b] buttons index: 1
2009-01-17 10:01:04.336 AlertsProgress[861:20b] buttons index: 2
```

Figure 11-19   A UIActionSheet in action

Figure 11-20   An application badge tells me I have 39 e-mails in my inbox.

Application Badges

The iPhone's Mail application illustrates using a badge. For instance, in Figure 11-20, I have
39 e-mails in my inbox. Using this functionality is easy. Simply access your application's
applicationBadgeNumber property and set it. A user's iPhone will remember the value between
uses of your program. To clear a badge, simply set its value to zero.

Try This Adding an Application Badge

1. Open the previous task in Xcode.

2. Modify the didDismissWithButtonIndex method to match Listing 11-13.

3. Click Build And Go to run the application.

4. Click the "Yes" button four or five times. Quit the application, but keep the simulator
   running. The application's icon is adorned with an application badge (Figure 11-21).

5. Start the application again; click the "No" button a few times. Quit the application, but
   keep the simulator running and notice the application's badge was decremented.

(continued)

Figure 11-21 The application has an application badge.

Listing 11-13 The didDismissWithButtonIndex method modified to use an application badge

```
- (void) actionSheet: (UIActionSheet *) actionSheet didDismissWith
ButtonIndex: (NSInteger) buttonIndex {
  if(buttonIndex == [actionSheet cancelButtonIndex])
    [UIApplication sharedApplication].applicationIconBadgeNumber =
    [UIApplication sharedApplication].applicationIconBadgeNumber - 1;
  else if (buttonIndex == [actionSheet destructiveButtonIndex])
    [UIApplication sharedApplication].applicationIconBadgeNumber =
    [UIApplication sharedApplication].applicationIconBadgeNumber + 1;
}
```

Summary

In this chapter you learned techniques for alerting users. Tasks that take time to complete should provide feedback to a user. When an application can estimate how long a task will take to complete, provide a UIProgressView. When an application cannot estimate how long a task will take to complete, provide a UIActivityView. When an unusual situation arises that requires a user decision, present a UIAlertView. When a user is making a decision that is potentially destructive, present a UIAlertView or a UIActionSheet, depending upon the uniqueness of the situation. If the situation is something commonly occurring while using an application, use a UIActionSheet. If it is an unusual situation, use a UIAlertView. But be careful not to overuse these two controls, as they interrupt an application's flow.

This chapter ended by presenting application badges. Application badges are useful to alert a user of unprocessed items or items needing a user's attention. Application badges are easy to incorporate into your application, but, like alerts and action sheets, should not be misused. You should not use an application badge to tell a user how many notes he or she has written in the Notes application. These notes do not require some action. Informing a user how many e-mails are in his or her inbox is an appropriate application badge use. Use your best judgment.

Chapter 12

Controls—Part One

Key Skills & Concepts

- Modifying buttons

- Understanding the UIToolbar

- Understanding the UISlider and UISwitch

- Understanding UITextField and UITextArea

- Understanding using a UIWebView

I n this chapter you learn how to use several of the iPhone SDK's available controls. You also learn about the toolbar and the web browser view. Although this chapter is not comprehensive, it will help you get started understanding the many controls you might use when creating an iPhone application. Several of the screenshots come directly from Apple's UICatalog example application (Figure 12-1). You can download this application at Apple's Web site. But note, the controls it illustrates are created programmatically, and not using Interface Builder.

Figure 12-1 Apple's UICatalog sample application

Figure 12-2   Apple's UICatalog's buttons screen

Buttons

The most rudimentary control is arguably the button. What can you say about buttons? You click them, or on an iPhone, you tap them, and something happens. The iPhone has several different button styles (Figure 12-02). Implementing a button is not hard. In the next few sections you examine the buttons available when programming an iPhone.

UIButton with a Background Image and Image

Although Apple's stock button, the rounded rectangular button, sometimes looks nice (Figure 12-3) it is usually rather ugly.

You are not limited to plain buttons though, and can make your buttons appear nicer. For instance, you can add a background image or an image. Creating custom buttons by adding an image or background image is not hard, but the artistic effort making the images appear correctly is time consuming. However, the results are usually worth the extra effort.

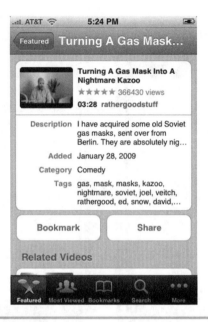

Figure 12-3 The YouTube App uses plain buttons.

Try This Using a Custom Button Background Image and Image

1. Create a new View-based Application. Name it ButtonsBackground.

2. Add outlets for two UIButtons to ButtonsBackgroundViewController (Listings 12-1 and 12-2).

3. Add an action called disableBut and add the code in Listing 12-2 to the method.

4. Add the butbackgray.png, butbackbluegray.png, butbackgraydisabled.png, power.png, and powerdisable.png to the Resources folder in Groups & Files. You will find these images in this book's resources folder.

5. Save and build.

6. Open ButtonsBackgroundViewController.xib in Interface builder.

7. Drag three buttons vertically aligned onto the view's canvas. Connect the second button to one of the outlets and connect the third button to one of the outlets.

8. Connect the disableBut action to the top button's Touch Up Inside.

9. Add the text Disable to the top button.

Figure 12-4   Ensure the Shows Touch on Highlight is checked.

10. For the second button, open the inspector to Buttons Attributes. Ensure the Shows Touch on Highlight is checked (Figure 12-4).

11. Notice the drop-down (Figure 12-5). Here you select the button's state and the related field's values will only apply to that state. Ensure Default State Configuration is selected.

12. Change Background to butbackgray.png and change Image to power.png.

13. Select Highlighted State Configuration and change Background to butbackbluegray.png and Image to power.png.

(continued)

Figure 12-5 Selecting a button's state

14. Select Disabled State Configuration and change Background to butbackgraydisabled.png and Image to powerdisabled.png.

15. For the third button, ensure Default State Configuration is selected and add the text "Shock" to Title. Select the butbackgray.png for Background.

16. Select Highlighted State Configuration and add the text "Shocking" to Title. Select butbackbluegray.png as the Background. Note: do not make any changes to the Disable setting.

17. Resize the buttons as necessary so they appear nice.

18. Click Build And Go to run the application.

Listing 12-1   ButtonsBackgroundViewController.h

```
#import <UIKit/UIKit.h>
@interface ButtonsBackgroundViewController : UIViewController {
  IBOutlet UIButton * clearButton;
  IBOutlet UIButton * smallButton;
}
@property (nonatomic, retain) IBOutlet UIButton * clearButton;
@property (nonatomic, retain) IBOutlet UIButton * smallButton;
- (IBAction) disableBut: (id) sender;
@end
```

Listing 12-2   ButtonsBackgroundViewController.m

```
#import "ButtonsBackgroundViewController.h"
@implementation ButtonsBackgroundViewController
@synthesize clearButton;
@synthesize smallButton;
- (IBAction) disableBut: (id) sender {
  if(clearButton.enabled == YES) {
    clearButton.enabled = NO;
    smallButton.enabled = NO;
    [((UIButton *) sender) setTitle:@"Enable" forState:
UIControlStateNormal];
  }
  else {
   clearButton.enabled = YES;
   smallButton.enabled = YES;
   [((UIButton *) sender) setTitle:@"Disable" forState:
UIControlStateNormal];
  }
}
- (void)dealloc {
  [clearButton release];
  [smallButton release];
  [super dealloc];
}
@end
```

Notice the results upon tapping the buttons. The buttons change the background image from grey to bluish-gray (Figure 12-6). The bottom button also changes its title. Click Disable, and the buttons are grayed out (Figure 12-7). The button with the image changes its background image and image to the choices made above. The button with the title text has this functionality built in. Making the button appear disabled was done automatically for you without you specifying images for the disabled state.

(continued)

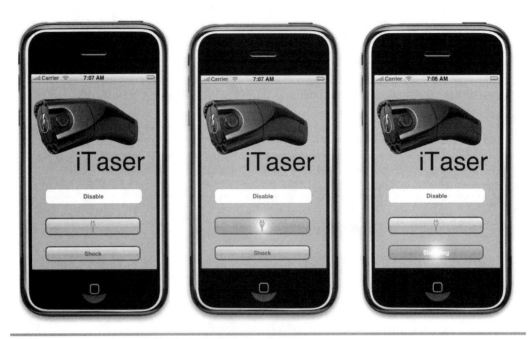

Figure 12-6 The buttons' background image changes

Figure 12-7 The buttons are grayed-out when disabled

TIP

Another way to create a custom button is by setting a button's type to custom. That technique is not shown here. It is not hard though. First, add an image to a button. Second, change the button's type to custom and only the image is visible. Note that you can use different images for different button states, exactly as you did in the previous example application.

Button Types

There are buttons types other than Round Rect and custom that you might use. Figure 12-8 illustrates creating a Detail Disclosure button. To create a Detail Disclosure button, select a Round Rect Button from the library in Interface Builder and then change its type to Detail Disclosure button.

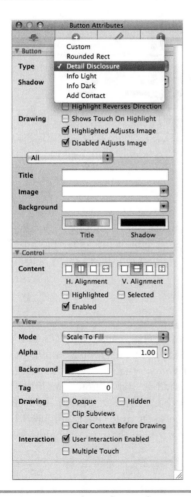
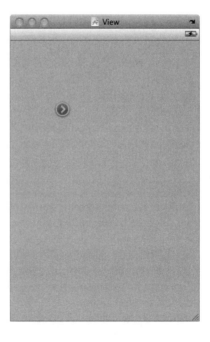

Figure 12-8 Detail Disclosure button

Figure 12-9 Info Light button, Info Dark button, and Add Contact button

You create the Info light and Info dark buttons, like the Detail Disclosure button, by selecting a Round Rect Button and changing its type to Info light or Info dark (Figure 12-9). You create a Contact button the same way you created the other button styles, by selecting a Round Rect Button and changing its type (Figure 12-9).

UIToolBar

Toolbars are for adding buttons of type UIBarButtonItem in a bar, usually along a view's bottom. With a little ingenuity, you can place just about anything on a toolbar, although some items you are not really adding to a toolbar, but rather you are placing over the toolbar (Figure 12-10). You can add the following controls to a toolbar: Bar Button Item, Fixed Space Bar Button Item, Flexible Space, Bar Button Item, Text Field, Switch, Slider, and Button. Placing other items above a toolbar require using a fixed or flexible spacer (Figure 12-11). Place a spacer on the toolbar at the location on the toolbar you wish to overlay with a control, and then place the control over the spacer.

Figure 12-10   You can go crazy with a toolbar.

Figure 12-11   Using spacers to place controls, such as labels on a toolbar

NOTE

Apple may or may not approve your application if you get too crazy with a toolbar. When in doubt; refer to Apple's user interface guidelines.

Try This Creating a UIToolbar

1. Create a new View-based Application. Name the application ToolBarProject.

2. Open ToolBarProjectViewController.xib in Interface Builder.

3. Drag a Toolbar from the library window to the view's canvas. Notice it placed one button on the toolbar for you (Figure 12-12).

4. Drag a Fixed Space Bar Button Item from the library window to the view's canvas. Enlarge the spacer's size. Add another Bar Button Item to the spacer's right (Figure 12-13).

5. Select the toolbar and open its Inspector window. Change the toolbar's style to Black Translucent (Figure 12-14).

6. Save and exit Interface Builder. Click Build And Go. The application displays the toolbar (Figure 12-15).

Figure 12-12 A toolbar on a view's canvas

Figure 12-13 Adding a spacer to a toolbar

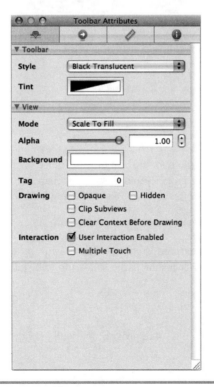

Figure 12-14 Two buttons separated by a spacer

(continued)

Figure 12-15 The sample application displaying a toolbar

UISwitch

A UISwitch, similar to a toggle button, is on or off. Figure 12-19 illustrates a UISwitch's appearance. A UISwitch has a property and method for changing its state. The Boolean property is on, when YES. The switch is off when NO. The following is the declaration for the on property.

```
@property(nonatomic, getter=isOn) BOOL on
```

Notice that the getter is entitled isOn, you can use this getter to obtain the on property's value or the property itself. For instance, the following two statements are equivalent.

```
if( ((UISwitch *) sender).on == YES)
if( [((UISwitch *) sender) isOn] == YES)
```

You can change the switch's value programmatically using the setOn method. This method's signature follows.

```
-(void) setOn: (BOOL) on animated: (BOOL) animated
```

UISlider

Sliders are a horizontal bar with a small round indicator that a user can move to the right or left to change the slider's value. Figure 12-16 contains a slider example.

Appearance

The UISlider class has several properties and methods you might use to modify a slider's appearance. You can modify the indicator using the setThumbImage method.

```
- (void) setThumbImage:(UIImage *)image forState: (UIControlState) state
```

This method allows you to provide the slider an image in place of the round indicator. Interface Builder does not provide a means to set this value, so you must do so programmatically when first loading the view containing the slider.

You can also specify a minimum and maximum image that appears directly to the slider's left and right. Set a slider's image appearing to the right using the maximumValueImage property.

```
@property(nonatomic, retain) UIImage *maximumValueImage
```

Set a slider's image appearing to the left using the minimumValueImage property.

```
@property(nonatomic, retain) UIImage *minimumValueImage
```

The next Try This example sets both properties using the Inspector pane in Interface Builder. There are more modifications you might make to a UISlider; refer to the UISlider Class Reference for a complete listing.

Values

By default, a UISlider's values begin with minimum of 0, a maximum of 1.00, and a .50 initial value. The slider's values are floats and you can set the value programmatically using the setValue method or the value property.

```
- (void) setValue:(float) value animated:(BOOL) animated
```

The minimum, maximum, and initial values are all properties that you can set programmatically or through Interface Builder.

Continuous Property

A slider changes its values continuously as a user adjusts the indicator. For instance, as a user moves the indicator from left to right, the slider is continuously firing value-changed events. You can change this behavior by changing the continuous property to NO. If the value is NO, the slider only fires the event when a user lifts his or her finger from the indicator. You can set this property programmatically, or through Interface Builder.

Try This Using a Switch and a Slider

1. Create a new View-based Application. Name the application SwitchSlider.

2. Drag the edit_add.png and edit_remove.png images from the resources folder to the Resources folder in Groups & Files.

3. Open SwitchSliderViewController.xib in Interface Builder.

4. Add a Slider and a Switch from the library. Resize the slider to be larger, set the edit_remove .png as the minimum image and edit_add.png as the maximum image (Figure 12-16).

5. Notice that the Slider's minimum value is zero and maximum is one. Leave the values unchanged.

6. Save and exit Interface Builder.

7. Open SwitchSliderViewController and implement a method named handleSwitch and a method named handleSlider (Listings 12-3 and 12-4). Also implement a property for the UISwitch named mySwitch.

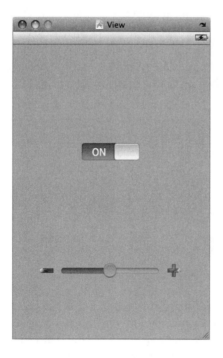
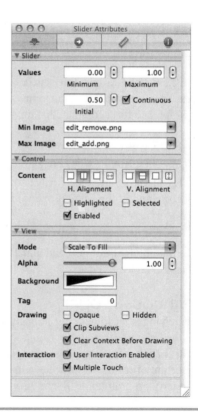

Figure 12-16 A view with a switch and a slider

8. Save and build.

9. Open SwitchSliderViewController.xib in Interface Builder.

10. Ensure File's Owner has a SwitchSliderViewController for its type (it should already).

11. Connect the mySwitch outlet to the switch on the canvas.

12. Connect the handleSlider action to the slider's Value Changed event.

13. Connect the handleSwitch action to the switch's Value Changed event.

14. Save and exit Interface Builder.

15. Click Build And Go (Figure 12-17). Click the switch and it logs to the Debugger Console. Change the slider's value to the far right. The switch's value changes to ON (Figure 12-18).

Figure 12-17 The application running in iPhone Simulator

(continued)

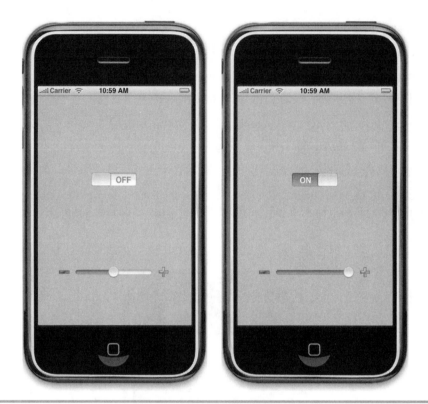

Figure 12-18 Moving the slider to maximum value changes the switch's value

Listing 12-3   SwitchSliderViewController.h

```
#import <UIKit/UIKit.h>
@interface SwitchSliderViewController : UIViewController {
  IBOutlet UISwitch * mySwitch;
}
@property(nonatomic, retain) UISwitch * mySwitch;
- (IBAction) handleSwitch: (id) sender;
- (IBAction) handleSlider: (id) sender;
@end
```

Listing 12-4   SwitchSliderViewController.m

```
#import "SwitchSliderViewController.h"
@implementation SwitchSliderViewController
@synthesize mySwitch;
- (IBAction) handleSwitch: (id) sender {
  if( [((UISwitch *) sender) isOn] == YES){
    NSLog(@"It's on");
  }
  else {
    NSLog(@"It's off");
  }
}
- (IBAction) handleSlider: (id) sender {
  NSLog(@"value: %f", ((UISlider *)sender).value);
  if( [((UISlider *) sender) value] == ((UISlider *) sender)
.maximumValue) {
    [mySwitch setOn:YES];
  }
}
- (void)dealloc {
  [mySwitch release];
  [super dealloc];
}
@end
```

UITextField

The iPhone uses the UITextField class to render text fields. A text field is associated with a keyboard that appears when a user taps in the text field. Keyboard styles include Number Pad, Phone Pad, URL, and several others. You can set the keyboard style programmatically or using Interface Builder (Figure 12-19).

Figure 12-20 illustrates several other text field properties you might set. You can specify how text should be capitalized. Valid choices are None, Words, Sentences, and All Characters. You can also specify if the text field should attempt to correct spelling errors by setting the correction property to YES. If you wish the text field to be a password, then check the Secure checkbox in Interface Builder. Other properties you might wish changing are the text field's

Figure 12-19 Setting a text field's keyboard type

border, background, font, and return key for the keyboard. Figure 12-20 shows the valid choices for a keyboard's return key. For a complete listing of properties and method available to you, refer to the UITextField Class Reference.

Figure 12-20   Valid choices for a keyboard's return key

Try This Using UITextField (with a Number Pad)

1. Create a new View-based Application named TextField.

2. Open TextViewController.xib in Interface Builder. Drag two UITextField controls from the library to the view's canvas and resize the text fields.

(continued)

3. Select the second text field and in its inspector, change its Keyboard to Number Pad.

4. Select the first text field and change its Return Key to Done.

5. Save and exit Interface Builder.

6. Open TextFieldViewController in Xcode and implement the textFieldDone action (Listings 12-5 and 12-6). Also, add an IBOutlet for the second text field and implement the numberFieldDone method.

7. Save and then open TextFieldViewController.xib in Interface Builder. Connect the textFieldDone action to the first text field's Did End on Exit event.

8. Save and exit Interface Builder.

9. Click Build And Go. Notice that when finished editing the first text field, upon clicking Done, the text pad disappears. The number pad, though, has no Done key (Figure 12-21).

Figure 12-21   The number pad has no Done key.

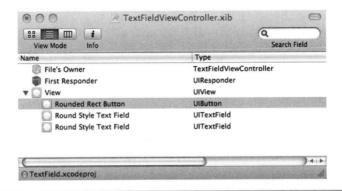

Figure 12-22 Button is under two textfields

10. Open TextFieldViewController.xib in Interface Builder and drag a button onto the view's canvas. Resize the button to cover the entire canvas.

11. In the Document window, expand the View and ensure the newly added button is behind the two text fields (Figure 12-22).

12. In the Inspector's Button Attributes pane, change the button's Type to custom and uncheck any checked drawing checkboxes (Figure 12-23).

13. Connect the numberField outlet to the second text field. Connect the numberFieldDone action to the Touch Up Inside event for the button added to the canvas (Figure 12-24).

14. Save and exit Interface Builder, then Click Build And Go. Click the second text field and the number pad appears. Click anywhere outside the second text field and the number pad disappears (Figure 12-25).

Listing 12-5   TextFieldViewController.h

```
#import <UIKit/UIKit.h>
@interface TextFieldViewController : UIViewController {
  IBOutlet UITextField * numberField;
}
@property(nonatomic, retain) UITextField * numberField;
- (IBAction) textFieldDone: (id) sender;
- (IBAction) numberFieldDone: (id) sender;
@end
```

(continued)

Figure 12-23 Changing button's type to Custom

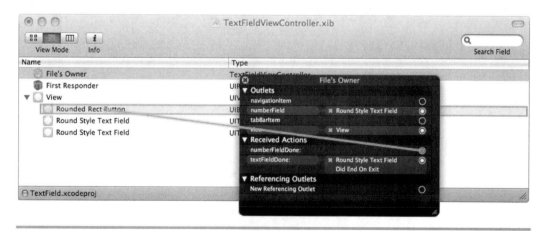

Figure 12-24 Connecting the numberFieldDone action to the button

Figure 12-25   The number pad appears and disappears from the application

---

Listing 12-6   TextFieldViewController.m

```
#import "TextFieldViewController.h"
@implementation TextFieldViewController
@synthesize numberField;
- (IBAction) textFieldDone: (id) sender {
  [sender resignFirstResponder];
}
- (IBAction) numberFieldDone: (id) sender {
  [numberField resignFirstResponder];
}
- (void)dealloc {
  [numberField release];
  [super dealloc];
}
@end
```

UITextView

Use a UITextView to capture multiple lines of text. Apple's reference documentation describes this control best: "The UITextView class implements the behavior for a scrollable, multiline text region." There is not really much more you can say about a text view, other than it's a text area, it is generally used for entering paragraphs of text rather than a single line. There are several properties you can set to customize the control's appearance; including, the font, textColor, editable, and textAlignment properties. You can also check if it has text using the hasText method. Figure 12-26 illustrates several properties you might wish setting for a UITextView in Interface Builder. For more information on the UITextView, refer to the UITextView Class Reference.

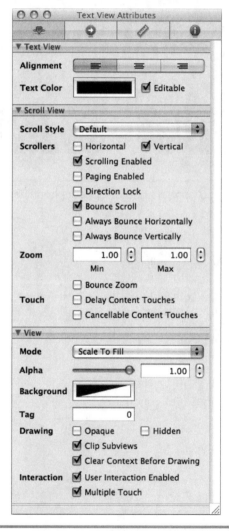

Figure 12-26   UITextView properties you might wish setting in Interface Builder

UISegmentedControl

A segmented control groups together two or more segments, where each segment acts as an independent button. The next task illustrates a segmented control.

Try This Using a UISegmentedControl

1. Create a new View-based Application named Segment.

2. Add the images colorize.png and wizard.png from the resources folder to the Resources folder in Groups & Files.

3. Open SegmentViewController.xib in Interface Builder.

4. Add a Segmented Control to the view's canvas.

5. Change the control so it has three segments. Change the zero segment's name to Kids, the first segment's image to colorize.png image, and the second segment's image to wizard .png (Figure 12-27). Change the control's style to Bordered.

Figure 12-27 Modifying the segmented control in Interface builder

(continued)

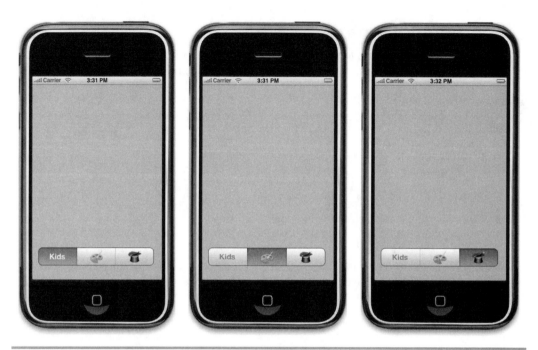

Figure 12-28 The application running in iPhone Simulator

6. Save and exit Interface Builder.

7. Open SegmentViewController and add an IBAction called handleSegment to SegmentViewController (Listings 12-7 and 12-8).

8. Save and then open SegmentViewController.xib in Interface Builder.

9. Connect the segment's Value Changed event to the File's Owner handleSegment method.

10. Click Build And Go. Figure 12-28 illustrates the application's appearance and Listing 12-9 contains the debugger console's logging.

Listing 12-7 SegmentViewController.h

```
#import <UIKit/UIKit.h>
@interface SegmentViewController : UIViewController {
}
- (IBAction) handleSegment: (id) sender;
@end
```

Listing 12-8 SegmentViewController.m

```
#import "SegmentViewController.h"
@implementation SegmentViewController
- (IBAction) handleSegment: (id) sender {
  UISegmentedControl * myseg = (UISegmentedControl *) sender;
  if(myseg.selectedSegmentIndex == 0) {
    NSLog(@"selected zero index...");
  }
  else if(myseg.selectedSegmentIndex == 1) {
    NSLog(@"selected one index...");
  }
  else {
    NSLog(@"selected two index...");
  }
}
- (void)dealloc {
  [super dealloc];
}
@end
```

Listing 12-9 The debugger console's logging for application

```
[Session started at 2009-03-15 15:31:19 -0400.]
2009-03-15 15:31:50.201 Segment[366:20b] selected one index...
2009-03-15 15:32:13.027 Segment[366:20b] selected two index...
2009-03-15 15:32:36.908 Segment[366:20b] selected zero index...
```

The Web View

This chapter wraps up its discussion of controls by discussing the web view. The UIWebView is the class you use to add a web browser to your application. It's based upon the same code foundation as Safari, and so you can use CSS and JavaScript. Using the web view can be easy, or more difficult, depending upon how much you wish your application to interact with the browser. In this chapter you keep it simple.

UIWebView

The UIWebView is responsible for the web view's display. It is an easy means of embedding web content in your application. The loadRequest: method is how you load web content. You can check on the control's progress loading a resource using the loading property. You might also wish moving forward or backward through the user's browsing history; you do this using the goBack and goForward methods. And of course, you can first check to see if the control can move backwards or forwards by checking the canGoBack or canGoForward properties.

If you own an iPhone, then I am certain you have noticed that you can tap telephone numbers in the Safari browser and it automatically dials the number. The UIWebView automatically implements this behavior unless you specifically inform it not to by setting the detectsPhoneNumbers property to NO. Another method that is subtle, yet powerful is the stringByEvaluatingJavaScriptFromString: method.

```
- (NSString *) stringByEvaluatingJavaScriptFromString: (NSString *) script
```

Why is this method so powerful? The stringByEvaluatingJavaScriptFromString: method allows evaluating any JavaScript string. You can access a page's Document Object Model (DOM) through JavaScript, and so you can manipulate an HTML page's content.

The HTML DOM is a W3C standard for manipulating HTML documents. HTML DOM is outside this book's scope, but for more information refer to the W3C School's HTML DOM Tutorial, available online at www.w3schools.com. If you wish programming using the web browser you would be well served by learning the HTML DOM. The following Try This example, illustrates using the stringByEvaluatingJavaScriptFromString: method to print a page's HTML content.

You navigate to a specific page by using the UIWebView's loadRequest method.

```
- (void) loadRequest: (NSURLRequest *) request
```

The loadRequest method takes a URL request as a parameter and navigates to the resource represented by the underlying URL. A NSURL class wraps the NSURLRequest's underlying URL. Both the NSURLRequest and NSURL are part of the Foundation framework. You use both in the next Try This example application.

UIWebViewDelegate

UIWebViews can also have a delegate. You create a delegate for a UIWebView by creating a class that adopts the UIWebViewDelegate protocol and then assigning the UIWebView's delegate property to the custom class. The UIWebViewDelegate handles key events when loading a web page. When an event occurs, the web view calls the appropriate delegate method. For instance, when a web view is about to load a page it calls the webView:should StartLoadWithRequest:navigationType: method.

```
- (BOOL)webView:(UIWebView *)webView shouldStartLoadWithRequest:(NSURL
Request *)
request navigationType:(UIWebViewNavigationType)navigationType
```

When a web view starts loading a page it calls the webViewDidStartLoad: method.

```
- (void)webViewDidStartLoad:(UIWebView *)webView
```

When a web view finishes loading a page it calls the webViewDidFinishLoad: method, unless an error occurs, and instead it calls the webView:didFailLoadWithError: method.

- (void)webViewDidFinishLoad:(UIWebView *)webView

- (void)webView:(UIWebView *)webView didFailLoadWithError:(NSError *)error

Try This Creating a Simple Web Browser

1. Create a new View-based Application named MyWeb.

2. Create a new class called MyWebViewDelegate and have it adopt the UIWebViewDelegate protocol (Listings 12-10 and 12-11).

3. Open MyWebViewController.xib in Interface Builder.

4. Add a Web View from the Library to the canvas. Also add a text field and a button (Figure 12-29).

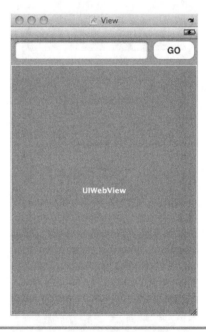

Figure 12-29 A simple web browser in Interface Builder

(continued)

5. Change the text field's keyboard type to URL.

6. Save and exit Interface Builder.

7. Open MyWebViewController and add IBOutlets for the text field and the web view (Listings 12-12 and 12-13). Add and IBAction called changeLocation. Add the MyWebViewDelegate as a property and implement the viewDidLoad method.

8. Save and return to Interface Builder.

9. Connect the button's Touch Up Inside action to the changeLocation action. Connect the text field and web view to their respective outlets.

10. Save and exit Interface Builder.

11. Build and Go.

12. Type http://www.apple.com in the text field and tap GO and the web page loads in the web view (Figure 12-30). The web page's HTML is also logged to the debugger console (not provided as a listing due to its length).

Figure 12-30 A simple web browser displaying Apple's home page

Listing 12-10   MyWebViewDelegate.h

```
#import <Foundation/Foundation.h>
@interface MyWebViewDelegate : NSObject <UIWebViewDelegate> {
}
@end
```

Listing 12-11   MyWebViewDelegate.m

```
#import "MyWebViewDelegate.h"
@implementation MyWebViewDelegate
- (void)webViewDidFinishLoad: (UIWebView *) webView {
  NSLog(@"%@", [webView stringByEvaluatingJavaScriptFromString:
@"document.documentElement.textContent"]);
}
@end
```

Listing 12-12   MyWebViewController.h

```
#import <UIKit/UIKit.h>
#import "MyWebViewDelegate.h"
@interface MyWebViewController : UIViewController {
  IBOutlet UITextField * myTextField;
  IBOutlet UIWebView * myWebView;
  MyWebViewDelegate * myWebViewDelegate;
}
@property(nonatomic, retain) UIWebView * myWebView;
@property(nonatomic, retain) UITextField * myTextField;
@property(nonatomic, retain) MyWebViewDelegate * myWebViewDelegate;
- (IBAction) changeLocation: (id) sender;
@end
```

Listing 12-13   MyWebViewController.m

```
#import "MyWebViewController.h"
@implementation MyWebViewController
@synthesize myWebView;
@synthesize myTextField;
@synthesize myWebViewDelegate;
- (void) viewDidLoad {
  myWebViewDelegate = [[MyWebViewDelegate alloc] init];
```

(continued)

```
  myWebView.delegate = myWebViewDelegate;
}
- (void)dealloc {
  myWebView.delegate = nil;
  [myWebViewDelegate release];
  [myTextField release];
  [myWebView release];
  [super dealloc];
}
- (IBAction) changeLocation: (id) sender {
  [myTextField resignFirstResponder];
  NSURL * url = [NSURL URLWithString: myTextField.text];
  NSURLRequest * request = [NSURLRequest requestWithURL:url];
  [myWebView loadRequest:request];
}
@end
```

Summary

This chapter discussed the controls available to you in the iPhone SDK. First you reviewed buttons. After reviewing buttons, you learned about the toolbar. Following the toolbar, you learned about switches, sliders, and text fields. Note the subtleties of using the keyboard; you must explicitly release the keyboard. Moreover, when using a number pad, if you wish releasing the keyboard you must resort to the "invisible button" hack. You then learned using the text view, segmented control, and to finish up you learned about the UIWebView.

Chapter 13

Controls—Part Two: Using Pickers and Using the Camera

Key Skills & Concepts

- Using a UIDatePicker to select dates

- Using a UIPickerView to select values

- Using a UIPickerView with multiple components

- Using a UIPickerView with UIImageView

- Using the UIImagePickerController to control the camera and access the photo library

- Using simple NSNotifications

What do the UIPickerView and the UIImagePicker classes have in common? Nothing, really, other than they are both ultimately UIViews. But they are both controls you might use in an iPhone application, and so they are covered together in this second chapter on iPhone controls. This chapter's first half covers using the UIDatePicker and UIPickerView classes. These classes create visual controls that appear similar to Las Vegas slot machines. This chapter's second half covers using the UIImagePickerController. This class allows programmatically accessing an iPhone's camera, camera roll, and photo library.

Using Pickers—Date Pickers and Pickers

You use pickers to select one of several values. There are two types of pickers: Date Pickers and Pickers. Date pickers are used for selecting a date, time, or countdown interval. Pickers are used for selecting one of many values.

Date Pickers

Date pickers pick dates and times, placing the selected values in an NSDate class, and are implemented using the UIDatePicker class. If using Interface Builder to develop an iPhone application, you drag a date picker onto your view's canvas from the library and modify the picker's properties in the Inspector. You then create an IBOutlet for the picker in your view's associated view controller and connect it to the picker on your view's canvas. The view controller uses this outlet to obtain the UIDatePicker object's selected date. The example later in this section illustrates this process.

UIDatePicker

A UIDatePicker has rotating wheels, allowing a user to select the date and time. If using a date picker to pick a date and time, valid modes are Date & Time, Time, and Date. If using a date picker to pick a countdown time, the valid mode is Timer. Figure 13-1 illustrates the picker's visual appearance for the different modes.

Figure 13-1 UIDatePicker has four modes: Date & Time, Time, Date, and Timer.

There are several attributes you might change from the default when using a UIDatePicker. Figure 13-2 illustrates the mode, locale, timeZone, date, minimumDate, maximumDate, and interval properties, as viewed in the Inspector.

The locale is an NSLocale. This class encapsulates how the date should be formatted for a different date or culture. The timeZone is an NSTimeZone; its default value is the operating system's time zone. The minuteInterval is the minute intervals displayed by the picker. For instance, Figure 13-3 illustrates a UIDatePicker using 30-minute intervals and a UIDatePicker using 1-minute intervals.

NSDate

UIDatePickers return values as an NSDate. You access a date picker's value through its date property. For instance, the following sets an NSDate from a UIDatePicker's date property.

```
NSDate * theDate = self.datePicker.date;
```

An NSDate is a date and time. Several NSDate methods you might use include isEqualToDate:, earlierDate:, compare:, and laterDate:. For a more complete understanding of date and time programming, refer to Apple's "Date and Time Programming Guide for Cocoa," available online.

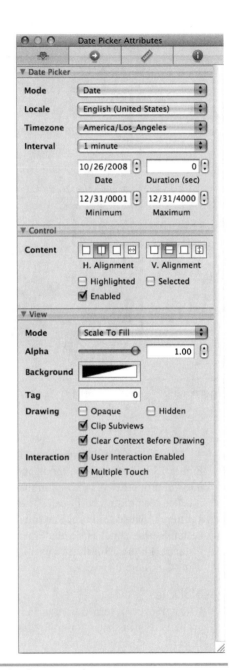

Figure 13-2 Several UIDatePicker properties you might change in the Inspector

Figure 13-3   A UIDatePicker showing 30-minute intervals and a UIDatePicker showing 1-minute intervals

NSDateFormatter

When you wish to display a date, you use an NSDateFormatter. An NSDateFormatter allows a date to be displayed as a formatted NSString. There are many formats you might use. For instance, consider the two formatters.

```
NSDateFormatter * dateFormatter = [[[NSDateFormatter alloc] init]
autorelease];
[dateFormatter setDateFormat:@"MM/dd/yyyy"];
```

The "MM/dd/yyyy" format outputs August 26, 2008, as "08/26/2008."

```
[dateFormatter setDateFormat:@"EEEE MMMM d',' yyyy"];
```

The "EEEE MMMM d',' yyyy" format outputs "Tuesday August 26, 2008," as the date. These are only two of many choices you might select to format dates and times. For more formats, refer to Apple's "Data Formatting Programming Guide for Cocoa," available online.

Try This Using a Date Picker

1. Create a new View-based Application. Name the application DatePickerProject.

2. Open DatePickerProjectViewController.xib in Interface Builder.

3. Add a date picker to the canvas and add a label (Figure 13-4).

4. Change the date picker's mode to Date (Figure 13-5).

5. Save and exit Interface Builder.

6. Open DatePickerProjectViewController and add an IBOutlet for the UIDatePicker and an IBOutlet for the UILabel (Listings 13-1 and 13-2). Also add an IBAction called changeValue. Don't forget to release the two outlets in the dealloc method.

7. Save and build. Open DatePickerProjectViewController.xib in Interface Builder.

8. Connect the File's Owner datePicker outlet to the UIDatePicker on the canvas. Connect the File's Owner theLabel to the UILabel on the canvas.

Figure 13-4 Adding a UIDatePicker and UILabel to the view

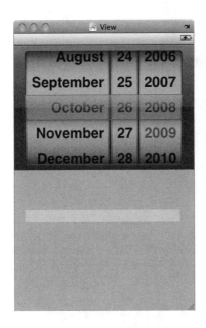

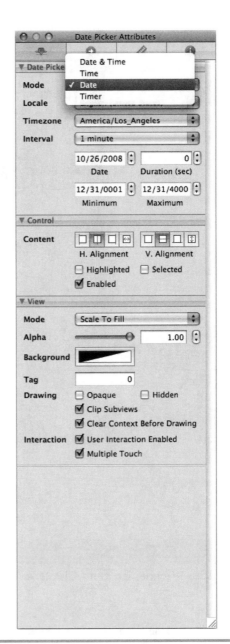

Figure 13-5 Change a UIDatePicker's mode to Date

(continued)

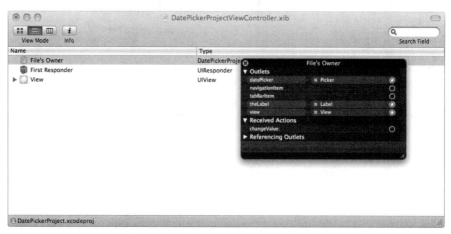

Figure 13-6 Connecting to the UIDatePicker's value changed event

9. Connect the File's Owner changeValue action to the UIDatePicker's Value Changed event (Figure 13-6).

10. Save and exit Interface Builder.

11. Click Build And Go and run the application in iPhone Simulator (Figure 13-7). The Debugger Console should have logging similar to Listing 13-3.

Figure 13-7 The application running in iPhone Simulator

Listing 13-1   DatePickerProjectViewController.h

```
#import <UIKit/UIKit.h>
@interface DatePickerProjectViewController : UIViewController {
  IBOutlet UIDatePicker * datePicker;
  IBOutlet UILabel * theLabel;
}
@property (nonatomic, retain) IBOutlet UIDatePicker * datePicker;
@property (nonatomic, retain) IBOutlet UILabel * theLabel;
- (IBAction) changeValue: (id) sender;
@end
```

(continued)

Listing 13-2   DatePickerProjectViewController.m

```
#import "DatePickerProjectViewController.h"
@implementation DatePickerProjectViewController
@synthesize datePicker;
@synthesize theLabel;
- (IBAction) changeValue: (id) sender {
  NSDate * theDate = self.datePicker.date;
  NSLog(@"the date picked is: %@", [theDate description]);
  NSDateFormatter * dateFormatter = [[[NSDateFormatter alloc] init]
autorelease];
  [dateFormatter setDateFormat:@"MM/dd/yyyy"];
  NSLog(@"formatted: %@", [dateFormatter stringFromDate:theDate]);
  [dateFormatter setDateFormat:@"EEEE MMMM d',' yyyy"];
NSLog(@"formatted: %@", [dateFormatter stringFromDate:theDate]);
  [theLabel setText:[theDate description]];
}
- (void)dealloc {
  [datePicker release];
  [theLabel release];
  [super dealloc];
}
@end
```

Listing 13-3   Debugger console output

```
2009-02-02 19:38:03.794 DatePickerProject[1033:20b] the date picked is:
2008-11-26 21:00:00 -0500
2009-02-02 19:38:03.795 DatePickerProject[1033:20b] formatted:
11/26/2008
2009-02-02 19:38:03.796 DatePickerProject[1033:20b] formatted:
Wednesday November 26, 2008
```

Try This Using a UIDatePicker in Timer Mode

UIDatePicker classes are also useful for selecting a duration for an NSTimer. A UIDatePicker selects an NSDate, which consists of a date and a time; therefore, you can create a timer using an NSDate's time. But a UIDatePicker does not implement a timer; it only provides a visual way to pick duration. You must then use this duration with an NSTimer. This task illustrates using a UIDatePicker to select a duration for an NSTimer and, in the process, illustrates using the NSCalendar, NSDateFormatter, and NSDateComponents classes.

1. Create a new View-based Application in Xcode named ATimer.

2. Create a new IBOutlet named timePicker for a UIDateTime and an IBAction called echoTime (Listing 13-4).

3. Implement the echoTime method so it implements an NSTimer that fires a timer every second (Listing 13-5).

4. Add a method called echoIt for the timer to call when firing.

5. Open ATimerViewController.xib in Interface Builder and place a UIDatePicker on the canvas. Set the interval to one minute. Place a button on the canvas (Figure 13-8).

6. Change the picker's mode to Timer in the Inspector.

7. Connect the file's owner timePicker property to the picker.

8. Connect the file's owner echoTime action to the button's Touch Up Inside event.

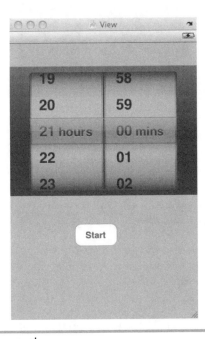

Figure 13-8 Adding a button to the canvas

(continued)

Figure 13-9 Running the application in iPhone Simulator

9. Save and exit Interface Builder.

10. Click Build And Go (Figure 13-9). The output to the Debugger Console should appear like Listing 13-6.

Listing 13-4 ATimerViewController.h

```
#import <UIKit/UIKit.h>
@interface ATimerViewController : UIViewController {
  IBOutlet UIDatePicker * timePicker;
}

@property (nonatomic, retain) IBOutlet UIDatePicker * timePicker;
- (IBAction) echoTime: (id) sender;
- (void) echoIt: (NSTimer *) timer;
@end
```

Listing 13-5   ATimerViewController.m

```
#import "ATimerViewController.h"
@implementation ATimerViewController
@synthesize timePicker;
NSInteger seconds = 0;
- (IBAction) echoTime: (id) sender {
  NSDate * time = timePicker.date;
  NSDateFormatter * dateFormatter = [[[NSDateFormatter alloc] init]
autorelease];
  [dateFormatter setDateFormat:@"HH:MM:SS"];
  NSLog(@"date: %@",[dateFormatter stringFromDate:time]);
  NSCalendar *gregorian = [[NSCalendar alloc] initWithCalendarIdentifier:
NSGregorianCalendar];
  NSDateComponents * comps = [gregorian components:(NSHourCalendarUnit |
NSMinuteCalendarUnit) fromDate:time];
  NSInteger hour = [comps hour];
  NSInteger minute = [comps minute];
  NSLog(@"Hour: %i", hour);
  NSLog(@"minute: %i", minute);
  NSInteger secs = hour * 60 * 60 + minute * 60;
  NSNumber * elapsedSeconds = [[NSNumber alloc] initWithInt:secs];
  NSDictionary * myDict = [NSDictionary dictionaryWithObject:
elapsedSeconds forKey:@"TotalSeconds"];
  [NSTimer scheduledTimerWithTimeInterval:1 target: self selector:
@selector(echoIt:) userInfo: myDict repeats: YES];
}
- (void) echoIt: (NSTimer *) timer {
  NSNumber * num = (NSNumber *) [[timer userInfo] valueForKey:@"Total
Seconds"];
  seconds++;
  NSInteger secs = [num integerValue] - seconds;
  NSLog(@"elapsed: %i, remaining: %i", seconds, secs);
}
- (void)dealloc {
  [timePicker release];
  [super dealloc];
}
@end
```

(continued)

Listing 13-6   The ATimer application logging to debugger console

```
2009-02-06 07:35:21.813 ATimer[540:20b] date: 01:12:00
2009-02-06 07:35:21.814 ATimer[540:20b] Hour: 1
2009-02-06 07:35:21.814 ATimer[540:20b] minute: 11
2009-02-06 07:35:22.815 ATimer[540:20b] elapsed: 1, remaining: 4259
2009-02-06 07:35:23.815 ATimer[540:20b] elapsed: 2, remaining: 4258
--- snip ---
2009-02-06 07:35:31.815 ATimer[540:20b] elapsed: 10, remaining: 4250
```

This example code involves several concepts not covered elsewhere in this book. Notice the NSDictionary, NSCalendar, and NSDateComponents classes. The UIDatePicker picks the hours and minutes for the timer. Upon clicking the button, the echoTime method creates an NSCalendar and obtains date components from the time. After obtaining the total seconds, echoTime adds the seconds to an NSDictionary and creates a timer that fires every second. When firing, the timer calls the echoIt method, passing itself and the dictionary as parameters. The echoIt method obtains the seconds from the userInfo parameter. The echoIt method then determines the elapsed seconds and logs it to the Debugger Console.

UIPickerView

A UIPickerView allows the selection of one or more value sets. A UIPickerView consists of rows and components. Think of the component as the column and the row as the row. So if you had a three-wheel UIPickerView, the third wheel is the third component. A UIPickerView must have an associated class that adopts the UIPickerViewDelegate and a class that adopts the UIPickerViewDataSource. The same class can adopt both protocols.

UIPickerViewDelegate

The UIPickerViewDelegate protocol dictates how a UIPickerView is to construct itself. This protocol contains five methods a class might implement when adopting this protocol: the pickerView:rowHeightForComponent:, pickerView:widthForComponent:, pickerView :titleForRow:forComponent:, pickerView:viewForRow:forComponent:reusingView, and pickerView:didSelectRow:inComponent: methods.

Width and Height   The pickerView:rowHeightForComponent: and pickerView:widthFor Component: methods set a picker's component dimensions. Remember, a picker's component can contain rows of strings or view controls, like a UIImageView. These methods accommodate controls by allowing you to set a component's height and width. Each method's signature follows.

```
- (CGFloat)pickerView:(UIPickerView *) pickerView rowHeightForComponent:
(NSInteger) component
- (CGFloat)pickerView:(UIPickerView *) pickerView widthForComponent:
(NSInteger) component
```

Content   The pickerView:titleForRow:forComponent: and pickerView:viewForRow:for
Component: methods provide a component's title or view. The title or the view is what is
displayed as the rows in a picker. You must implement one of the two methods. If using a string,
implement the pickerView:titleForRow:forComponent: method; if using a view, implement the
pickerView:viewForRow:forComponent: method. Each method's signature follows.

```
- (NSString *)pickerView:(UIPickerView *)pickerView titleForRow:
(NSInteger) row forComponent: (NSInteger) component
- (UIView *)pickerView:(UIPickerView *)pickerView
viewForRow:(NSInteger) row forComponent:(NSInteger)component
reusingView:(UIView *)view
```

Selecting   The UIPickerView calls the pickerView:didSelectRow:inComponent: method
when a user selects a component's row. It takes the component's index number and the
row's index number as parameters, so you can determine the component selected and the
component's row. The method's signature follows.

```
- (void)pickerView:(UIPickerView *)pickerView didSelectRow:(NSInteger)row
inComponent:(NSInteger)component
```

UIPickerViewDatasource

A UIPickerViewDatasource handles a UIPickerView's data. It contains two methods you
should define when adopting this protocol: the numberOfComponentsInPickerView: and
pickerView:numberOfRowsInComponent: methods. The numberOfComponentsInPickerView:
method returns how many components, or columns, a picker must display.

```
- (NSInteger)pickerView:(UIPickerView *)pickerView
numberOfRowsInComponent: (NSInteger) component
```

The pickerView:numberOfRowsInComponent: method returns a component's row count.

```
- (NSInteger)pickerView:(UIPickerView *)pickerView
numberOfRowsInComponent: (NSInteger) component
```

Try This   **Using a Picker**

1. Create a new View-based Application named APicker.

2. Open APickerViewController.xib in Interface Builder.

3. Drag a picker view from the library to the canvas. Right-click and notice that the control
   doesn't have the choices a UIDatePicker has (Figure 13-10).

(continued)

Figure 13-10 A UIPickerView has less outlets and actions than a UIDatePicker

4. Add a button to the canvas.

5. Save and exit Interface Builder.

6. Create a new NSObject named MyPickerDelegate and change it to adopt the
   UIPickerViewDelegate and UIPickerViewDataSource protocols. Have MyPickerDelegate
   implement the needed methods (Listings 13-7 and 13-8).

7. Open APickerViewController and add IBOutlets for UIPickerView and MyPickerDelegate
   (Listing 13-9). Add an IBAction called changeColor.

8. Implement the changeColor action (Listing 13-10).

9. Save and build. Open APickerViewController.xib in Interface Builder.

10. Connect File's Owner changeColor action to the button's Touch Up Inside event.

11. Connect File's Owner myPicker outlet to the UIPickerView.

12. Drag an object from the library to the document window. Change the object's type to
    MyPickerDelegate.

13. Connect the File's Owner myPickerDelegate outlet to the object just added.

14. Connect the UIPickerView's dataSource and delegate outlets to the newly added object.

Figure 13-11   Running the application in iPhone Simulator

15. Save and exit Interface Builder.

16. Click Build And Go to run the application in iPhone Simulator. Upon pushing the button, the debugger console logs the picker's chosen color (Figure 13-11 and Listing 13-11).

Listing 13-7   MyPickerDelegate.h

```
#import <Foundation/Foundation.h>
@interface MyPickerDelegate : NSObject <UIPickerViewDelegate,
UIPickerViewDataSource> {
  NSArray * myData;
}
@property (nonatomic, retain) NSArray * myData;
@end
```

(continued)

Listing 13-8 MyPickerDelegate.m

```
#import "MyPickerDelegate.h"
@implementation MyPickerDelegate
@synthesize myData;
- (id) init {
  if([super init] == nil) return nil;
  myData = [[NSArray alloc]
initWithObjects:@"Red",@"Yellow",@"Green",@"Blue", @"Purple", @"Orange",
@"Black", @"Gray", @"Tan", @"Pink", @"Coral", nil];
  return self;
}
- (void)pickerView:(UIPickerView *)pickerView didSelectRow:(NSInteger)row
inComponent:(NSInteger)component {
  NSLog(@"picked row: %i, component: %i", row, component);
  NSLog(@"the value: %@", [self.myData objectAtIndex:row]);
}
- (NSInteger) numberOfComponentsInPickerView: (UIPickerView *) pickerView {
  return 1;
}
- (NSInteger) pickerView: (UIPickerView *) pickerView
numberOfRowsInComponent: (NSInteger) component {
  return [self.myData count];
}
- (NSString *) pickerView: (UIPickerView *) pickerView titleForRow:
(NSInteger) row forComponent: (NSInteger) component {
  return [self.myData objectAtIndex:row];
}
- (void)dealloc {
  [myData release];
  [super dealloc];
}
@end
```

Listing 13-9 APickerViewController.h

```
#import <UIKit/UIKit.h>
#import "MyPickerDelegate.h"
@interface APickerViewController : UIViewController {
  IBOutlet UIPickerView * myPicker;
  IBOutlet MyPickerDelegate * myPickerDelegate;
}
```

```
@property (nonatomic, retain) IBOutlet UIPickerView * myPicker;
@property (nonatomic, retain) IBOutlet MyPickerDelegate *
myPickerDelegate;
- (IBAction) changeColor: (id) sender;
@end
```

Listing 13-10   APickerViewController.m

```
#import "APickerViewController.h"
@implementation APickerViewController
@synthesize myPicker;
@synthesize myPickerDelegate;
- (IBAction) changeColor: (id) sender {
  NSLog(@"the color is: %@", (NSString *)[myPickerDelegate.myData
objectAtIndex: [myPicker selectedRowInComponent:0]]);
}
- (void)dealloc {
  [myPickerDelegate release];
  [myPicker release];
  [super dealloc];
}
@end
```

Listing 13-11   Debug console output from running APicker application

```
[Session started at 2009-02-06 22:57:09 -0500.]
2009-02-06 22:57:13.007 APicker[429:20b] picked row: 1, component: 0
2009-02-06 22:57:13.008 APicker[429:20b] the value: Yellow
2009-02-06 22:57:14.687 APicker[429:20b] picked row: 3, component: 0
2009-02-06 22:57:14.687 APicker[429:20b] the value: Blue
2009-02-06 22:57:16.540 APicker[429:20b] picked row: 8, component: 0
2009-02-06 22:57:16.541 APicker[429:20b] the value: Tan
2009-02-06 22:57:17.499 APicker[429:20b] the color is: Tan
2009-02-06 22:57:21.215 APicker[429:20b] picked row: 10, component: 0
2009-02-06 22:57:21.215 APicker[429:20b] the value: Coral
2009-02-06 22:57:22.547 APicker[429:20b] the color is: Coral
```

A UIPickerView must have helper classes adopting the UIPickerViewDelegate and UIPickerViewDataSource protocols. In this example, you had one class, MyPickerDelegate, adopt both protocols. The delegate uses a simple NSArray to hold NSString objects. Because the data is simple strings, the delegate implements the titleForRow method. When a user selects a row, the didSelectRow method logs the row, component, and value to the debugger console.

Try This Using a UIPickerView with Two Components

1. Open APicker application in Xcode.

2. Modify MyPickerDelegate's numberOfComponentsInPickerView to return the number 2 (Listing 13-13).

3. Click Build And Go. Notice the picker now shows two independent spinning wheels (Figure 13-12).

4. Add a second value array. Call the array myData2 and initialize it in the init method, as you did before with myData (Listings 13-12 and 13-13).

5. Create two constants representing the different wheels: COLOR_WHEEL for the wheel containing the myData values and SHADE_WHEEL for the wheel containing the myData2 values. Remember, you define constants in a class's header file (Listing 13-12).

6. Modify the numberOfRowsInComponent method and titleForRow method to reflect the newly added wheel.

7. Open APickerViewController.m and modify the changeColor method to reflect the second wheel (Listing 13-14).

Figure 13-12 A UIPickerView with two components

Figure 13-13   Running the application in iPhone Simulator

8. Click Build And Go. The application shows two wheels. Upon clicking the button, the debugger console logs the first wheel's color and the second wheel's shade (Figure 13-13 and Listing 13-15).

Listing 13-12   MyPickerDelegate.h modified to reflect two wheels

```
#import <Foundation/Foundation.h>
#define COLOR_WHEEL 0
#define SHADE_WHEEL 1
@interface MyPickerDelegate : NSObject <UIPickerViewDelegate,
UIPickerViewDataSource> {
  NSArray * myData;
  NSArray * myData2;
}
@property (nonatomic, retain) NSArray * myData;
@property (nonatomic, retain) NSArray * myData2;
@end
```

(continued)

Listing 13-13 MyPickerDelegate.m modified to reflect two wheels

```objc
#import "MyPickerDelegate.h"
@implementation MyPickerDelegate
@synthesize myData;
@synthesize myData2;
- (id) init {
  if([super init] == nil) return nil;
  myData = [[NSArray alloc]initWithObjects: @"Red", @"Yellow", @"Green",
@"Blue",
@"Purple", @"Orange", @"Black", @"Gray", @"Tan", @"Pink", @"Coral", nil];
  myData2 = [[NSArray alloc] initWithObjects: @"Very Dark", @"Dark", @"Normal",
@"Light", @"Very Light", nil];
  return self;
}
- (NSInteger) numberOfComponentsInPickerView: (UIPickerView *) pickerView {
  return 2;
}
- (void)pickerView:(UIPickerView *)pickerView didSelectRow:(NSInteger)row
inComponent:(NSInteger)component {
  NSLog(@"picked row: %i, component: %i", row, component);
  if(component == COLOR_WHEEL)
    NSLog(@"the value: %@", [self.myData objectAtIndex:row]);
  else
    NSLog(@"the value: %@", [self.myData2 objectAtIndex:row]);
}
- (NSInteger) pickerView: (UIPickerView *) pickerView numberOfRowsInComponent:
(NSInteger) component {
  if(component == COLOR_WHEEL)
    return [self.myData count];
  else
    return [self.myData2 count];
}
- (NSString *) pickerView: (UIPickerView *) pickerView titleForRow: (NSInteger)
row forComponent: (NSInteger) component {
  if(component == COLOR_WHEEL)
    return [self.myData objectAtIndex:row];
  else
    return [self.myData2 objectAtIndex:row];
}
- (void)dealloc {
  [myData release];
  [myData2 release];
  [super dealloc];
}
@end
```

Listing 13-14   The changeColor method modified to reflect two wheels

```
- (IBAction) changeColor: (id) sender {
  NSLog(@"the color is: %@ and the shade is: %@", (NSString *)
[myPickerDelegate.myData objectAtIndex: [myPicker
selectedRowInComponent: COLOR_WHEEL]], (NSString *)[myPickerDelegate
.myData2 objectAtIndex: [myPicker selectedRowInComponent:SHADE_
WHEEL]]);
}
```

Listing 13-15   Debugger console logging from running APicker application

```
[Session started at 2009-02-06 23:01:29 -0500.]
2009-02-06 23:01:32.630 APicker[550:20b] picked row: 7, component: 0
2009-02-06 23:01:38.632 APicker[550:20b] the value: Orange
--- snip ---
2009-02-06 23:01:39.508 APicker[550:20b] the color is: Orange and the
shade is: Very Light
```

Using more components involves adding code to check which component was selected. But note, rather than using the raw integers, in this task, you created constants for both components. Each delegate's method then checks which component the user selected.

```
if(component == COLOR_WHEEL)
  return [self.myData objectAtIndex:row];
else
  return [self.myData2 objectAtIndex:row];
```

Try This # Loading UIImageViews into a UIPickerView

1. Open the APicker application created earlier—not the project with two components, but the earlier project with only one component.

2. Replace the pickerView:titleForRow:forComponent: method in MyPickerDelegate with pickerView:viewForRow:forComponent: (Listing 13-16).

3. Add the images money.png, wizard.png, and tux.png to the project. You can find these images in the book's resources folder.

(continued)

4. Modify the MyPickerDelegate's init: method so it loads UIImageViews rather than strings into myData (Listing 13-16).

5. Modify the pickerView:didSelectRow:inComponent: so it only logs the row and component to the debugger console (Listing 13-16).

6. Save and build.

7. Open APickerViewController.xib and remove the button.

8. Save and exit Interface Builder.

9. Click Build And Go. The application loads the images into the UIPickerView (Figure 13-14).

NOTE

Notice that the pickerView:viewForRow:forComponent method takes a UIView. So, similar to custom table cells, you can also create custom picker rows using a UIView.

Figure 13-14 A UIPickerView that uses UIImageView objects as its components

Listing 13-16   MyPickerDelegate.m modified to load images into the UIPickerView

```
#import "MyPickerDelegate.h"
@implementation MyPickerDelegate
@synthesize myData;
- (id) init {
  if([super init] == nil) return nil;
  UIImageView * one = [[UIImageView alloc] initWithImage:[[UIImage alloc]
initWithContentsOfFile: [[[NSBundle mainBundle] resourcePath]
stringByAppendingPathComponent:@"wizard.png"]]];
  UIImageView * two =[[UIImageView alloc] initWithImage:[[UIImage alloc]
initWithContentsOfFile: [[[NSBundle mainBundle] resourcePath]
stringByAppendingPathComponent: @"tux.png"]]];
  UIImageView * three =[[UIImageView alloc] initWithImage:[[UIImage
alloc] initWithContentsOfFile: [[[NSBundle mainBundle] resourcePath]
stringByAppendingPathComponent:@"money.png"]]];

  myData = [[NSArray alloc] initWithObjects:one,two,three,nil];
  return self;
}
- (void)pickerView:(UIPickerView *)pickerView didSelectRow:(NSInteger)row
inComponent: (NSInteger)component {
  NSLog(@"picked row: %i, component: %i", row, component);
}
- (NSInteger) numberOfComponentsInPickerView: (UIPickerView *)
pickerView {
  return 1;
}
- (NSInteger) pickerView: (UIPickerView *) pickerView
numberOfRowsInComponent: (NSInteger) component {
  return [self.myData count];
}
- (UIView *)pickerView:(UIPickerView *)pickerView viewForRow:(NSInteger)
row forComponent:(NSInteger)component reusingView:(UIView *)view {
  return [self.myData objectAtIndex:row];
}
@end
```

Using the Camera—UIImagePickerController

Rather than working directly with an iPhone's camera, you use the UIImagePickerController to manipulate an iPhone's camera and photo library. Using the UIImagePickerController, you take, or select, a photo, optionally edit the photo, and then dismiss the UIImagePickerController, returning control back to your application.

UIImagePickerController

The UIImagePickerController is different from other view controllers. Rather than developers creating the controller's view and adding components to the view's canvas, the UIImage PickerController's views are already created and are part of the UIKit library. Developers simply determine the controller's source type and implement a delegate for the controller. The controller creates and manages the views while the delegate responds to the view being dismissed by a user.

Source

The iPod touch, as of this book's publication, does not have a camera. The iPhone Simulator also lacks a camera. If you attempted to use an iPod touch's nonexistent camera, you would obtain an exception. Attempting to use the camera on an iPhone Simulator results in a nonresponsive application after it logs a message to the debugger console (Figure 13-15).

```
2009-02-09 06:50:30.164 CameraProject[216:20b] photos can only be
captured on HW
```

To avoid an exception or nonresponsive application, the UIImagePickerController provides the isSourceTypeAvailable: method.

```
+ (BOOL)isSourceTypeAvailable:(UIImagePickerControllerSourceType)
sourceType
```

This method returns YES if a source type is available and NO if unavailable. Valid source types are UIImagePickerControllerSourceTypePhotoLibrary, for selecting images from the photo library; UIImagePickerControllerSourceTypeCamera, for selecting images from the camera; and UIImagePickerControllerSourceTypeSavedPhotosAlbum, for selecting images from a camera roll, or from the photo library if the device doesn't have a camera.

After ensuring a device has a source type, you set the UIImagePickerController's sourceType property. This property determines what controls the UIImagePickerController displays. Allowable source types are the same as with the isSourceTypeAvailable: method.

Editing and Delegating

The controller also has an allowsImageEditing property and delegate property. The allowsImageEditing property determines if a user should be allowed to edit an image after taking or selecting the image. The delegate property specifies the class's UIImagePicker ControllerDelegate.

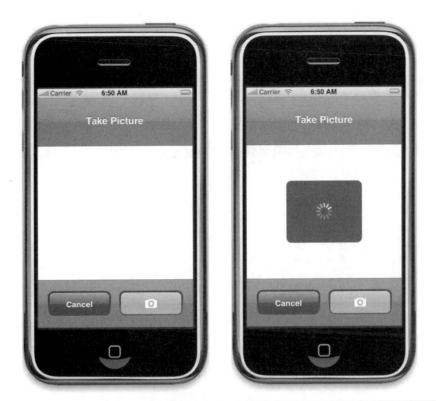

Figure 13-15   Using a camera on the iPhone Simulator results in a nonresponsive application.

UIImagePickerControllerDelegate

The UIImagePickerControllerDelegate's protocol has two methods your delegate should implement for the image picker. The imagePickerController:didFinishPickingMediaWithInfo :info: method is called after a user selects an image. This could be selecting an image from a camera roll or photo library, or after taking a photo using the camera. The method's signature follows.

```
- (void)imagePickerController:(UIImagePickerController *) picker
didFinishPickingMediaWithInfo: (NSDictionary *) info;
```

If you cancel a photo selected, the imagePickerControllerDidCancel: method is called. The method's signature follows.

```
- (void)imagePickerControllerDidCancel:(UIImagePickerController *)picker
```

The imagePickerController:didFinishPickingMediaWithInfo: info: has three parameters. The first parameter holds a reference to the image picker, the second to the image picked, and the third parameter references an NSDictionary containing editing information. If editing is disabled, the third parameter holds nil. If editing is enabled, the parameter holds the unedited image and the cropped rectangle. For more information on the imagePickerController:didFinish PickingMediaWithInfo:info method, refer to Apple's online UIImagePickerControllerDelegate Reference.

Try This   Using the UIImagePickerController

NOTE

Using the camera or camera roll requires having an iPhone, a developer's membership, and a provision for this example application. You can select a photo from a photo album using the iPhone Simulator, however. To accommodate more readers, this task limits itself to the iPhone Simulator's photo library.

1. Create a new View-based Application. Name the project CameraProject.

2. Open CameraProjectViewController.xib in Interface Builder.

3. Drag a toolbar from the library onto the view's canvas.

4. Rename the first button Take Photo. Add another button to the toolbar and call it Select Photo. Add a UIImageView to the canvas (Figure 13-16).

Figure 13-16   The application's canvas

5. Save and quit Interface Builder.

6. Create a new NSObject called MyImagePickerDelegate. Modify the class so it adopts the UINavigationControllerDelegate and UIImagePickerControllerDelegate protocols (Listing 13-17). Add a property that contains the UIImage that the image picker will select.

7. Implement the imagePickerController methods (Listing 13-18).

8. Open CameraProjectViewController.h and import MyImagePickerDelegate. Add an IBOutlet for MyImagePickerDelegate and add an IBOutlet for the UIImageView added to the canvas (Listing 13-19).

9. Add two IBActions to CameraProjectViewController. Name one action takePicture and the other selectPicture (Listing 13-20). Implement both methods as shown in Listing 13-20.

10. Implement the viewDidLoad method in CameraProjectViewController so the method ensures the camera is supported (Listing 13-20).

NOTE

If running on the iPhone Simulator, comment the code in viewDidLoad that checks if a camera is available. Be certain to only click the Select Photo button.

11. Save and build.

12. Open CameraProjectViewController.xib in Interface Builder.

13. Connect the File's Owner theImageView outlet to the UIImageView on the canvas.

14. Connect the selectPicture action to the Select Photo button and the takePicture action to the Take Photo button.

15. Drag an object from the library to the Document window. Change its type to MyImagePickerDelegate.

16. Connect the File's Owner imagePickerDelegate outlet to the newly created object.

17. Save and exit Interface Builder.

18. If you wish to use the camera, follow the necessary steps to register and provision the application so you can install it on your iPhone. Otherwise, use the Select Photo button and select a photo from the SDK's photo albums.

19. Run the application. Everything works as expected, except notice that the view's image is not set to the image selected by the image picker.

(continued)

Listing 13-17   MyImagePickerDelegate.h

```
#import <Foundation/Foundation.h>
@interface MyImagePickerDelegate : NSObject <UINavigationController
Delegate, UIImagePickerControllerDelegate> {
  UIImage * selectedImage;
}
@property (nonatomic, retain) UIImage * selectedImage;
@end
```

Listing 13-18   MyImagePickerDelegate.m

```
#import "MyImagePickerDelegate.h"
@implementation MyImagePickerDelegate
@synthesize selectedImage;
- (void) imagePickerControllerDidCancel: (UIImagePickerController *)
picker {
  [picker.parentViewController dismissModalViewControllerAnimated:
YES];
  [picker release];
}
- (void)imagePickerController:(UIImagePickerController *) picker
didFinishPickingMediaWithInfo:(NSDictionary *) info {
  self.selectedImage = (UIImage*)[info
objectForKey:UIImagePickerControllerOriginalImage];
  [picker.parentViewController dismissModalViewControllerAnimated:
YES];
  [picker release];
}
- (void) dealloc {
  [selectedImage release];
  [super dealloc];
}
@end
```

Listing 13-19   CameraProjectViewController.h

```
#import <UIKit/UIKit.h>
#import "MyImagePickerDelegate.h"
@interface CameraProjectViewController : UIViewController {
  IBOutlet MyImagePickerDelegate * imgPickerDelegate;
  IBOutlet UIImageView * theImageView;
}
```

```
@property (nonatomic, retain) MyImagePickerDelegate *
imgPickerDelegate;
@property (nonatomic, retain) UIImageView * theImageView;
- (IBAction) takePicture: (id) sender;
- (IBAction) selectPicture: (id) sender;
@end
```

Listing 13-20   CameraProjectViewController.m

```
#import "CameraProjectViewController.h"
@implementation CameraProjectViewController
@synthesize imgPickerDelegate;
@synthesize theImageView;
- (void) viewDidLoad {
  [super viewDidLoad];
  if(!([UIImagePickerController isSourceTypeAvailable:
UIImagePickerControllerSourceTypeCamera]))
  {
    NSLog(@"Camera not supported....quitting application");
    UIAlertView * myAlert = [[UIAlertView alloc]
initWithTitle:@"Camera Error" message:@"Camera Not Supported.
Application will terminate." delegate:nil cancelButtonTitle:nil
otherButtonTitles:@"OK", nil];
    [myAlert show];
    [myAlert release];
    //warning - terminate is undocumented api
    [[UIApplication sharedApplication] terminate];
  }
}
- (IBAction) takePicture: (id) sender {
  UIImagePickerController * pickCont = [[UIImagePickerController
alloc] init];
  pickCont.delegate = imgPickerDelegate;
  pickCont.allowsImageEditing = YES;
  pickCont.sourceType = UIImagePickerControllerSourceTypeCamera;
  [self presentModalViewController:pickCont animated:YES];
  NSLog(@"heynow");
}
- (IBAction) selectPicture: (id) sender {
  UIImagePickerController * pickCont = [[UIImagePickerController
alloc] init];
  pickCont.delegate = imgPickerDelegate;
```

(continued)

```
    pickCont.allowsImageEditing = YES;
    pickCont.sourceType = UIImagePickerControllerSourceTypePhotoLibrary;
    [self presentModalViewController:pickCont animated:YES];
    NSLog(@"heynow");
    if(self.imgPickerDelegate.selectedImage != nil)
    self.theImageView.image = self.imgPickerDelegate.selectedImage;
}
- (void)dealloc {
    [theImageView release];
    [imgPickerDelegate release];
    [super dealloc];
}
@end
```

Nothing happens after selecting or taking a photo, unless you click one of the application's buttons a second time. The photo previously selected is then displayed (Figure 13-17). What is supposed to happen is that the theImageView in CameraProjectViewController should display the newly taken photo. You might think that placing the following lines in the selectPicture would solve the problem, but they do not.

```
if(self.imgPickerDelegate.selectedImage != nil)
    self.theImageView.image = self.imgPickerDelegate.selectedImage;
```

Notice the "heynow" logging added to the delegate's methods. Immediately after displaying the image picker, the debugger console logs "heynow." If the logging does not wait for the image picker to finish, the two lines setting the image don't wait either, and so the image isn't set correctly until the next time you push one of the application's two buttons.

CameraProjectController must be changed so it is notified when a picture is taken so it can update its view. There are two ways you might fix the image not displaying. First, you could add a reference to the CameraProjectViewController in MyImagePickerDelegate, but I dislike this solution. Why? Adding a CameraProjectViewController to MyImagePickerDelegate as a property introduces close coupling between the two classes. You can never again reuse MyImagePickerDelegate, unless you reuse CameraProjectViewController. Unacceptable. A better solution, in my humble opinion, is using a notification.

Notifications

If you have ever used Java listeners, you already know a notification's basic workings. Cocoa's notifications are similar to Java's listeners, only easier and more flexible. Every Cocoa application has a notification center, NSNotificationCenter. Classes in your application can post notifications, NSNotification, to the notification center. Other classes can register with the notification center to listen for notifications. Through notifications, classes can communicate with each other without even knowing about one another's existence. Although this book doesn't present notifications with any detail, in the next few steps, you add a notification to the CameraProjectViewController.

Figure 13-17 Running the application in iPhone Simulator and using the provided photo library

(continued)

NOTE

Refer to Apples *Introduction to Notification Programming Topics* for more information on using notifications.

1. Open CameraProject in Xcode.

2. Modify the imagePickerController;didFinishPickingMediaWithInfo:info: method to post a notification (Listing 13-21).

3. Add a method called changeImage to CameraProjectViewController (Listing 13-22).

4. Modify viewDidLoad so it observes the notification (Listing 13-23). Also, modify dealloc so it unregisters itself as a notification listener.

5. Click Build And Go. Now the application sets the UIImageView's image as expected.

Listing 13-21 The didFinishPickingMediaWithInfo modified to post a notification

```
- (void)imagePickerController:(UIImagePickerController *) picker
didFinishPickingMediaWithInfo:(NSDictionary *) info {
  self.selectedImage = (UIImage*)[info
objectForKey:UIImagePickerControllerOriginalImage];
  [[NSNotificationCenter defaultCenter] postNotificationName:@"Image
Picked" object:nil];
  [picker.parentViewController dismissModalViewControllerAnimated:YES];
  [picker release];
}
```

Listing 13-22 The changeImage method

```
- (void) changeImage {
  NSLog(@"IMAGE CHANGED");
  self.theImageView.image = self.imgPickerDelegate.selectedImage;
}
```

Listing 13-23 The viewDidLoad method modified to have CameraViewController observe the notification

```
- (void) viewDidLoad {
  [super viewDidLoad];
  if(!([UIImagePickerController isSourceTypeAvailable:
UIImagePickerControllerSourceTypeCamera]))
  {
    NSLog(@"Camera not supported....quitting application");
    UIAlertView * myAlert = [[UIAlertView alloc]
```

```
initWithTitle:@"Camera Error" message:@"Camera Not Supported.
Application will terminate." delegate:nil cancelButtonTitle:nil
otherButtonTitles:@"OK", nil];
    [myAlert show];
    [myAlert release];
    //warning - terminate is undocumented api
    [[UIApplication sharedApplication] terminate];
  }
  [[NSNotificationCenter defaultCenter] addObserver:self selector:
@selector(changeImage) name:@"ImagePicked" object:nil];
}
 - (void) dealloc {
 [super dealloc];
 [theImageView release];
 [imgPickerDelegate release];
 [ [NSNotificationCenter defaultCenter] removeObserver:self];
}
```

In this task, you created an application that uses the UIImagePickerController to control an iPhone's camera. You created two buttons, one for taking a photo using the camera and one for selecting an image from the photo library. If you obtained provisioning for the application and installed the provisioning on your iPhone, you could install the application on your iPhone and use the camera (Figure 13-18). But instead, you selected photos from the photo library and ran the application on the iPhone Simulator.

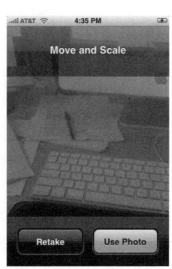

Figure 13-18   Using the camera on an iPhone

Summary

In this chapter, you used a UIDatePicker, a UIPickerView, and a UIImagePickerController. A UIDatePicker is for selecting a date and time. You used a UIDatePicker to select a date, and you used a UIDatePicker to select a time. After the UIDatePicker, you learned about UIPickerViews. A UIPickerView is for selecting a string value or an object descending from UIView. You used a UIPickerView with one component and a UIPickerView with two components. You then modified the one-component UIPickerView to display images rather than strings. After examining the UIDatePicker and UIPickerView controls, you learned about the UIImagePickerController. This class allows you to select images from an iPhone's camera, camera roll, or photo album. Only the third option, selecting from a photo album, works on the iPhone Simulator or iPod touch, as neither has a camera. In this chapter's final task, you used a UIImagePickerController to select a photo from the iPhone Simulator's photo album.

Chapter 14

Application Settings

Key Skills & Concepts

- Creating a settings bundle

- Understand settings field types

- Initializing an application with a settings bundle's values

You set your iPhone or iPod touch's settings through the Settings application (Figure 14-1). For instance, you can set your device's brightness, Wi-Fi settings, and wallpaper settings using the Settings application. Different applications can also use the Settings application for setting its user's configuration preferences. In this chapter, you learn how to add an application's settings to the Settings application.

Figure 14-1   The iPhone Settings application

The Settings Application

The Settings application is used for setting both a device's preferences and different applications' preferences. When using the Settings application for an application's preferences, use it only for an application's configuration settings and not for settings that change frequently. Change volatile preferences through the application's interface and not the Settings application.

The Settings Bundle

An application's preferences are stored in an Extended Markup Language (XML) file called Root.plist. Root.plist is stored in a bundle called Settings.bundle. A settings bundle is not automatically added to your project, and so you must add a settings bundle to your application if you wish to use the Settings application (Figure 14-2). Besides a Root.plist, a setting bundle contains any additional .plist files, any images used for sliders, and one or more .lproj files. Additional .plist files are for any child preference panes your application might require. Figure 14-15 illustrates a child preference pane. The .lproj files are for localized string resources (not covered in this chapter). You can also store 16 × 16 pixel images you might wish to use in your preference panes, as the minimumImage and maximumImage on a slider pane should also be stored in the settings bundle.

NOTE

You can also specify an icon for your application in the Settings application. Create a 29 × 29 pixel Portable Network Graphics (PNG) image and name it Icon-Settings.png. This file should be placed in your Xcode project's Resources folder in Groups & Files.

Try This   Creating a Settings Bundle

1. Create a new View-based Application named MySettings.

2. Expand the Resources folder and add a new settings bundle (Figure 14-2). Accept the default name. Note that Settings.bundle is added to Resources.

3. Expand Settings.bundle and click Root.plist.

(continued)

Figure 14-2 Adding a settings bundle

4. Click Build And Go. Tap the Home button to end the application, and tap the Settings Application's icon. The Settings application includes MySettings (Figure 14-3). Tap the arrow, and Settings displays the MySettings application's default settings screen (Figure 14-4).

NOTE
To change this example's title displayed in Settings, change the application's Bundle Display Name in the MySettings-Info.plist file (Figure 14-5).

Figure 14-3   Settings application with MySettings

Figure 14-4   MySettings application's settings

(continued)

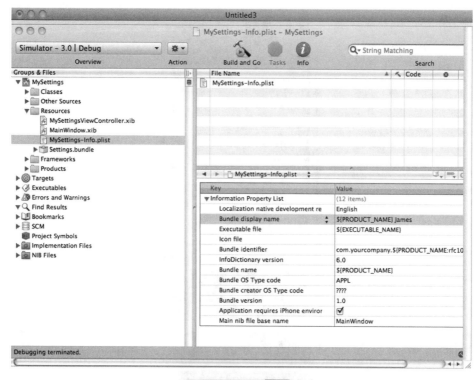

Figure 14-5 Changing the application's name

Key	Purpose	Type	Valid Values	Required
Type	Specifies preference type.	String	PSGroupSpecifier	Yes
Title	Specifies the title displayed by Settings application.	String	Any string value.	Yes

Table 14-1 PSGroupSpecifier Settings

Settings Field Types

TIP
I dislike jargon. I use the word "expand" rather than "disclose" throughout this book. In this chapter, you will notice you "expand" rows; you don't "disclose" them. The little arrows, called Disclosure buttons, when clicked, are said to "disclose" their content.

You add preferences to the settings bundle through Root.plist. Different settings display differently in the Settings application. Possible values for settings are PSTextFieldSpecifier, PSTitleValueSpecifier, PSToggleSwitchSpecifier, PSMultiValueSpecifier, PSGroupSpecifier, and PSChildPaneSpecifier. This section considers each setting in turn.

PSGroupSpecifier
The PSGroupSpecifier groups settings into a group. If you have many settings, consider using this specifier to group your settings into logical groupings. Table 14-1 summarizes the PSGroupSpecifier's settings.

PSTextFieldSpecifier
The PSTextFieldSpecifier is for a preference whose value is a string. Table 14-2 summarizes a PSTextFieldSpecifier's settings.

Key	Purpose	Type	Valid Values	Required
Type	Specifies preference type.	String	PSTextFieldSpecifier	Yes
Title	Specifies the title displayed by the Settings application.	String	Any string value	Yes
Key	Specifies the preference's key used for storage and retrieval.	String	Any string value	Yes
DefaultValue	Specifies adefault value for the preference.	String	Any string value	No
IsSecure	Specifies if preference should be treated as password.	Boolean	Yes or No	No
KeyboardType	Specifies type of keyboard to display when tapped.	String	Alphabet, NumbersAndPunctuation, NumberPad, URL, EmailAddress	No
AutoCapitalizationType	Specifies if autocapitalization should occur.	String	None, Sentences, Words, AllCharacters; default is None	No
AutoCorrectionType	Specifies if should spelling should be automatically corrected.	String	Default, Yes, No	Default

Table 14-2 PSTextFieldSpecifier Settings

Try This Adding a PSTextFieldSpecifier

1. Open MySettings in Xcode. Open Root.plist in the Editor window.

2. Expand PreferenceSpecifiers and delete Item 2, Item 3, and Item 4.

3. Select Item 1 and click the plus sign to its right. It adds a new row. Note, this row is a child of PreferenceSpecifiers.

4. Select Item 2 and change its type to Dictionary.

5. Expand Item 2 and then click the button with three lines to the row's right. A new child row should be added. Note that this row is a child of Item 2. Add two more new child rows; ensure that they are children of Item 2, not the newly added row. Change each row to match Figure 14-6.

6. Save the .plist file.

7. Click Build And Go. Navigate to Settings and MySettings settings. Click the text field, and your Simulator should match Figure 14-7.

Key	Type	Value
▼ Root	Dictionary	(3 items)
Title	String	Settings Project
StringsTable	String	Root
▼ PreferenceSpecifiers	Array	(2 items)
▶ Item 1	Dictionary	(2 items)
▼ Item 2	Dictionary	(3 items)
Type	String	PSTextFieldSpecifier
Title	String	My Text Field
Key	String	keyOne

Figure 14-6 Root.plist with PSTextFieldSpecifier

Figure 14-7   Settings reflecting the new setting

PSMultiValueSpecifier

The PSMultiValueSpecifier is for selecting one of many alternative choices. Table 14-3 summarizes the PSMultiValueSpecifier's settings. Note that you create entries below Values and Titles for each value and for each title.

Key	Purpose	Type	Valid Values	Required
Type	Specifies preference type.	String	PSMultiValueSpecifier	Yes
Title	Specifies the title displayed by the Settings application.	String	Any string value	Yes
Key	Specifies the preference's key used for storage and retrieval.	String	Any string value	Yes
Values	Specifies an array of values.	Array	Array of Key-Value entries	Yes
Titles	Specifies titles for array of values.	Array	Array of Key-Value entries	Yes
DefaultValue	Specifies a default value for the preference.	String	Any value from the Values array	Yes

Table 14-3   PSMultiValueSpecifier Settings

Try This Adding a PSMultiValueSpecifier

1. Return to MySettings in Xcode. Open the Root.plist in the editor.

2. Create an Item 3 below PreferenceSpecifiers and ensure its type is Dictionary.

3. Expand Item 3 and add six new child rows.

4. Change the first child row to have Type for the key, String for the type, and PSMultiValueSpecifier for the value (Figure 14-8).

5. Change the next child row to have Title for the Key, String for the type, and Colors for the value.

6. Change the next child row to have DefaultValue for the Key, String for the type, and blue for the value.

7. Change the next child row to have Key for the Key, String for the type, and keyTwo for the value.

8. Change the next two child rows to have Titles and then Values for the Keyom and Array for the type.

9. Expand Titles and then add three child rows to it. Do the same for Values (see Figure 14-8). Assign the three child Titles the values Red, Blue, and Orange. Assign the three child Values the values red, blue, and orange.

Key	Type	Value
▼ Root	Dictionary	(3 items)
Title	String	Settings Project
StringsTable	String	Root
▼ PreferenceSpecifiers	Array	(3 items)
▼ Item 1	Dictionary	(2 items)
Type	String	PSGroupSpecifier
Title	String	Group
▼ Item 2	Dictionary	(3 items)
Type	String	PSTextFieldSpecifier
Title	String	My Text Field
Key	String	keyOne
▼ Item 3	Dictionary	(6 items)
Type	String ‡	PSMultiValueSpecifier
DefaultValue	String	blue
Title	String	Colors
Key	String	keyTwo
▼ Titles	Array	(3 items)
Item 1	String	Red
Item 2	String	Blue
Item 3	String	Orange
▼ Values	Array	(3 items)
Item 1	String	red
Item 2	String	blue
Item 3	String	orange

Figure 14-8 Root.plist with the PSMultiValueSpecifier added

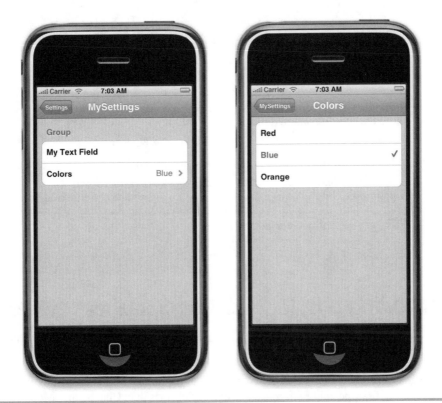

Figure 14-9 Settings reflecting the new setting

10. Save the .plist file.

11. Click Build And Go. Navigate to the Settings application, and the new setting appears (Figure 14-9).

PSToggleSwitchSpecifier

The PSToggleSwitchSpecifier is for selecting a Boolean value. The toggle switch displayed in the Settings application for this specifier is On or Off. Table 14-4 summarizes the PSToggleSw itchSpecifier's settings.

Key	Purpose	Type	Valid Values	Required
Type	Specifies preference type.	String	PSToggleSwitchSpecifier	Yes
Title	Specifies the title displayed by the Settings application.	String	Any string value	Yes
Key	Specifies the preference's key used for storage and retrieval.	String	Any string value	Yes
TrueValue	The value for true.	Boolean	A Boolean	Yes
FalseValue	The value for false.	Boolean	A Boolean	No
DefaultValue	Specifies a default value for the preference.	String	String value from TrueValue or FalseValue	

Table 14-4 PSToggleSwitchSpecifier Settings

Try This Adding a PSToggleSwitchSpecifier

1. Return to Root.plist and add a fourth item below PreferenceSpecifiers (i.e., highlight Item 3 and click the plus sign on the right). Change the new item's type to Dictionary.

2. Expand Item 4 and add six new child rows. Change the first child row to have a Type for key, String for type, and PSToggleSwitchSpecifier for value. Change the second child row to have Title for key, String for type, and Use Colors? for value. Change the third child row to have Key for key, String for type, and keyThree for value. Change the fourth child row to have TrueValue for key, String for type, and YES for value. Change the fifth child row to have FalseValue for key, String for type, and NO for value. Finally, change the sixth child row to have DefaultValue for key, String for type, and NO for value (Figure 14-10).

3. Save the .plist file.

4. Click Build And Go. Navigate to Settings, and the new value appears (Figure 14-11).

NOTE

Notice I keep stating to "save the .plist file" as its own step. The reason for this is that Build And Go does not automatically save the .plist file, like it does for source files.

Key	Type	Value
▼ Root	Dictionary	(3 items)
Title	String	Settings Project
StringsTable	String	Root
▼ PreferenceSpecifiers	Array	(4 items)
▶ Item 1	Dictionary	(2 items)
▶ Item 2	Dictionary	(3 items)
▼ Item 3	Dictionary	(6 items)
Type	String	PSMultiValueSpecifier
DefaultValue	String	blue
Title	String	Colors
Key	String	keyTwo
▶ Titles	Array	(3 items)
▶ Values	Array	(3 items)
▼ Item 4	Dictionary	(6 items)
Type	String	PSToggleSwitchSpecifier
Title	String	Use Colors?
Key	String	keyThree
TrueValue	String	YES
FalseValue	String ‡	NO
DefaultValue	String	NO

Figure 14-10   Root.plist with the PSToggleSwitchSpecifier added

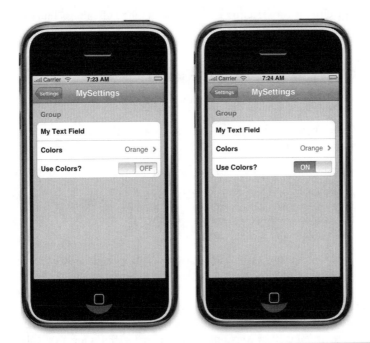

Figure 14-11   Settings reflecting the new setting

Key	Purpose	Type	Valid Values	Required
Type	Specifies preference type	String	PSSliderSpecifier	Yes
Title	Specifies the title displayed by the Settings application	String	Any string value	Yes
Key	Specifies the preference's key used for storage and retrieval	String	Any string value	Yes
DefaultValue	Specifies a default value for the preference	Number	Any number between minimum and maximum values	Yes
MinimumValue	Minimum value for slider	Number	Any number	Yes
MaximumValue	Maximum value for slider	Number	Any number	Yes
MinimumValueImage	Path to image (21 × 21 pixels)	String	Valid path	No
MaximumValueImage	Path to image (21 × 21) pixels	String	Valid path	No

Table 14-5 PSSliderSpecifier Settings

PSSliderSpecifier

The PSSliderSpecifier is for selecting a value from a range of values. Table 14-5 summarizes PSSliderSpecifier's settings.

Try This Adding a PSSliderSpecifier

1. Return to Root.plist and add a new item below Item 4.

2. Change the newly added item to a Dictionary type. Expand the item and add two child rows below it.

3. Assign the first child item's key to Type, type to String, and value to PSGroupSpecifier.

4. Assign the second child item's key to Title, type to String, and value to Intensity.

5. Close Item 5 and add another item after it. Change the item's type to Dictionary. Expand the newly added item and add six child rows.

6. Change the first child row's key to Type, type to String, and value to PSSliderSpecifier. Change the second child row's key to Title, type to String, and value to Intensity. Change the third child row's key to Key, type to String, and value to keyFour. Change the fourth child row's key to DefaultValue, type to Number, and value to 5. Change the fifth child row's key to MinimumValue, type to Number, and value to 0. Change the sixth child row's key to MaximumValue, type to Number, and value to 10. Figure 14-12 shows Root.plist after making the changes.

7. Save the .plist file.

8. Click Build And Go, and the changes appear in the Settings application (Figure 14-13).

Key	Type	Value
▼ Root	Dictionary	(3 items)
Title	String	Settings Project
StringsTable	String	Root
▼ PreferenceSpecifiers	Array	(6 items)
▶ Item 1	Dictionary	(2 items)
▶ Item 2	Dictionary	(3 items)
▶ Item 3	Dictionary	(6 items)
▶ Item 4	Dictionary	(6 items)
▼ Item 5	Dictionary	(2 items)
Type	String	PSGroupSpecifier
Title	String	Intensity
▼ Item 6	Dictionary	(6 items)
Type	String	PSSliderSpecifier
Title	String	Intensity
Key	String	keyFour
DefaultValue	Number	5
MinimumValue	Number	0
MaximumValue	Number	10

Figure 14-12 Root.plist with the PSSliderSpecifier added

Figure 14-13 Settings reflects the new setting

Key	Purpose	Type	Valid Values	Required
Type	Specifies preference type.	String	PSChildPaneSpecifier	Yes
Title	Specifies the title displayed by the Settings application.	String	Any string value	Yes
File	Specifies the file used for the child pane.	String	The .plist file name without the extension	Yes

Table 14-6 PSChildPaneSpecifier Settings

PSChildPaneSpecifier

The PSChildPaneSpecifier is for specifying a child pane in the Settings application. You define the settings in this pane in a separate .plist file. Table 14-6 summarizes PSChildSpecifier's settings.

Try This Adding a PSChildPaneSpecifier

1. Return to Root.plist and add a seventh item. Change its type to Dictionary. Expand and add three child rows.

2. Change the first child row's key to Type, type to String, and value to PSChildPaneSpecifier. Change the second child row's key to Title, type to String, and value to Shade. Change the third child row's key to File, type to String, and value to Shades (Figure 14-14).

Key	Type	Value
▼ Root	Dictionary	(3 items)
Title	String	Settings Project
StringsTable	String	Root
▼ PreferenceSpecifiers	Array	(7 items)
▶ Item 1	Dictionary	(2 items)
▶ Item 2	Dictionary	(3 items)
▶ Item 3	Dictionary	(6 items)
▶ Item 4	Dictionary	(6 items)
▶ Item 5	Dictionary	(2 items)
▶ Item 6	Dictionary	(6 items)
▼ Item 7	Dictionary	(3 items)
Type	String	PSChildPaneSpecifier
Title	String	Shade
File	String	Shades

Figure 14-14 Root.plist with the PSChildPaneSpecifier added

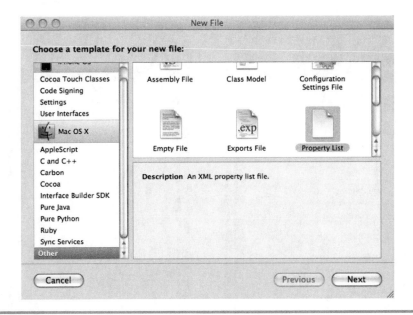

Figure 14-15 Creating a new property list

3. Save.

4. Create a new property list (Figure 14-15). Name the file Shades.

5. Open Shades.plist in the editor and add one row. Change the row's key to Title, type to String, and value to Shades (Figure 14-16).

6. Save.

7. Click Build And Go. The change is reflected in the Settings application (Figure 14-17).

Key	Type	Value
▼ Root	Dictionary	(1 item)
Title	String	Shades

Figure 14-16 The Shades.plist settings

(continued)

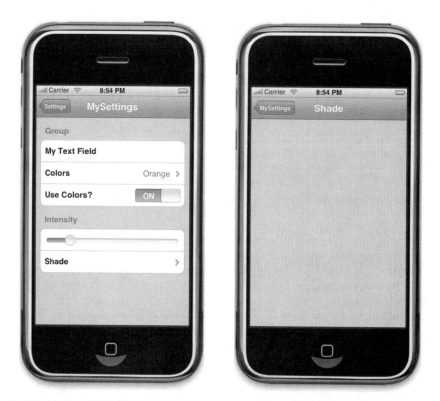

Figure 14-17 Application's settings pane shows the new sub-pane

Reading Settings Using NSUserDefaults

You use the NSUserDefaults class to access the default system. An application with default values is loaded at startup time and cached. You access these values using the NSUserDefaults class's methods. Methods for obtaining values include arrayForKey:, boolForKey:, dataForKey:, dictionaryForKey:, floatForKey:, integerForKey:, objectForKey:, stringArrayForKey:, and stringForKey:. For instance, to obtain a string value from a key holding a string, you use the stringForKey: method.

```
NSString* value = [[[NSUserDefaults standardUserDefaults]
stringForKey:@"myKey"] retain];
```

Try This Reading the Settings Bundle

1. Open MySettingsAppDelegate.m and modify applicationDidFinishLaunching: to log the application's settings (Listing 14-1). Notice that you also initialize the application's settings.

Listing 14-1 The applicationDidFinishLaunching method in MySettingsAppDelegate

```
- (void)applicationDidFinishLaunching:(UIApplication *)application {
  NSString *testValue = [[NSUserDefaults standardUserDefaults]
  stringForKey:@"keyOne"];
  if (testValue == nil) {
    NSDictionary *appDefaults = [NSDictionary
dictionaryWithObjectsAndKeys: @"keyOneValue", @"keyOne",
@"keyTwoValue", @"keyTwo",@"0", @"keyThree", @"keyFourValue",
@"keyFour", nil];
    [[NSUserDefaults standardUserDefaults] registerDefaults:
appDefaults];
    [[NSUserDefaults standardUserDefaults] synchronize];
  }
  NSUserDefaults * defaults = [NSUserDefaults standardUserDefaults];
  NSLog([defaults stringForKey:@"keyOne"]);
  NSLog([defaults stringForKey:@"keyTwo"]);
  NSLog([defaults stringForKey:@"keyThree"]);
  NSLog([defaults stringForKey:@"keyFour"]);
}
```

2. Click Build And Go. The Debugger Console logs the default values (Listing 14-2).

Listing 14-2 Debugger Console logging settings

```
[Session started at 2009-03-11 20:44:26 -0400.]
2009-03-11 20:44:27.981 MySettings[361:20b] keyOneValue
2009-03-11 20:44:27.982 MySettings[361:20b] keyTwoValue
2009-03-11 20:44:27.982 MySettings[361:20b] 0
2009-03-11 20:44:27.982 MySettings[361:20b] keyFourValue

[Session started at 2009-03-11 20:45:24 -0400.]
2009-03-11 20:45:25.897 MySettings[368:20b] test
2009-03-11 20:45:25.898 MySettings[368:20b] blue
2009-03-11 20:45:25.899 MySettings[368:20b] YES
2009-03-11 20:45:25.899 MySettings[368:20b] 3.784314
```

(continued)

3. Without terminating, tap the Home button and navigate to the Settings application. Change MySetting's values. Exit the Settings application. Terminate the iPhone Simulator.

4. Click Build And Go again, and this time, the default values from the Settings application should appear in the debugger console (see Listing 14-2).

Notice the console does not log the text value represented by keyOne. This is because you did not specify a default value. If you navigate to the Settings application, add a value for the text field, and then exit Settings, the next time you start the application, keyOne will log a value.

Although not well documented, in Apple's AppSettings sample application, code is provided that handles uninitialized preferences. Listing 14-1 uses the sample application's logic to first check if the first setting was set. If not, it creates default settings for the user settings values. Note that it doesn't save these values, though. Until a user actually goes into the Settings application and changes the settings, the MySettings application's user preferences will always default to the values set in the applicationDidFinishLaunching: method.

Summary

It is important to remember that application preferences are for preferences that will not change often. For instance, a user's username, password, and e-mail address are not likely to change often. An application's preferences are set using the Root.plist and zero or more plists for child panes. Users modify an application's preferences through the Settings application. The application can access its preferences through the NSUserDefault class. Again, application preferences are for relatively static preferences, not dynamic preferences that might change often.

Chapter 15

Property Lists and Archiving

Key Skills & Concepts

● Understanding the iPhone directory structure

● Persisting a collection as a property list

● Archiving an object hierarchy

In this chapter, you learn how to persist your data to a file using properties and then how to persist your data using archiving. However, before learning about these two topics, you briefly explore the iPhone's file system.

An iPhone Application's Directory Structure

Persisting and archiving requires writing data to a file, but an iPhone application can only read and write to files in the application's sandbox. When installed, an application is placed in its own home directory. This directory is the application's root directory and should be left untouched, lest you risk corrupting your application. Under the application's home directory are the directories you may write to. These directories are the Documents, Preferences, Caches, and tmp directories.

```
<application home directory>/Documents
<application home directory>/Library/Preferences
<application home directory>/Library/Caches
<application home directory>/tmp
```

The Documents directory is where you should write your application's data files. The Preferences directory is where your application's preferences are stored. These are the preferences set through the iPhone's AppSettings, using the NSUserDefaults class, not preferences you might create programmatically. The Caches directory, like the Documents directory, is another location you can persist files to, although, as the name implies, this directory should be reserved for caching data rather than storing an application's files. The tmp directory is a temporary directory for writing files that do not need persisting between application launches. Your application should remove files from this directory when not needed, but the iPhone operating system also removes files from this folder when an application is not running.

Directories

You will mostly read and write from two directories only: the Documents directory and the tmp directory. Files you wish persisting between application instances should go in the Documents directory. These files are also backed up by iTunes when an iPhone or iPod touch is synchronized with a user's computer. Files placed in the tmp folder are temporary and should be deleted when an application terminates. If the application does not clean the folder, the iPhone's operating system might delete them, depending upon some algorithm the iPhone operating system uses to clean up temporary files. You should never hardcode a path in your code to either folder. When using the Documents folder, you should use the NSHomeDirectory method combined with the NSSearchPathForDirectoriesInDomain method. When obtaining the tmp directory, you should use the NSTemporaryDirectory method.

NSHomeDirectory

The NSHomeDirectory is how you should obtain an application's root directory.

```
NSString * NSHomeDirectory (void);
```

Obtain the path to your Documents directory using the NSHomeDirectory. By itself, this method isn't very useful, as you usually wish obtaining the Documents directory.

NSSearchPathForDirectoriesInDomains

Obtain the path to your application's Documents directory using the NSSearchPathFor DirectoriesInDomains.

```
NSArray * NSSearchPathForDirectoriesInDomains ( NSSearchPathDirectory
directory,
NSSearchPathDomainMask domainMask, BOOL expandTilde );
```

The method takes three parameters: the directory to begin the search, the search path domain mask, and a flag indicating if tildes should be converted to actual paths. The method returns an array of paths. Although on a desktop or laptop there might be multiple elements in the array, on the iPhone, there will only be one result in the array. The following code illustrates obtaining an application's Documents directory on an iPhone:

```
NSArray * myPaths = NSSearchPathForDirectoriesInDomains
(NSDocumentDirectory, NSUserDomainMask, YES);
NSString * myDocPath = [myPaths objectAtIndex:0];
```

Values you might use for the directory parameter on an iPhone include NSDocumentDirectory, NSApplicationDirectory, NSCachesDirectory, and NSApplication SupportDirectory.

NSTemporaryDirectory

The NSTemporaryDirectory method returns the path to your application's tmp directory.

```
NSString * NSTemporaryDirectory (void);
```

Unlike the NSHomeDirectory method, the NSTemporaryDirectory method is useful by itself, as it is the most direct way to obtain a path to your application's tmp directory.

Property Lists

The easiest way to save your application's settings is using a property list. If an object can be serialized, you can persist it to a file using a path or URL. You can also reconstitute the object by reading it from the file.

Simple Serialization

The NSDictionary, NSArray, NSString, NSNumber, and NSData classes, and their mutable equivalents, can all be saved as a property list using the writeToFile: or writeToURL: method.

```
- (BOOL)writeToFile:(NSString *) path atomically:(BOOL)flag
- (BOOL)writeToURL:(NSURL *) aURL atomically:(BOOL)flag
```

The first parameter is the path, or URL, to save the file as. The second parameter is a flag indicating if the file should first be saved to an auxiliary file. If the flag is YES, the data is written to an auxiliary file that is then renamed to the file indicated by the path or URL. Writing to an auxiliary file prevents the file system from becoming corrupt should writing the file fail midstream.

NOTE

You can refer to the NSDictionary, NSArray, NSString, NSNumber, or NSData classes, or one of their mutable equivalents, as a property list object. So you could say "the property list objects" all contain..." rather than naming each property list object individually.

Reading a property list back into the object uses the initWithContentsOfFile: or initWithContentsOfURL: method.

```
- (id)initWithContentsOfFile:(NSString *)path
- (id)initWithContentsOfURL:(NSURL *)aURL
```

The initWithContentsOfFile: method takes a path to the property file, while the initWithContentsOfURL: takes a URL. Both return an id.

Try This   Preserving an NSArray

1. Create a new View-based Application named SimpleArray.

2. Open SimpleArrayAppDelegate.m and modify applicationDidFinishLaunching to match Listing 15-1.

3. Click Build And Go (Listing 15-2).

4. After running the application, navigate to properties.plist and open it in TextEdit (Listing 15-3).

Listing 15-1 The applicationDidFinishLaunching method in SimpleArrayAppDelegate.m

```
- (void)applicationDidFinishLaunching:(UIApplication *)application {
  NSMutableArray * dataArray = [[NSMutableArray alloc] initWithObjects:
@"First", @"Second", @"Third", nil];
  NSString * path = [(NSString *) [NSSearchPathForDirectoriesInDomains
(NSDocumentDirectory, NSUserDomainMask, YES) objectAtIndex:0]
stringByAppendingPathComponent:@"properties.plist"];
  [dataArray writeToFile:path atomically:YES];
  NSArray * dataArray2 = [[NSArray alloc] initWithContentsOfFile:path];
  NSLog(@"objects: %@, %@, %@", [dataArray2 objectAtIndex:0],
[dataArray2 objectAtIndex:1], [dataArray2 objectAtIndex:2]);
  [window addSubview:viewController.view];
  [window makeKeyAndVisible];
  [dataArray release];
  [dataArray2 release];
}
```

The application first gets a path to its Documents directory and adds the filename to the path. After creating the path, the application persists the array to a file. Immediately after persisting the file, it creates a new array from the file's content and logs the array's values to the Debugger Console.

Listing 15-2 Logging to the Debugger Console

```
[Session started at 2009-02-15 15:38:39 -0500.]
2009-02-15 15:38:42.081 SimpleArray[841:20b] objects: First, Second,
Third
```

One thing interesting to note is that the application persists the array in an XML format. If you wished, you could easily modify the data in any text editor. You could also persist the application to a URL, and since it is XML with a published document type definition (DTD), you could process the file with almost any back-end programming language that had libraries for parsing XML and DTD files. However, note that the writeToURL: atomically: method is synchronous and your application will halt processing until the data is successfully written to the URL, so you are better off using a more "official" way via the NSURLConnection class.

(continued)

Listing 15-3   The properties.plist file is saved as XML.

```
<?xml version="1.0" encoding="UTF-8"?>
<!DOCTYPE plist PUBLIC "-//Apple//DTD PLIST 1.0//EN"
"http://www.apple.com/DTDs/PropertyList-1.0.dtd">
<plist version="1.0">
<array>
  <string>First</string>
  <string>Second</string>
  <string>Third</string>
</array>
</plist>
```

NSPropertyListSerialization

Using the writeToFile: method to save a property list object as a simple property list is usually sufficient, but another way you can persist a property list object to a property list is by using the NSPropertyListSerialization class.

Serializing

To serialize a property list object, use the dataFromPropertyList:format:errorDescription: method.

```
+ (NSData *)dataFromPropertyList:(id)plist format:
(NSPropertyListFormat *)format
errorDescription:(NSString **) errorString
```

This method's first parameter is an id that references the property list data, and must be a property list object. Note that the dataFromPropertyList:format:errorDescription: method doesn't open and read a file's content; you must first obtain the data using the initWithContentsOfFile: or initWithContentsOfURL: method. The method's second parameter is the property list's desired format. This parameter is one of the valid NSPropertyListFormat types: NSPropertyListOpen StepFormat, NSPropertyListXMLFormat_v1_0, or NSPropertyListBinaryFormat_v1_0. The method's final parameter is a string to place an error description should something fail. As an aside, you must release this string should an error occur. The method returns an NSData object. You can then write this object to disk, using the writeToFile: or writeToURL: method.

Deserializing

To deserialize a property list, use the propertyListFromData:mutabilityOption:format: errorDescription: method.

```
+ (id)propertyListFromData:(NSData *)data mutabilityOption:(
NSPropertyListMutabilityOptions) opt format:
(NSPropertyListFormat *)format
errorDescription:(NSString **) errorString
```

This method's first parameter is the data to deserialize. The method's second parameter indicates if the properties should be immutable or mutable. The method's third parameter indicates the format to make the property list, and the fourth parameter is the error description. Valid values for the second parameter are NSPropertyListImmutable, NSPropertyListMutable Containers, and NSPropertyListMutableContainersAndLeaves. Valid values for the third parameter are NSPropertyListOpenStepFormat, NSPropertyListXMLFormat_v1_0, and NSPropertyListBinaryFormat_v1_0. Note that as with the dataFromPropertyList: method, should something fail, you must release the NSString holding the error description.

NOTE

Do not take this task's more complex data structure as implying you cannot use a property list object's writeToFile: or writeToURL: method to persist complex data structures. You can, provided all items in a data structure are a property list object. For instance, if an NSArray's elements each contained an NSDictionary, you could serialize the entire data structure at once by writing the NSArray to a file.

`Try This` Preserving to an XML Property List

1. Create a new View-based Application named Properties.

2. Open PropertiesAppDelegate.m and modify the applicationDidFinishLaunching method (Listing 15-4).

3. Click Build And Go.

Listing 15-4   The PropertiesAppDelegate's applicationDidFinishLaunching method

```
- (void)applicationDidFinishLaunching:(UIApplication *)application {
  NSString * errorDescription;
  NSString *pathToFile = [[NSSearchPathForDirectoriesInDomains (
NSDocumentDirectory, NSUserDomainMask,YES) objectAtIndex:0]
stringByAppendingPathComponent:@"properties.plist"];
  NSData * myData;
  NSLog(pathToFile);
  if([[NSFileManager defaultManager] fileExistsAtPath:pathToFile] ==
NO) {
    NSMutableDictionary * dict2Serialize = [[[NSMutableDictionary
alloc] init] autorelease];
    NSString * name = @"James";
    NSArray * kids = [NSArray arrayWithObjects:@"Nicolas",
@"Juliana", nil];
    NSNumber * age = [NSNumber numberWithInt:40];
    [dict2Serialize setObject:name forKey:@"name"];
```

(continued)

```
    [dict2Serialize setObject:kids forKey:@"kids"];
    [dict2Serialize setObject:age forKey:@"age"];
    myData = [NSPropertyListSerialization dataFromPropertyList:(id)
dict2Serialize format:NSPropertyListXMLFormat_v1_0
errorDescription:&errorDescription];
    if(myData)
      [myData writeToFile:pathToFile atomically:YES];
    else {
      NSLog(@"Error writing to myData, error: %@", errorDescription);
      [errorDescription release];
    }
}
  else {
    NSLog(@"property file exists....");
    NSPropertyListFormat format;
    NSData * plistData = [NSData dataWithContentsOfFile:pathToFile];
    NSDictionary * props = (NSDictionary *)[NSPropertyListSerialization
propertyListFromData:plistData mutabilityOption:NSPropertyListImmutable
format:&format errorDescription:&errorDescription];
    NSLog(@"name: %@", [props objectForKey:@"name"]);
    NSLog(@"age: %i", [(NSNumber *)[props objectForKey:@"age"]
intValue]);
    NSLog(@"kid: %@", (NSString *)[(NSArray *)[props
objectForKey:@"kids"] objectAtIndex:0]);
    NSLog(@"kid: %@", (NSString *)[(NSArray *)[props
objectForKey:@"kids"] objectAtIndex:1]);
  }
  [window addSubview:viewController.view];
  [window makeKeyAndVisible];
}
```

The first time you run the application, there will be no debugger output. The second time, however, the application logs to the Debugger Console. Notice that rather than writing the NSDictionary directly to disk, you first transformed it into an NSData object representing the property list. Had this first step of converting to XML gone awry, you would have the error description informing you (hopefully) where the problem occurred. This error handling is not provided using the NSMutableDictionary's writeToFile: method. After converting to a property list, you then persisted it using the NSData's writeToFile method. Listing 15-5 lists the file's XML content. Upon running the application a second time, you read the property list as an NSData object and converted it to an NSDictionary. To prove that the data was in fact reconstituted correctly, you logged the output to the Debugger Console (Listing 15-6).

Listing 15-5   The application's plist saved as XML

```xml
<?xml version="1.0" encoding="UTF-8"?>
<!DOCTYPE plist PUBLIC "-//Apple//DTD PLIST 1.0//EN"
"http://www.apple.com/DTDs/PropertyList-1.0.dtd">
<plist version="1.0">
<dict>
  <key>age</key>
  <integer>40</integer>
  <key>kids</key>
  <array>
    <string>Nicolas</string>
    <string>Juliana</string>
  </array>
  <key>name</key>
  <string>James</string>
</dict>
</plist>
```

Listing 15-6   The application's Debugger Console logging

```
[Session started at 2009-02-15 14:25:19 -0500.]
2009-02-15 14:25:21.487 Properties[729:20b]
/Users/jamesbrannan/Library/Application Support/iPhone
Simulator/User/Applications/01AB70B1-26C5-4DE5-B222
-264710477218/Documents/properties.plist
2009-02-15 14:25:21.488 Properties[729:20b] property file exists....
2009-02-15 14:25:21.492 Properties[729:20b] name: James
2009-02-15 14:25:21.497 Properties[729:20b] age: 40
2009-02-15 14:25:21.497 Properties[729:20b] kid: Nicolas
2009-02-15 14:25:21.499 Properties[729:20b] kid: Juliana
```

Archiving

You can only serialize and deserialize property list objects. Moreover, all of a property list object's constituent objects must also be property list objects. This limitation hinders the usefulness of property lists. Thus, rather than using a property list, you can use archiving. Archiving is a more flexible approach to persisting an object than a property list.

You create an archive using an NSKeyedArchiver. This class persists any object that adopts the NSCoding protocol. You reconstitute an object by using NSKeyedArchiver's complement, the NSKeyedUnarchiver class. In this section, you learn how to create a class that adopts the NSCoding protocol. You then learn how to archive and unarchive this class.

Protocols to Adopt

Archiving a class requires that a class adopt the NSCoding protocol. The class should also adopt the NSCopying protocol when creating a class that adopts the NSCoding protocol.

NSCoding

Classes that adopt this protocol must implement the encodeWithCoder: and initWithCoder: methods. The encodeWithCoder: method encodes the object and the object's instance variables so they can be archived.

```
-  (void)encodeWithCoder:(NSCoder *)encoder
```

The initWithCoder: method decodes the object and the object's instance variables.

```
-  (id)initWithCoder:(NSCoder *)decoder
```

You use both methods in the example task that follows.

NSCopying

When implementing the NSCoding protocol, best practices dictate that you also implement the NSCopying protocol. Classes that implement the NSCopying protocol must implement the copyWithZone method. Remember, when you set one object to another, you are merely creating another reference to the same underlying physical object. For instance, in the following code, both A and B are pointing to the same Foo that was originally allocated and initialized by A.

```
Foo * A = [[Foo alloc] init];
Foo * B = A;
```

When you copy an object, you obtain a distinct physical object, as if the object obtaining the copy actually allocated and initialized the object.

```
Foo * A = [[Foo alloc] init];
Foo * B = [A copy];
```

The method that allows copying is the copyWithZone: method.

```
-  (id)copyWithZone:(NSZone *)zone
```

You can use either this method or NSObject's copy method to obtain what is called a "deep copy" of an object. For more information, refer to Apple's "Memory Management Programming Guide for Cocoa," available online.

NOTE

This chapter only discusses NSCopying briefly, as it is not used in this chapter. It is included because best practices dictate that if a class implements the NSCoding protocol for archiving, it must also implement the NSCopying protocol.

NSKeyedArchiver and NSKeyedUnarchiver

The NSKeyedArchiver class archives objects, while the NSKeyedUnarchiver class unarchives objects.

NSKeyedArchiver

NSKeyedArchiver stores one or more objects to an archive using the initForWritingWith MutableData method. To be archived, an object must implement the NSCoding protocol.

```
- (id)initForWritingWithMutableData:(NSMutableData *)data
```

This method takes a writable data object and returns the archived object as an id. You can then write the archive to disk.

The steps for creating and writing an archive to disk are as follows. First, create an NSMutableData object.

```
NSMutableData * theData = [NSMutableData data];
```

After creating the data object, create an NSKeyedArchiver, passing the newly created data object as a parameter.

```
NSKeyedArchiver * archiver = [[NSKeyedArchiver alloc]
initForWritingWithMutableData:theData];
```

After initializing the NSKeyedArchiver, encode the objects to archive. If you wish, you can encode multiple objects using the same archiver, provided all archived objects adopt the NSCoding protocol. The following code snippet illustrates.

```
[archiver encodeObject:objectA forKey:@"a"];
[archiver encodeObject:objectB forKey:@"b"];
[archiver encodeObject:objectC forKey:@"c"];
[archiver finishEncoding];
```

After archiving, write the data object, which now contains the archived objects, to a file.

```
[theData writeToFile:"myfile.archive" atomically:YES]
```

NSKeyedUnarchiver

You use NSKeyedUnarchiver to unarchive an archive. NSKeyedUnarchiver reconstitutes one or more objects from a data object that was initialized with an archive. To be unarchived, an object must implement the NSCoding protocol. When programming for the iPhone, you use the initForReadingWithData: method.

```
- (id)initForReadingWithData:(NSData *)data
```

The steps to unarchive are similar to archiving. First, create an NSData object from the previously archived file.

```
NSData * theData =[NSData dataWithContentsOfFile:"myfile.archive"];
```

After creating the data object, create and initialize an NSKeyedUnarchiver instance.

```
NSKeyedUnarchiver * uarchiver = [[NSKeyedUnarchiver alloc]
initForReadingWithData:theData];
```

After initializing the NSKeyedUnarchiver, unarchive the objects previously archived.

```
A * objA = [[unarchiver decodeObjectForKey:@"a"] retain];
B * objB = [[unarchiver decodeObjectForKey:@"b"] retain];
C * objC = [[unarchiver decodeObjectForKey:@"c"] retain];
[unarchiver finishDecoding];
[unarchiver release];
```

Try This Archiving and Unarchiving an Object

1. Create a new View-based Application called Encoding.

2. Create a new Objective-C class called Foo.

3. Add two properties to Foo. Make one property an NSString and name it "name" and make the other property an NSNumber and name it "age."

4. Have Foo adopt the NSCopying and NSCoding protocols (Listings 15-7 and 15-8). Remember, Foo must get deep copies of name and age.

5. Modify Foo so it implements the encodeWithCoder:, initWithCoder:, and copyWithZone: methods.

6. Add Foo as a property to EncodingAppDelegate (Listings 15-9 and 15-10).

7. Implement the applicationWillTerminate: method and modify the applicationDidFinish Launching: methods to decode and encode Foo.

8. Click Build And Go.

Listing 15-7 Foo.h

```
#import <Foundation/Foundation.h>
@interface Foo : NSObject <NSCoding, NSCopying> {
```

```
  NSString * name;
  NSNumber * age;
}
@property (nonatomic, retain) NSString * name;
@property (nonatomic, retain) NSNumber * age;
@end
```

Listing 15-8   Foo.m

```
#import "Foo.h"
@implementation Foo
@synthesize name;
@synthesize age;
- (id) copyWithZone: (NSZone *) zone {
  Foo * aFoo = [[Foo allocWithZone:zone] init];
  aFoo.name = [NSString stringWithString: self.name];
  aFoo.age = [NSNumber numberWithInt:[self.age intValue]];
  return aFoo;
}
- (void) encodeWithCoder: (NSCoder *) coder {
  [coder encodeObject: name forKey: @"name"];
  [coder encodeObject:age forKey: @"age"];
}
- (id) initWithCoder: (NSCoder *) coder {
  self = [super init];
  name = [[coder decodeObjectForKey:@"name"] retain];
  age = [[coder decodeObjectForKey:@"age"] retain];
  return self;
}
- (void) dealloc {
  [name release];
  [age release];
  [super dealloc];
}
@end
```

Listing 15-9   EncodingAppDelegate.h

```
#import <UIKit/UIKit.h>
@class Foo;
@class EncodingViewController;
```

(continued)

```
@interface EncodingAppDelegate : NSObject <UIApplicationDelegate> {
  UIWindow *window;
  EncodingViewController *viewController;
  Foo * myFoo;
}
@property (nonatomic, retain) Foo * myFoo;
@property (nonatomic, retain) IBOutlet UIWindow *window;
@property (nonatomic, retain) IBOutlet EncodingViewController
*viewController;
@end
```

Listing 15-10   EncodingAppDelegate.m

```
#import "EncodingAppDelegate.h"
#import "EncodingViewController.h"
#import "Foo.h"
@implementation EncodingAppDelegate
@synthesize window;
@synthesize viewController;
@synthesize myFoo;
- (void)applicationDidFinishLaunching:(UIApplication *)application {
  NSString *pathToFile = [[NSSearchPathForDirectoriesInDomains(
NSDocumentDirectory, NSUserDomainMask,YES) objectAtIndex:0]
stringByAppendingPathComponent:@"foo.archive"];
  NSLog(pathToFile);
  NSData * theData =[NSData dataWithContentsOfFile:pathToFile];
  if([theData length] > 0) {
    NSKeyedUnarchiver * archiver = [[[NSKeyedUnarchiver alloc]
initForReadingWithData:theData] autorelease];
    myFoo = [archiver decodeObjectForKey:@"myfoo"];
    [archiver finishDecoding];
    NSLog(@"nth run - name: %@ age: %i", myFoo.name, [myFoo.age
intValue]);
  }
  else {
    NSLog(@"first run: no name or age");
    myFoo =[[Foo alloc] init];
    myFoo.name = @"James";
    myFoo.age = [NSNumber numberWithInt:40];
  }
  [window addSubview:viewController.view];
  [window makeKeyAndVisible];
}
- (void) applicationWillTerminate: (UIApplication *) application {
  NSString *pathToFile = [[NSSearchPathForDirectoriesInDomains(
```

```
NSDocumentDirectory, NSUserDomainMask,YES) objectAtIndex:0]
stringByAppendingPathComponent:@"foo.archive"];
  NSMutableData * theData = [NSMutableData data];
  NSKeyedArchiver * archiver = [[[NSKeyedArchiver alloc]
initForWritingWithMutableData:theData] autorelease];
  [archiver encodeObject:self.myFoo forKey:@"myfoo"];
  [archiver finishEncoding];
if( [theData writeToFile:pathToFile atomically:YES] == NO)
   NSLog(@"writing failed....");
}
- (void)dealloc {
  [myFoo release];
  [viewController release];
  [window release];
  [super dealloc];
}
@end
```

Try This Archiving and Unarchiving an Object Hierarchy

1. Open the previous application, Encoding, in Xcode.

2. Create a new Objective-C class and name it Bar. Have it adopt the NSCoding and NSCopying protocols (Listings 15-11 and 15-12).

3. Add an NSMutableArray as a property in Bar.

4. Override init to add a couple of Foo objects to the array (Listing 15-13).

5. Implement the initWithCoder:, encodeWithCoder:, and copyWithZone: methods (Listing 15-14).

6. Add Bar as a property to EncodingAppDelegate. Remember, you must import the class, add it as a property to the header, and synthesize the property in the implementation.

7. Modify EncodingAppDelegate's applicationDidFinishLaunching: and applicationWill Terminate: methods to include the newly created Bar property.

8. Navigate to the application's Documents directory and delete the previous foo.archive file.

9. Click Build And Go.

(continued)

Listing 15-11 Bar.h

```
#import <Foundation/Foundation.h>
#import "Foo.h"
@interface Bar : NSObject <NSCoding, NSCopying> {
  NSMutableArray * foos;
}
@property (nonatomic, retain) NSMutableArray * foos;
@end
```

Listing 15-12 Bar.m

```
#import "Bar.h"
@implementation Bar
@synthesize foos;
- (id) init {
  if([super init] == nil) return nil;
  Foo * foo1 = [[Foo alloc] init];
  foo1.name = @"Juliana";
  foo1.age = [NSNumber numberWithInt:7];
  Foo * foo2 = [[Foo alloc] init];
  foo2.name = @"Nicolas";
  foo2.age = [NSNumber numberWithInt:3];
  foos = [[NSMutableArray alloc] initWithObjects:foo1, foo2, nil];
  return self;
}
- (void) encodeWithCoder: (NSCoder *) coder {
  [coder encodeObject: foos forKey:@"foos"];
}
- (id) initWithCoder: (NSCoder *) coder {
  self = [super init];
  foos = [[coder decodeObjectForKey:@"foos"] retain];
  return self;
}
- (id) copyWithZone: (NSZone *) zone {
  Bar * aBar = [[Bar allocWithZone:zone] init];
  NSMutableArray *newArray = [[[NSMutableArray alloc] initWithArray:
self.foos copyItems:YES] autorelease];
  aBar.foos = newArray;
  return aBar;
}
- (void) dealloc {
  [foos release];
  [super dealloc];
}
@end
```

Listing 15-13 EncodingAppDelegate.h

```
#import <UIKit/UIKit.h>
#import "Bar.h"
@class Foo;
@class EncodingViewController;
@interface EncodingAppDelegate : NSObject <UIApplicationDelegate> {
  UIWindow *window;
  EncodingViewController *viewController;
  Foo * myFoo;
  Bar * myBar;
}
@property (nonatomic, retain) Foo * myFoo;
@property (nonatomic, retain) Bar * myBar;
@property (nonatomic, retain) IBOutlet UIWindow *window;
@property (nonatomic, retain) IBOutlet EncodingViewController
*viewController;
@end
```

Listing 15-14 EncodingAppDelegate.m

```
#import "EncodingAppDelegate.h"
#import "EncodingViewController.h"
#import "Foo.h"
@implementation EncodingAppDelegate
@synthesize window;
@synthesize viewController;
@synthesize myFoo;
@synthesize myBar;
- (void)applicationDidFinishLaunching:(UIApplication *)application {
  NSString *pathToFile = [[NSSearchPathForDirectoriesInDomains(
NSDocumentDirectory, NSUserDomainMask,YES) objectAtIndex:0]
stringByAppendingPathComponent:@"foo.archive"];
  NSLog(pathToFile);
  NSData * theData =[NSData dataWithContentsOfFile:pathToFile];
  if([theData length] > 0) {
    NSKeyedUnarchiver * archiver = [[[NSKeyedUnarchiver alloc]
initForReadingWithData:theData] autorelease];
    myFoo = [archiver decodeObjectForKey:@"myfoo"];
    myBar = [archiver decodeObjectForKey:@"mybar"];
    [archiver finishDecoding];
  NSLog(@"nth run - name: %@ age: %i", myFoo.name, [myFoo.age
intValue]);
```

(continued)

```
    NSArray * array = myBar.foos;
    for(Foo * aFoo in array) {
       NSLog(@"Foo: name: %@, age: %i", aFoo.name, [aFoo.age
intValue]);
     }
  }
  else {
    NSLog(@"first run: no name or age");
    myFoo =[[Foo alloc] init];
    myFoo.name = @"James";
    myFoo.age = [NSNumber numberWithInt:40];
    myBar = [[Bar alloc] init];
  }
  [window addSubview:viewController.view];
  [window makeKeyAndVisible];
}
- (void) applicationWillTerminate: (UIApplication *) application {
  NSString *pathToFile = [[NSSearchPathForDirectoriesInDomains(
NSDocumentDirectory, NSUserDomainMask,YES) objectAtIndex:0]
stringByAppendingPathComponent:@"foo.archive"];
  NSMutableData * theData = [NSMutableData data];
  NSKeyedArchiver * archiver = [[[NSKeyedArchiver alloc]
initForWritingWithMutableData:theData] autorelease];
  [archiver encodeObject:myFoo forKey:@"myfoo"];
  [archiver encodeObject:myBar forKey:@"mybar"];
  [archiver finishEncoding];
if( [theData writeToFile:pathToFile atomically:YES] == NO)
    NSLog(@"writing failed....");
}
- (void)dealloc {
  [myFoo release];
  [myBar release];
  [viewController release];
  [window release];
  [super dealloc];
}
@end
```

When the application starts, it loads the archive file into a data object. If the data object is null, the file doesn't exist. If the file does exist, the data is unarchived. When the application terminates, it archives Foo. Because Bar contains constituent Foo objects in an array, it also archives those objects. The key for the archived Foo is "myfoo," and "mybar" for the archived Bar object. Both Foo and Bar implement the NSCoding protocol. This allows them to be archived. Notice that Bar contains an NSMutableArray of Foo objects. Because NSMutableArray adopts the NSCoding protocol, NSMutableArray can be encoded and decoded. Moreover, the NSMutableArray knows to encode or decode its constituent elements.

Now examine Bar's copyWithZone method. Because Bar contains an NSMutableArray of Foo objects, when copying a Bar you must also copy the Bar's Foo array. But you cannot just set the new Bar's array to the old Bar's array, as the new Bar's array will simply be a pointer to the old Bar's array. Instead you must create a new NSMutableArray and initialize the new array with the old array, being certain to specify copyItems as YES. By taking this step, the new Bar obtains a deep copy of the old Bar's array of Foo objects.

NOTE

For more information on archiving, refer to "Apple's Archives and Serializations Programming Guide for Cocoa."

Summary

In this chapter, you learned how to persist an application's data using property lists and archiving. Personally, I do not advocate using these techniques to persist more than a few objects to a file. Large object hierarchies are much better persisted using SQLite or the Core Data framework. But for small data amounts, persisting to a property list or archiving is fine. In this chapter, you learned methods for doing both. As a rule of thumb, if persisting variables not tied to particular objects, simply place them in a collection and persist the collection as a property list. But if persisting variables that are object properties, have the objects adopt the NSCoding protocol and archive the objects. If persisting a moderate to large amount of data, use SQLite or use the Core Data framework. If you wish using the data outside of an iPhone or Cocoa application, you should use SQLite.

Chapter 16

Data Persistence
Using SQLite

Key Skills & Concepts

- Creating a database and adding data to it
- Including the database in Xcode
- Reading from a database
- Making a database writable
- Inserting a record
- Updating a record
- Deleting a record

The SQLite database is a popular open-source database written in C. The database is small and designed for embedding in an application. Unlike a database such as Oracle, SQLite is a C library included when compiling a program. SQLite is part of the standard open-source Linux/BSD server stack, and as OS X is essentially FreeBSD, it was only natural Apple chose SQLite as the iPhone's embedded database.

Adding a SQLite Database

Adding a SQLite database to your project involves two steps. First, you must create the database. In this chapter's first task, you create a database using the Firefox SQLite Manager plug-in. Second, you must add the SQLite library to your Xcode project. The first task also illustrates adding the SQLite library to your Xcode project. After creating the database and loading it, you can then use the database programmatically using its C programming interface.

Try This Creating a Simple Database Using FireFox SQLite Manager

1. If you don't already have Firefox, download and install it.
2. Select Add-ons from the Tools menu (Figure 16-1).
3. Select Get Add-ons, type **SQLite** in the search box, and install SQLite Manager.
4. Once installed and you have restarted Firefox, select Tools | SQLite Manager.

Figure 16-1 Adding SQLite Manager to Firefox

5. Select the New icon (the blank paper graphic), and create a new database named myDatabase. Note SQLite Manager automatically adds the .sqlite extension.

6. Click Create Table and create a new table named photos.

7. Add three columns: id, name, and photo. Make id an INTEGER and check Primary Key and Autoinc check boxes.

8. Make name a VARCHAR and check only Allow Null.

9. Make photo a BLOB and check only Allow Null.

10. Your screen should resemble Figure 16-2.

11. Click OK and the SQLite Manager generates the database table.

(continued)

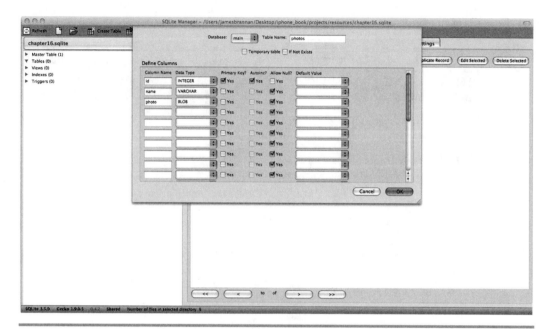

Figure 16-2 Creating a database using SQLite Manager

NOTE

SQLite does not enforce foreign key relationships. You must instead write triggers manually to enforce foreign key relationships. SQLite does not support right outer joins or full outer joins. SQLite views are read-only.

1. Click the Browse & Search tab, and then click the Add Record button.

2. In the action sheet, leave id blank. Name the name Icon One. Notice the small paperclip beside photo. Move your mouse over the paperclip, and the tooltip should say "Add File as a Blob" (Figure 16-3). Click the paperclip and add a photo from the book's Resources folder. If the photo column doesn't say something like BLOB (Size: 65984), the file was not added as a blob.

3. Click OK, and the record is added. Add another record, selecting any image from this book's Resources folder.

4. From the menu, select Database | Close Database and close the database. Exit and quit Firefox.

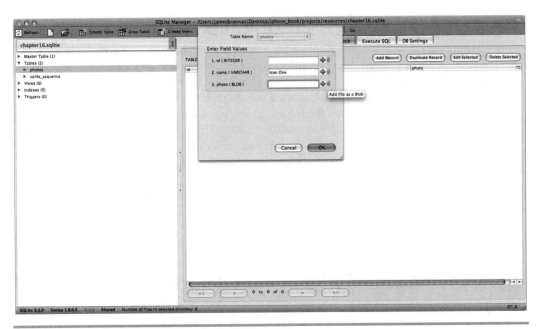

Figure 16-3 Adding a record using SQLite Manager

5. Open Xcode and create a new View-based Application. Name the application MyDBProject.

6. Select Frameworks in Groups & Files. Right-click Frameworks and select Add | Existing Frameworks from the pop-up menu.

7. Navigate to your iPhone Simulator's sdk folder.

8. Navigate to usr/lib and add libsqlite3.0.dylib to the project.

9. Add the database file to the Resources in Groups & Files. Like a photo, check the Copy Items check box.

10. This task is completed. Do not delete the project or database, as you use them for this chapter's remainder.

NOTE

On my computer, adding binary data using SQLite Manager is buggy. Sometimes it works, sometimes not. If getting the file's content added is problematic, a workaround is to add the record and insert Null for the blob's value. After inserting, update the row, and add the file's content. Updating the blob seems more stable in SQLite Manager.

Basic SQLite Database Manipulation

If you have ever used a database from within a programming language, SQLite database manipulation using C should seem intuitive. You open the database. You create a prepared statement containing an SQL string. That statement might have one or more parameters you bind values to. After binding, you execute the statement. If the statement returns results, you loop through each record and load the record's column values into your program's variables. After looping through all records, you finalize the statement, and, if you are finished with the database, you close the database. The steps are similar for most languages and databases.

Opening the Database

You open a database using the sqlite3_open, sqlite_open16, or sqlite3_open_v2 commands. This chapter uses the sqlite3_open command exclusively. The sqlite3_open command takes a database filename as a UTF-8 string and opens the database. Listing 16-1, taken from the SQLite's online documentation, lists the sqlite_open3 method signature.

Listing 16-1   The sqlite3_open method signature (from SQLite online documentation)

```
int sqlite3_open(
  const char *filename, /* Database filename (UTF-8) */
  sqlite3 **ppDb /* OUT: SQLite db handle */
);
```

The method returns an integer as the method's success or failure code. Listing 16-2, from the SQLite online documentation, lists several common result codes.

Listing 16-2   SQLite return codes (taken from SQLite online documentation)

```
#define SQLITE_OK            0    /* Successful result */
#define SQLITE_ERROR         1    /* SQL error or missing database */
#define SQLITE_READONLY      8    /* Attempt to write a readonly
database */
#define SQLITE_INTERRUPT     9    /* Operation terminated by
#define SQLITE_IOERR        10    /* Some kind of disk I/O error
occurred */
#define SQLITE_CANTOPEN     14    /* Unable to open the database file */
#define SQLITE_MISMATCH     20    /* Data type mismatch */
#define SQLITE_ROW         100    /* sqlite3_step() has another row
ready */
#define SQLITE_DONE        101    /* sqlite3_step() has finished
executing */
```

Statements, Preparing Statements, and Executing Statements

There are two primary ways of executing SQL statements using SQLite's C interface. One method is the sqlite3_exec method. Although a powerful method, it is more advanced C programming, and so this chapter uses the sqlite3_stmt structure and the sqlite3_prepare_v2 and sqlite3_step statements instead of the sqlite3_exec function.

The SQLite sqlite3_stmt

The sqlite3_stmt encapsulates a SQL statement. For instance, "select * from photos" is a SQL statement. In your program, you encapsulate this SQL string using a statement. For instance, the following code snippet illustrates creating a SQL string, initializing a statement, and loading the statement (Listing 16-3).

Listing 16-3   Using a sqlite3_stmt in a C program

```
const char *sqlselect = "SELECT id,name,photo FROM photos";
static sqlite3_stmt *statement = nil;
sqlite3_prepare_v2(database, sqlselect, -1, &statement, NULL);
```

The SQLite sqlite3_prepare_v2 Method

You load a SQL string into a statement using sqlite3_prepare methods. The prepare methods are sqlite3_prepare, sqlite3_prepare_v2, sqlite3_prepare_16, and sqlite3_prepare16_v2. This chapter uses only the sqlite3_prepare_v2 method. Notice the prepare statement takes a C string, not an NString, but getting the C string from an NString is not difficult—simply call the NSString's UTF8String method. The sqlite3_prepare_v2 method's signature is in Listing 16-4. Notice, like the open statements, the prepare statement returns an integer result code you should check when calling the method.

Listing 16-4   The sqlite3_prepare_v2 method signature (taken from the SQLite online documentation)

```
int sqlite3_prepare_v2(
  sqlite3 *db,            /* Database handle */
  const char *zSql,       /* SQL statement, UTF-8 encoded */
  int nByte,              /* Maximum length of zSql in bytes. */
  sqlite3_stmt **ppStmt,  /* OUT: Statement handle */
  const char **pzTail     /* OUT: Pointer to unused portion of zSql */
);
```

After preparing the statement, you execute it and step through the results.

The SQLite sqlite3_step Method

The sqlite3_step method executes a prepared statement. You must call this method at least once. For instance, when calling insert or update, you call sqlite3_step once. You only call it once because these statements do not result in a record set being returned from the database. When selecting data, you typically call this method multiple times until you receive no more results. The following is the method's signature.

```
int sqlite3_step(sqlite3_stmt*);
```

Like the other SQLite methods, this method returns a response code you should check after calling the method.

Select

You select one or more records from a SQL database using a select statement. Because a select statement usually returns multiple rows, you must loop through the row set if you wish to obtain all records.

```
while (sqlite3_step(statement) == SQLITE_ROW){
  //process row here
}
```

Obtaining SQLite Column Values

You obtain column values through a method in Listing 16-5. Using these methods will become more apparent after the next task.

Listing 16-5   Methods for obtaining column data (from SQLite online documentation)

```
const void *sqlite3_column_blob(sqlite3_stmt*, int iCol);
int sqlite3_column_bytes(sqlite3_stmt*, int iCol);
int sqlite3_column_bytes16(sqlite3_stmt*, int iCol);
double sqlite3_column_double(sqlite3_stmt*, int iCol);
int sqlite3_column_int(sqlite3_stmt*, int iCol);
sqlite3_int64 sqlite3_column_int64(sqlite3_stmt*, int iCol);
const unsigned char *sqlite3_column_text(sqlite3_stmt*, int iCol);
const void *sqlite3_column_text16(sqlite3_stmt*, int iCol);
int sqlite3_column_type(sqlite3_stmt*, int iCol);
sqlite3_value *sqlite3_column_value(sqlite3_stmt*, int iCol);
```

Try This Opening and Querying a Database

1. Open MyDBProject in Xcode. Open MyDBProjectAppDelegate.h.

2. In Classes, create a new group called Model.

3. Add a new Objective-C class called PhotosDAO to Model. Create another Objective-C class called PhotoDAO.

4. Add a name, photoID, and photo property to PhotoDAO.h and PhotoDAO.m (Listings 16-6 and 16-7).

5. Open PhotosDAO.h and import SQLite3 and PhotoDAO. Add a reference to the database you will use (Listing 16-8).

6. Add a getAllPhotos method to PhotosDAO and implement the method (Listing 16-9).

7. Open MyDBProjectViewController.h and import PhotosDAO and PhotoDAO (Listing 16-10).

8. Add an NSMutableArray property to hold the photos. Add an IBOutlet for a UIImageView. Add a UILabel named theLabel, add an IBAction, and name the method changeImage.

9. Open MyDBProjectViewController.m and synthesize photos and theImageView (Listing 16-11).

10. Implement the viewDidLoad and changeImage methods so they match Listing 16-11.

11. Save or build the application.

Listing 16-6   PhotoDAO.h

```
#import <Foundation/Foundation.h>
@interface PhotoDAO : NSObject {
  NSString * name;
  NSInteger photoID;
  UIImage * photo;
}
@property (nonatomic, retain) NSString * name;
@property (nonatomic, assign) NSInteger photoID;
@property (nonatomic, retain) UIImage * photo;
@end
```

(continued)

Listing 16-7   PhotoDAO.m

```
#import "PhotoDAO.h"
@implementation PhotoDAO
@synthesize name;
@synthesize photoID;
@synthesize photo;
- (void) dealloc {
  [name release];
  [photo release];
  [super dealloc];
}
@end
```

Listing 16-8   PhotosDAO.h

```
#import <Foundation/Foundation.h>
#import <sqlite3.h>
#import "PhotoDAO.h"
@interface PhotosDAO : NSObject {
  sqlite3 *database;
}
- (NSMutableArray *) getAllPhotos;
@end
```

Listing 16-9   PhotosDAO.m

```
#import "PhotosDAO.h"
@implementation PhotosDAO
- (NSMutableArray *) getAllPhotos {
  NSMutableArray * photosArray = [[NSMutableArray alloc] init];
  @try {
    NSFileManager *fileManager = [NSFileManager defaultManager];
    NSString *theDBPath = [[[NSBundle mainBundle] resourcePath]
stringByAppendingPathComponent:@"myDatabase.sqlite"];
    BOOL success = [fileManager fileExistsAtPath:theDBPath];
    if (!success) { NSLog(@"Failed to find database file '%@'.",
theDBPath);}
    if (!(sqlite3_open([theDBPath UTF8String], &database) == SQLITE_
OK)) {
      NSLog(@"An error opening database, normally handle error
here.");
    }
```

```
    const char *sql = "SELECT id,name,photo FROM photos";
    sqlite3_stmt *statement;
    if (sqlite3_prepare_v2(database, sql, -1, &statement, NULL) !=
SQLITE_OK){
        NSLog(@"Error, failed to prepare statement, normally handle
error here.");
    }
    while (sqlite3_step(statement) == SQLITE_ROW) {
        PhotoDAO * aPhoto = [[PhotoDAO alloc] init];
        aPhoto.photoID = sqlite3_column_int(statement, 0);
        aPhoto.name = [NSString stringWithUTF8String:(char *)
        sqlite3_column_text(statement, 1)];
        const char * rawData = sqlite3_column_blob(statement, 2);
        int rawDataLength = sqlite3_column_bytes(statement, 2);
        NSData *data = [NSData dataWithBytes:rawData length:
rawDataLength];
        aPhoto.photo = [[UIImage alloc] initWithData:data];
        [photosArray addObject:aPhoto];
        [aPhoto release];
    }
    if(sqlite3_finalize(statement) != SQLITE_OK){
        NSLog(@"Failed to finalize data statement, normally error
handling here.");
    }
    if (sqlite3_close(database) != SQLITE_OK) {
        NSLog(@"Failed to close database, normally error handling
here.");
    }
  }
  @catch (NSException *e) {
    NSLog(@"An exception occurred: %@", [e reason]);
    return nil;
  }
  return photosArray;
}
@end
```

Listing 16-10   MyDBProjectViewController.h

```
#import <UIKit/UIKit.h>
#import "PhotoDAO.h";
#import "PhotosDAO.h";
```

(continued)

```
@interface MyDBProjectViewController : UIViewController {
  NSMutableArray * photos;
  IBOutlet UIImageView * theImageView;
  IBOutlet UILabel * theLabel;
}
@property (nonatomic, retain) NSMutableArray * photos;
@property (nonatomic, retain) IBOutlet UIImageView * theImageView;
@property (nonatomic, retain) IBOutlet UILabel * theLabel;
- (IBAction) changeImage: (id) sender;
@end
```

Listing 16-11   MyDBProjectViewController.m

```
#import "MyDBProjectViewController.h"
@implementation MyDBProjectViewController
@synthesize photos;
@synthesize theImageView;
@synthesize theLabel;
- (void)viewDidLoad {
  PhotosDAO * myPhotos = [[PhotosDAO alloc] init];
  self.photos = [myPhotos getAllPhotos];
  [self.theImageView setImage:((PhotoDAO *)[self.photos
objectAtIndex:0]).photo];
  [self.theLabel setText:((PhotoDAO *)[self.photos objectAtIndex:0]).
name];
  [myPhotos release];
  [super viewDidLoad];
}
- (IBAction) changeImage: (id) sender {
  static NSInteger currentElement = 0;
  if(++currentElement == [self.photos count]) currentElement = 0;
  PhotoDAO * aPhoto = (PhotoDAO *) [self.photos objectAtIndex:
currentElement];
  [self.theLabel setText:aPhoto.name];
  [self.theImageView setImage:aPhoto.photo];
}
- (void)dealloc {
  [photos release];
  [theImageView release];
  [theLabel release];
  [super dealloc];
}
@end
```

Figure 16-4   Adding a UIImageView and a UIToolBar to the view's canvas

12. Open MyDBProjectViewController.xib in Interface Builder. Add a toolbar, a label, and a UIImageView (Figure 16-4). Change the button's title to Next. Remove the text from the label.

13. Connect the File's Owner theLabel outlet to the label added to the toolbar. Connect the theImageView outlet to the UIImageView. Connect the changeImage action to the Next button. Save and exit Interface Builder.

14. Build and run the application in iPhone Simulator. As I am a registered developer, I deployed the application to my iPhone and ran the application (Figures 16-5 and 16-6). Aren't they cute? Excuse my obligatory computer book author's inclusion of his or her kids into the book.

NOTE

You should never load an entire database at once when creating a real application, especially when using a large blob, like this example. Only load what you need. But for simplicity, you loaded all records in this task.

(continued)

Figure 16-5 Running the application on my iPhone (first image)

Figure 16-6 Running the application on my iPhone (second image)

The Model-View-Controller

When writing a program for any platform, you should adhere to the MVC design pattern as closely as possible. Rather than placing the database logic in a view or view controller, you created separate classes, insulating the view and controller layers from the database layer. The MyDBProjectViewController knows nothing about the underlying SQLite3 library; the view controller only knows about PhotosDAO and PhotoDAO. Notice you further separated the code by placing it in its own group, Model, under Classes. All this separation makes debugging and maintaining the program easier. It also makes reading and understanding this chapter's example code easier.

Opening the Database

To keep the task's length manageable and focused, rather than creating several data access methods in PhotosDAO, you only created one.

```
- (NSMutableArray *) getAllPhotos;
```

This method returns an array of PhotoDAO objects. The getAllPhotos method first finds the database and opens it. Because the database is in the resources folder, you can access it directly using the bundle's resourcePath.

```
NSFileManager *fileManager = [NSFileManager defaultManager];

NSString *theDBPath = [[[NSBundle mainBundle] resourcePath]
stringByAppendingPathComponent: @"chapter18.sqlite"];
```

After obtaining the database's path, you open it.

```
if (!(sqlite3_open([theDBPath UTF8String], &database) == SQLITE_OK))
```

Notice that you obtain the UTF8String from the NSString before passing the sqlite3_open method the path.

Querying the Data

After opening the database, you query it for the photo records. If you have ever worked with a database using code, for instance, Java Database Connectivity (JDBC), then this code should look familiar. The getAllPhotos method first creates the SQL select string. Next, the method places the string in a statement and then queries the database. After obtaining the data, getAllPhotos loops through each record.

For each new record, getAllPhotos creates a new PhotoDAO. The newly created PhotoDAO object's values are then set to the appropriate values from the current record. After initializing the PhotoDAO object, getAllPhotos places the object into PhotosDAO's photosArray.

Loading a Blob into NSData

This code snippet is useful. It shows you a quick, easy way to load a blob, any blob, into an NSData object. First, load the blob into a C string.

```
const char * rawData = sqlite3_column_blob(statement, 2);
```

Second, obtain the blob's byte size.

```
int rawDataLength = sqlite3_column_bytes(statement, 2);
```

Third, create an NSData class using the C string and size variables.

```
NSData *data = [NSData dataWithBytes:rawData length:rawDataLength];
```

As you already know the database blob is an image, you initialize the PhotoDAO's photo property using the UIImage's initWithData method.

```
aPhoto.photo = [[UIImage alloc] initWithData:data];
```

This same technique works for other binary data as well (replacing UIImage with the appropriate class).

Closing the Database

When finished using a statement, you release its resources by finalizing the statement.

```
if(sqlite3_finalize(statement) != SQLITE_OK)
```

After you no longer need the database, you close it.

```
if (sqlite3_close(database) != SQLITE_OK)
```

Selecting all records only has limited value. Rarely will you use SQL statements where you do not wish to limit the results returned. For this, you typically add parameters to your SQL statements and then replace the parameters with values in your program. This is called binding your program's values to the statements' parameters. Programs must also usually allow more than simply selecting data; most applications allow users to add, edit, and delete records. In the next section, you learn about binding, inserting, updating, and deleting records.

SQLite Binding, Inserting, Updating, and Deleting

SQL allows limiting data to only the data needed via the where clause. For instance, the following statement only selects records whose age column is greater than 30.

```
select * from mytable where age > 30
```

When placing SQL statements like this into a SQLite statement, you can parameterize the where clause's value. For instance, to parameterize age's value, write the following code.

```
select * from mytable where age > ?
```

You then bind your program's value to the SQL statement's parameter.

Binding

You bind one of your program's values to a SQL statement's parameter using a bind method (Listing 16-12). Different data types have different bind methods.

Listing 16-12   SQLite bind methods (from the SQLite online documentation)

```
int sqlite3_bind_blob(sqlite3_stmt*, int, const void*, int n,
void(*)(void*));
int sqlite3_bind_double(sqlite3_stmt*, int, double);
int sqlite3_bind_int(sqlite3_stmt*, int, int);
int sqlite3_bind_int64(sqlite3_stmt*, int, sqlite3_int64);
int sqlite3_bind_null(sqlite3_stmt*, int);
int sqlite3_bind_text(sqlite3_stmt*, int, const char*, int n,
void(*)(void*));
int sqlite3_bind_text16(sqlite3_stmt*, int, const void*, int,
void(*)(void*));
int sqlite3_bind_value(sqlite3_stmt*, int, const sqlite3_value*);
int sqlite3_bind_zeroblob(sqlite3_stmt*, int, int n);
```

NOTE
Bindings start with 1 rather than 0.

For instance, the following code snippet shows a SQL statement and its subsequent binding.

```
const char * select_statement = "Select * from photos where name = ?";
sqlite3_bind_text(select_statement, 1, [photo.name UTF8String], -1,
SQLITE_TRANSIENT);
```

The first argument is a pointer to the prepared statement. The second argument is the SQL statement's parameter number. The third argument is the value that should be bound to the SQL statement's parameter. The fourth argument is the number of bytes in the value—if negative, the length is automatically determined from the C string

Insert, Update, and Delete
There is little difference between the steps for inserting, updating, or deleting records using the SQLite C library. The primary difference is you only call the sqlite3_step method once. Usually, you use insert, update, or delete with binding. For instance,

```
insert into customers (name, age, company, location) values (?, ?, ?,?);
```

or

```
update customers set location = ? where company = ?;
```

or

```
delete customers where company = ?;
```

In the following task, you insert, update, and delete a record.

Try This Inserting, Updating, and Deleting Records

Making a Database Writable

1. Open the MYDBProject project in Xcode.

2. Add a class method named moveDatabase to PhotosDAO. Remember, a class method uses a plus rather than a minus.

3. Implement the method in PhotosDAO.m as in Listing 16-13.

4. Modify the getAllPhotos method in PhotosDAO to obtain the records from the documents directory.

5. Open MYDBProjectViewController.m and add a call to the moveDatabase method to the first line of viewDidLoad (Listing 16-14).

Listing 16-13 The moveDatabase and getAllPhotos methods

```
+ (void) moveDatabase {
  NSFileManager *fileManager = [NSFileManager defaultManager];
  NSString *theDBPath = [[[NSBundle mainBundle] resourcePath]
stringByAppendingPathComponent:@"myDatabase.sqlite"];
  NSError *error;
  BOOL success;
  NSArray * paths = NSSearchPathForDirectoriesInDomains
(NSDocumentDirectory, NSUserDomainMask, YES);
  NSString * docsDir = [paths objectAtIndex:0];
  NSString * newPath = [docsDir
stringByAppendingPathComponent:@"chapter18.sqlite"];
  [fileManager removeItemAtPath:newPath error: &error];
  success = [fileManager copyItemAtPath:theDBPath toPath:newPath
error: &error];
  if (!success) {
    NSLog(@"Failed to copy database...error handling here %@.", [error
localizedDescription]);
  }
}
- (NSMutableArray *) getAllPhotos {
  NSMutableArray * photosArray = [[NSMutableArray alloc] init];
  @try {
    NSFileManager *fileManager = [NSFileManager defaultManager];
    NSArray * paths = NSSearchPathForDirectoriesInDomains
(NSDocumentDirectory, NSUserDomainMask, YES);
    NSString * docsDir = [paths objectAtIndex:0];
```

```
    NSString * theDBPath = [docsDir stringByAppendingPathComponent:
@"myDatabase.sqlite"];
    BOOL success = [fileManager fileExistsAtPath:theDBPath];
    if (!success) {
      NSLog(@"Failed to find database file '%@'.");
    }
    if (!(sqlite3_open([theDBPath UTF8String], &database) ==
SQLITE_OK)) {
      NSLog(@"An error opening database, normally handle error
here.");
    }
    const char *sql = "SELECT id,name,photo FROM photos";
    sqlite3_stmt *statement;
    if (sqlite3_prepare_v2(database, sql, -1, &statement, NULL) !=
SQLITE_OK) {
      NSLog(@"Error, failed to prepare statement, normally handle
error here.");
    }
    while (sqlite3_step(statement) == SQLITE_ROW) {
      PhotoDAO * aPhoto = [[PhotoDAO alloc] init];
      aPhoto.photoID = sqlite3_column_int(statement, 0);
      aPhoto.name = [NSString stringWithUTF8String:(char *)
sqlite3_column_text(statement, 1)];
      const char * rawData = sqlite3_column_blob(statement, 2);
      int rawDataLength = sqlite3_column_bytes(statement, 2);
      NSData *data = [NSData dataWithBytes:rawData length:
rawDataLength];
      aPhoto.photo = [[UIImage alloc] initWithData:data];
      [photosArray addObject:aPhoto];
    }
    if(sqlite3_finalize(statement) != SQLITE_OK)
    { NSLog(@"Failed to finalize data statement, normally error
handling here."); }
    if (sqlite3_close(database) != SQLITE_OK) {
      NSLog(@"Failed to close database, normally error handling
here."); }
  }
  @catch (NSException *e) {
    NSLog(@"An exception occurred: %@", [e reason]);
    return nil;
  }
  return photosArray;
}
```

(continued)

Listing 16-14   The viewDidLoad method

```
- (void) viewDidLoad {
  [PhotosDAO moveDatabase];
  PhotosDAO * myPhotos = [[PhotosDAO alloc] init];
  self.photos = [myPhotos getAllPhotos];
  [self.theImageView setImage:((PhotoDAO *)[self.photos
objectAtIndex:0]).photo];
  [self.theLabel setText:((PhotoDAO *)[self.photos objectAtIndex:0])
.name];
  [myPhotos release];
  [super viewDidLoad];
}
```

The first thing you do is make the database writeable. The Resources folder is read-only. Saving changes requires the database to be writable, so you copied the database to your documents directory. You also modified the getAllPhotos method so it obtained the database from the application's document directory rather than the resources directory.

Inserting Records

1. Add kids.png to the project's Resources group. You can find this photo in the book's Resources folder.

2. Add a new method to PhotosDAO called addPhoto. Implement the method (Listing 16-15).

3. Create a new IBAction in MyDBProjectViewController called addKidPhoto (Listing 16-16).

4. Build and save the application.

5. Open MyDBProjectViewController.xib and add a new Bar Button item to the toolbar. Change the bar button's title to Add.

6. Connect the addKidPhoto action to the Add button. \

7. Save and exit Interface Builder.

8. Click Build And Go to run the application in the iPhone Simulator (Figure 16-7).

Listing 16-15   The addPhoto method

```
- (void) addPhoto : (PhotoDAO *) photo {
  const char * sql = "insert into photos (name, photo) values (?, ?)";
  sqlite3_stmt *insert_statement = nil;
  NSArray * paths = NSSearchPathForDirectoriesInDomains
(NSDocumentDirectory, NSUserDomainMask, YES);
```

Figure 16-7   Running the application on my iPhone

```
    NSString * docsDir = [paths objectAtIndex:0];
    NSString * thePath = [docsDir stringByAppendingPathComponent:
@"myDatabase.sqlite"];
    sqlite3_open([thePath UTF8String], &database);
    sqlite3_prepare_v2(database, sql, -1, &insert_statement, NULL);
    sqlite3_bind_text(insert_statement, 1, [photo.name UTF8String], -1,
SQLITE_TRANSIENT);
    NSData * binData = UIImagePNGRepresentation(photo.photo);
    sqlite3_bind_blob(insert_statement, 2, [binData bytes], [binData
length], SQLITE_TRANSIENT);
    sqlite3_step(insert_statement);
    sqlite3_finalize(insert_statement);
    sqlite3_close(database);
  }
```

Listing 16-16   The addKidPhoto IBAction

```
- (IBAction) addKidPhoto: (id) sender {
    static BOOL wasAdded;
```

(continued)

```
if(!wasAdded) {
    PhotosDAO * myPhotos = [[PhotosDAO alloc] init];
    PhotoDAO * aPhoto = [[PhotoDAO alloc] init];
    NSString * imgPath = [[[NSBundle mainBundle] resourcePath]
stringByAppendingPathComponent:@"kids.png"];
    aPhoto.name = @"Kids Both";
    aPhoto.photo = [[UIImage alloc] initWithContentsOfFile:imgPath];
    [myPhotos addPhoto:aPhoto];
    [self.photos release];
    self.photos = [myPhotos getAllPhotos];
    [myPhotos release];
    wasAdded = YES;
  }
}
```

The addPhoto method (Listing 16-15) allows new photos to be inserted. As it is a simple example, the method merely gets the photo from your resources group. The addPhoto method first creates a SQL string with parameters. The method then replaces the question marks by binding them to the appropriate value. For instance, the name column is text, so addPhoto binds it to a C string. The UIImage is binary, so it is bound to a blob. After binding, addPhoto then inserts the record by calling the sqlite3_step method. This method is called only once, as no data is returned from the insert statement. Notice, for brevity, an examination of the return code is omitted, as is other error handling from Listing 16-6 forward.

Updating Records

1. Return to the Xcode project.

2. Drag woman.png from the book's Resources folder to the Resources group in Xcode.

3. Add a new NSInteger called currentID to MyDBProjectViewController.m. Change the changeImage method to update this new variable with the current photo's id from the database (Listing 16-17).

4. Add a new method called changeAPhotoImage to PhotosDAO (Listing 6-18).

5. Add a new IBAction called changePhotosImage to MyDBProjectViewController (Listing 16-19). Save and build the application.

6. Open MyDBProjectViewController.xib in Interface Builder and add another bar button to the toolbar. Change the button's title to Change.

7. Connect the changePhotosImage action to the Change button.

8. Save and exit Interface Builder. Click Build And Go to run the application in the iPhone Simulator (Figure 16-8).

Figure 16-8   Changing the image

Listing 16-17   The currentID variable, and modified changeImage

```
NSInteger currentID = 0;
- (IBAction) changeImage: (id) sender {
  static NSInteger currentElement = 0;
  if(++currentElement == [self.photos count]) currentElement = 0;
  PhotoDAO * aPhoto = (PhotoDAO *) [self.photos objectAtIndex:
currentElement];
  currentID = aPhoto.photoID;
  [self.theLabel setText:aPhoto.name];
  [self.theImageView setImage:aPhoto.photo];
}
```

Listing 16-18   The changeAPhotoImage method

```
- (void) changeAPhotoImage: (UIImage *) image theID: (NSInteger) photoID {
  const char * sql = "update photos set photo = ? where id = ?";
  sqlite3_stmt *update_statement = nil;
  NSArray * paths = NSSearchPathForDirectoriesInDomains(NSDocumentDirectory,
NSUserDomainMask, YES);
  NSString * docsDir = [paths objectAtIndex:0];
  NSString * thePath = [docsDir
```

(continued)

```
stringByAppendingPathComponent:@"chapter18.sqlite"];
  sqlite3_open([thePath UTF8String], &database);
  sqlite3_prepare_v2(database, sql, -1, &update_statement, NULL);
  NSData * binData = UIImagePNGRepresentation(image);
  sqlite3_bind_blob(update_statement, 1, [binData bytes], [binData length],
SQLITE_TRANSIENT);
  sqlite3_bind_int(update_statement, 2, photoID);
  sqlite3_step(update_statement);
  sqlite3_finalize(update_statement);
  sqlite3_close(database);
}
```

Listing 16-19   The changePhotosImage method

```
-(IBAction) changePhotosImage: (id) sender {
  PhotosDAO * myPhotos = [[PhotosDAO alloc] init];
  NSString * imgPath = [[[NSBundle mainBundle] resourcePath]
stringByAppendingPathComponent:@"woman.png"];
  [myPhotos changeAPhotoImage:[[UIImage alloc] initWithContentsOfFile:
imgPath] theID: currentID];
  [self.photos release];
  self.photos = [myPhotos getAllPhotos];
  [myPhotos release];
}
```

Updating a record is as straightforward as inserting it. The changeAPhotoImage first creates a SQL string with parameters. It then binds a file's binary data to photo and an integer to id. After binding, it then calls the step function once, finalizes the statement, and closes the database. Notice that updating requires the record's id, as SQLite uses the id to update the correct record. To accommodate this requirement, you added a currentID variable and changed the changeImage method to set the currentID with the currently selected photo record.

Deleting Records

1. Quit the application and return to Xcode.

2. Add a new method called deletePhoto to PhotosDAO (Listing 16-20).

3. Create a new IBAction called deletePhoto to MyDBProjectViewController (Listing 16-21).

4. Move the static NSInteger currentElement from the changeImage method in Listing 16-11 to just below the currentID variable (Listing 16-22). Remove the static qualifier.

5. Save and build.

6. Open MyDBProjectViewController.xib in Interface Builder.

Figure 16-9   The MyDBProjectViewController view's canvas

7. Add another button to the toolbar and change its title to Delete.

8. Resize the image and move the label to above the toolbar, as you are running out of space on the toolbar (Figure 16-9).

9. Connect the button to the deletePhoto action.

10. Click Build And Go and try deleting a photo.

Listing 16-20   The deletePhoto method in PhotosDAO

```
- (void) deletePhoto: (NSInteger) photoID {
  const char * sql = "delete from photos where id = ?";
  sqlite3_stmt *delete_statement = nil;
  NSArray * paths = NSSearchPathForDirectoriesInDomains(NSDocumentDirectory,
NSUserDomainMask, YES);
  NSString * docsDir = [paths objectAtIndex:0];
  NSString * thePath = [docsDir stringByAppendingPathComponent:
@"chapter18.sqlite"];
  sqlite3_open([thePath UTF8String], &database);
  sqlite3_prepare_v2(database, sql, -1, &delete_statement, NULL);
  sqlite3_bind_int(delete_statement, 1, photoID);
```

(continued)

```
    sqlite3_step(delete_statement);
    sqlite3_finalize(delete_statement);
    sqlite3_close(database);
}
```

Listing 16-21   The deletePhoto IBAction in MyDBProjectViewController

```
- (IBAction) deletePhoto : (id) sender {
  PhotosDAO * myPhotos = [[PhotosDAO alloc] init];
  [myPhotos deletePhoto:currentID];
  [self.photos release];
  self.photos = [myPhotos getAllPhotos];
  currentElement = 0;
  [myPhotos release];
}
```

Listing 16-22   Placing currentElement at the class's top so it shared in the class

```
@implementation MyDBProjectViewController
@synthesize photos;
@synthesize theImageView;
@synthesize theLabel;
NSInteger currentID = 0;
NSInteger currentElement = 0;
```

The delete statement follows the same pattern as insert and update. The only real difference is the SQL string.

```
const char * sql = "delete from photos where id = ?";
```

Summary

If you ever obtain a permanent position programming the iPhone, this chapter covered material you will use everyday. Trust me, after 15 years of programming, I know. Doesn't matter if it's Java, Visual Basic, ColdFusion, ASP, or Objective-C—if you are programming for the "man," then you are probably moving data from point A to point B. Forget interesting programming problems; reading, writing, updating, and deleting values from a database probably accounts for at least 80 percent of all code I have ever written. Translation: You must understand database manipulation to get a job, so if you skipped this chapter's details, you should reconsider and go over the chapter again. SQLite is the database chosen by Apple for iPhone programming, so you should know SQLite if you wish to program the iPhone.

Chapter 17

Core Data

Key Skills & Concepts

- Understanding Core Data's basics

- Creating a Core Data model

- Understanding how to load, fetch, and save a model's data

- Knowing where to obtain more Core Data information

With its release as part of the iPhone OS X 3.0 SDK, Core Data is arguably the best choice for persisting an application's data. It is more robust than using properties and is easier than using SQLite. You can visually lay out your application's data model, much as you would when using a database-modeling tool. Moreover, it provides the infrastructure for managing the objects you create, freeing you from writing the typical object management code. As this chapter will demonstrate, using Core Data is a natural choice for persisting an application's data. Core Data allows you to focus on the application rather than on the code persisting the application's data.

Core Data in Brief

Core Data is a framework used to easily manage an application's data objects. Core Data consists of managed object models, managed object contexts, and persistent data stores. A managed object model contains an object graph. The object graph is a collection of objects and their relationships with one another. You create a graph using Xcode's data modeler. The data modeler is where you visually add entities and create relationships between them.

A managed object context contains the objects created from the entities in the managed object model. A managed object context has a persistent store coordinator that manages one or more persistent stores. A persistent data store persists objects created by the managed object context. Although an application can have multiple persistent stores, in this chapter, you restrict yourself to one persistent store. Figure 17-1 illustrates Core Data's architecture.

Creating a Model

A model contains entities. Entities contain attributes. Relationships model how one or more entities relate to one another. You model these concepts using Xcode's data modeler. You add a model to your application by creating a file with an .xcdatamodel extension through Xcode's New File dialog (Figure 17-2). It is best to place the model file in a project's Resources folder. After creating the model, when you select the file, Xcode should automatically display the data modeler in the Editor window.

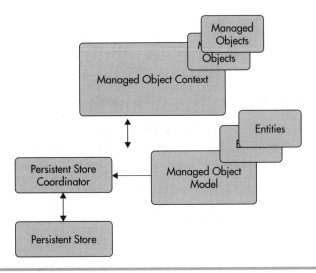

Figure 17-1   Core Data's architecture (simplified)

Entities

Entities, represented by the NSEntityDescription class, are patterns describing NSManagedObject instances. NSManagedObjects are what you persist. For Core Data to know how to instantiate new object instances and persist the instances, it needs a pattern. Entities in the model provide those

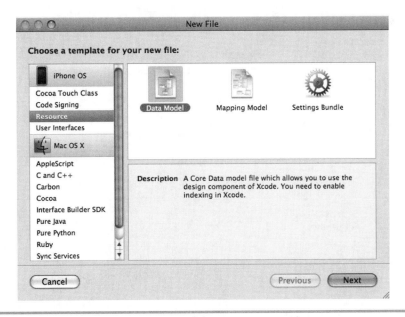

Figure 17-2   Creating a new Core Data model

patterns. For instance, you might have an application containing fruit stands, crates, apples, and oranges. A fruit stand contains one or more crates. A crate contains an apple and orange mixture. You model these objects using entities.

Try This Adding Entities to a Core Data Model

In this first task, you add entities to a data model. There is nothing to run in this task, as you will add attributes and relationships, generate classes, and then write the code to manage the object model in future tasks. In this task, you simply create entities in the data modeler.

1. Create a new View-based Application named FruitStand.

2. Add the CoreData.framework framework to your project's frameworks.

3. Add a new NSObject named FruitStand to the project.

4. Add an NSMutableArray to FruitStand as a property. Name the property crates. Add another NSString property named standName. Do not forget to synthesize both properties in FruitStand's implementation. Save or compile the application.

5. Add a new data model to Resources by selecting File | New File and then selecting Data Model. Click Next. Name the data model FruitStandModel. Click Next.

6. The next dialog asks you if you wish to add any pre-existing objects to the data model. Add FruitStand (Figure 17-3).

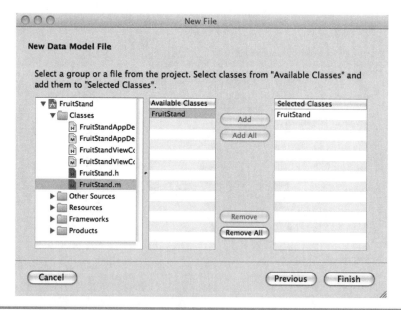

Figure 17-3 Adding FruitStand to data model

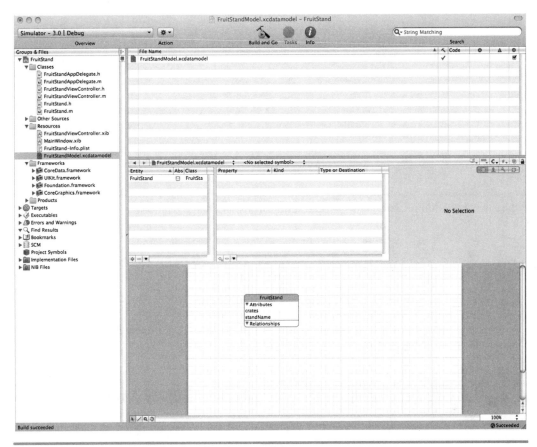

Figure 17-4   FruitStand added to the data model

7. Xcode adds the FruitStand class, and its attributes, to the newly created data model (Figure 17-4).

8. Create a new entity called Crate, a new entity called Apple, and one called Orange. Also, add an entity named Fruit (Figure 17-5). You create a new entity by CONTROL-clicking in the model and selecting Add Entity, or by clicking the plus sign at the bottom of the entity pane.

9. Save the model and compile. Notice the build fails because FruitStand contains an undefined attribute type. The crates property is an NSMutableArray, designed to hold zero or more crates. However, as you shall see in a later task, this is not how you model relationships using Core Data.

10. Delete the crates property from FruitStand and compile.

(continued)

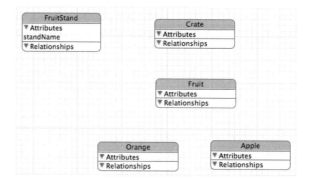

Figure 17-5   Adding Crate, Fruit, Apple, and Orange to the data model

Attributes

Entities can have attributes. While entities are NSEntityDescription objects, attributes are NSAttributeDescription objects. Consider an attribute as an object's property. Attributes provide further information about the entity. For instance, an apple might have a color attribute or a radius attribute.

Try This   Adding Attributes to a Core Data Model

1. Open FruitStandModel in Xcode. Open the data model in Xcode's data modeler.

2. Suspend disbelieve and assume all fruit is round and has a radius. CONTROL-click the Fruit entity and select Add Attribute from the pop-up menu.

3. Highlight the newly added attribute; change its Name to "radius" and its Type to Float (Figure 17-6).

4. Build and exit Xcode.

Relationships

Entities can have relationships with other entities. For instance, an apple and an orange are both types of fruit, a crate might hold one or more apples and oranges, and a fruit stand might contain one or more crates.

The Apple and Orange entities are subentities of Fruit, or Fruit is the parent of Apple and Orange. This relationship between Fruit and its two subentities is inheritance. Inheritance between entities is exactly like inheritance between classes. The child entities, Apple and

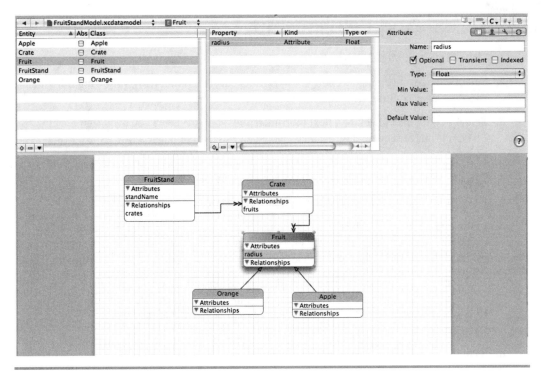

Figure 17-6 Adding a radius attribute to Fruit

Orange, inherit their parent's attributes and relationships. You can also make a parent abstract by selecting the Abstract check box next to the parent's name in the data modeler (Figure 17-7).

A Crate aggregates zero or more Fruit. A crate does not care if the fruit is an apple or an orange, and so it merely aggregates fruit. A FruitStand aggregates zero or more Crate entities. The following task illustrates adding these relationships to the data model.

Figure 17-7 Entities can be declared abstract.

Try This Modeling Relationships

1. Open FruitStandModel in Xcode. Open the data model in Xcode's data modeler.

2. Select Orange and change its parent to Fruit; repeat for Apple. Arrows showing inheritance should appear pointing from the child classes to their parent (Figure 17-8).

3. Select the Abstract check box next to Fruit. Think about it: Have you ever seen a fruit? I haven't; I have seen apples, bananas, pears, and so on, but never a fruit. Make Fruit abstract.

4. Click the small line in the lower-left corner of the modeling window.

5. Drag from Crate to Fruit to create a relationship between them.

6. In the upper-right pane, change the relationship's Name to "fruits" and select the To-Many Relationship check box. Ensure the Optional check box is selected and the Inverse says No Inverse Relationship. Change the Delete Rule to Cascade (Figure 17-9).

7. Add another relationship for FruitStand's relationship with Crate. Change the relationship's Name to "crates" and select the To-Many Relationship check box. Change the Delete Rule to Cascade. Ensure the Optional check box is selected and the Inverse is No Inverse Relationship.

8. Save the model and then Build the application.

TIP

After creating the relationships between FruitStand and Crate, and Crate and Fruit, there are two build warnings stating that there isn't an inverse relationship between those same entities. What that means is that in the case of the crate-to-fruit relationship, not only should you say that one crate can hold multiple fruit, but that one fruit can only be in one crate at a time. For simplicity, ignore this inverse relationship, but realize that in reality, these warnings are both correct: a crate can only be in one FruitStand and a Fruit can only be in one Crate.

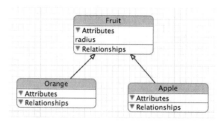

Figure 17-8 Adding inheritance

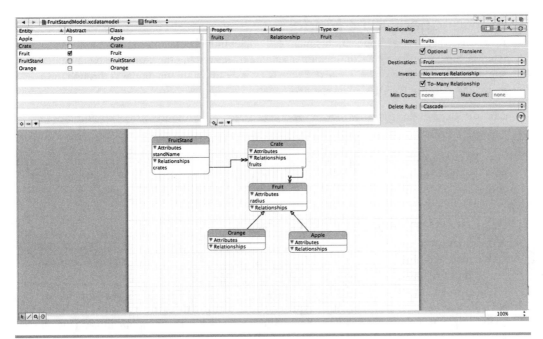

Figure 17-9   Changing Delete Rule to Cascade

Notice you specified all relationships have a Cascade Delete Rule. This rule informs the model that when an object containing a reference to another object is deleted, delete the referenced object. For instance, FruitStand references one or more Crate entities. The relationship is cascade, and so when you delete a FruitStand, the context deletes all the stand's referenced crates. Other delete rules you might specify include Nullify, Deny, and No Action.

NOTE

For more information on creating models using Xcode, refer to Apple's "Creating a Managed Object Model with Xcode."

Model, Context, and Store

The previous three tasks created the model used to create entities and their relationships in a managed object context. When an application runs, it needs a model instance, the context, and the persistent store. The persistent store and the model are largely transparent to you when coding your application. You simply obtain both these items and then set properties referencing them in the managed object context.

NSManagedObjectModel

As discussed earlier, an application's managed object model contains entities and their relationships. It serves as an application's schema by describing the entities used in an application's managed object context. The easiest way to obtain the model is through the mergedModelFromBundles: class method.

```
managedObjectModel = [[NSManagedObjectModel mergedModelFromBundles:
nil] retain];
```

This method creates a data model by merging all the models it finds into a bundle. Because the previous code specifies nil, the method simply finds all the models in the application's Resources folder and merges them into one NSManagedObjectModel instance.

NSPersistentStoreCoordinator

A persistent store coordinator coordinates one or more persistent stores and associates them with a managed object model. Although advanced applications might have more than one persistent store, this chapter limits consideration to single store applications. Core Data can persist data in several different ways. Store types you might use to persist data include NSSQLiteStoreType, NSBinaryStoreType, or NSInMemoryStoreType. Consider the following code snippet. It defines a store by loading a SQLite database from an application's Documents directory.

```
NSURL *storeUrl = [NSURL fileURLWithPath: [[self applicationDocuments
Directory]
stringByAppendingPathComponent: @"CoreTemplateApp.sqlite"]];
```

After obtaining the URL to the store, you create an NSPersistentStoreCoordinator instance. The coordinator initializes the store coordinator using a managed object model instance. The persistent store contains the data, while the model defines how to interpret that data.

```
persistentStoreCoordinator = [[NSPersistentStoreCoordinator alloc]
initWithManagedObjectModel: [self managedObjectModel]];
```

NSManagedObjectContext

The NSManagedObjectContext represents an application's managed object context. This is where you add entity instances (NSManagedObject classes) to your application. It is where you fetch managed objects to and from the persistent store, and it is where you modify the objects. =Apple describes the context as a big "scratch-pad" because no manipulations to a context are persisted until code explicitly tells the context to persist the changes.

You obtain an application's managed context by allocating and initializing a new NSManagedObjectContext instance. You then set its persistent store coordinator.

```
managedObjectContext = [[NSManagedObjectContext alloc] init];

[managedObjectContext setPersistentStoreCoordinator: coordinator];
```

NSManagedObject

The NSManagedObjectContext manages NSManagedObject instances. NSManagedObjects are not entities, but rather, created from entities. An application obtains data from the persistent store and uses the entities in the model to create the NSManagedObjects placed in the context. Consider NSEntityDescriptions as the classes and NSManagedObjects as the objects.

The previous Try This tasks created entities in the xcdatamodel file. Although the NSManagedObjectModel uses these entities, the NSManagedObjectContext does not; it manages NSManagedObjects. Before you can use the entities in an application, you must generate classes that extend the NSManagedObject class. After creating the NSManagedObjects, you can then work with them programmatically. The following task illustrates creating NSManagedObjects from entities.

Try This Generating NSManagedObjects from Entities

1. Open FruitStandProject in Xcode. Open the FruitStandModel data model.

2. Select all entities in the model. Click File | New File, and then select Managed Object Class. Click Next, and on the next screen ensure that FruitStand is selected and the other values are correct. Click Next and ensure that all classes are checked (Figure 17-10).

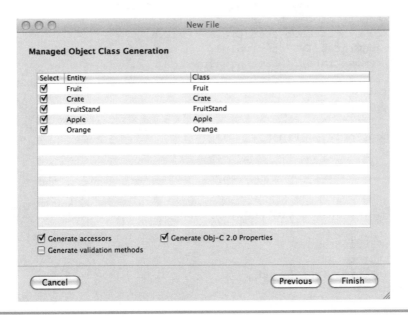

Figure 17-10 Generating classes from entities

(continued)

3. If Xcode generated the classes in your Resources folder, move the classes to the Classes folder. Delete the old FruitStand.h and FruitStand.m, as you generated new versions. For brevity, only the generated FruitStand and Apple interfaces and implementations are listed in Listings 17-1 and 17-2.

4. Select File | New File, and create a new C Header File. Name the file MyObjects.h and import all the generated headers (Listing 17-3).

5. Save and then Build the application.

In this task, you generated NSManagedObject subclasses. Open Crate.h and notice that Crate contains an NSSet of fruits. It also has accessor methods called addFruitsObject, removeFruitsObject, addFruits, and removeFruits. Open several of the other generated classes, and you see similar accessors.

Listing 17-1   Generated class interfaces

```
#import <CoreData/CoreData.h>
@class Crate;
@interface FruitStand :  NSManagedObject {
}
@property (retain) NSString * standName;
@property (retain) NSSet* crates;
@end
@interface FruitStand (CoreDataGeneratedAccessors)
- (void)addCratesObject:(Crate *)value;
- (void)removeCratesObject:(Crate *)value;
- (void)addCrates:(NSSet *)value;
- (void)removeCrates:(NSSet *)value;
@end

#import <CoreData/CoreData.h>
#import "Fruit.h"
@interface Apple :  Fruit {
}
@end
```

Listing 17-2   Generated class implementations

```
#import "FruitStand.h"
#import "Crate.h"
@implementation FruitStand
@dynamic standName;
@dynamic crates;
@end
```

```
#import "Apple.h"
@implementation Apple
@end
```

Listing 17-3 MyObjects.h

```
#import "Orange.h"
#import "FruitStand.h"
#import "Fruit.h"
#import "Crate.h"
#import "Apple.h"
```

NOTE

NSManagedObjects have no dealloc methods, as the Core Data framework manages their life cycle. Core Data is also responsible for generating NSManagedObjects' accessor methods at runtime.

Try This Adding Core Data to the Application's Code

1. Open FruitStand in Xcode, open FruitStandAppDelegate.h, and import the Core Data header file (Listing 17-4). Create a property called managedObjectContext for the NSManagedObjectContext class.

2. Create a new method called loadCoreData and implement it (Listing 17-5).

3. Add code that calls the loadCoreData method in applicationDidFinishLaunching.

4. Open FruitStandController.h and import Core Data in FruitStandController's header file. Add a property referencing NSManagedObjectContext and name the property managedObjectContext (Listings 17-6 and 17-7).

5. Return to the applicationDidFinishLaunching method in FruitStandAppDelegate.m and add code that sets the FruitStandViewController's managedObjectContext property.

6. Build the application.

Listing 17-4 FruitStandAppDelegate.h

```
#import <UIKit/UIKit.h>
#import <CoreData/CoreData.h>
@class FruitStandViewController;
```

(continued)

```
@interface FruitStandAppDelegate : NSObject <UIApplicationDelegate> {
  UIWindow *window;
  FruitStandViewController *viewController;
  NSManagedObjectContext * managedObjectContext;
}
@property (nonatomic, retain) IBOutlet UIWindow *window;
@property (nonatomic, retain) IBOutlet FruitStandViewController
*viewController;
@property (nonatomic, retain) NSManagedObjectContext *
managedObjectContext;
-(void) loadCoreData;
@end
```

Listing 17-5   FruitStandAppDelegate.m

```
#import "FruitStandAppDelegate.h"
#import "FruitStandViewController.h"
@implementation FruitStandAppDelegate
@synthesize window;
@synthesize viewController;
@synthesize managedObjectContext;
- (void) loadCoreData {
  NSArray *paths = NSSearchPathForDirectoriesInDomains(NSDocument
Directory, NSUserDomainMask, YES);
  NSString *basePath = ([paths count] > 0) ? [paths objectAtIndex:0] :
nil;
  NSLog(@"%@", basePath);
  NSURL *storeUrl = [NSURL fileURLWithPath: [basePath
stringByAppendingPathComponent: @"FruitStand.sqlite"]];
  NSError *error;
  NSPersistentStoreCoordinator * persistentStoreCoordinator =
[[NSPersistentStoreCoordinator alloc] initWithManagedObjectModel:
[NSManagedObjectModel mergedModelFromBundles:nil]];
  if (![persistentStoreCoordinator addPersistentStoreWithType:
NSSQLiteStoreType configuration:nil URL:storeUrl options:nil
error:&error]) {
    NSLog(@"error loading persistent store...");
  }
  managedObjectContext = [[NSManagedObjectContext alloc] init];
  [managedObjectContext setPersistentStoreCoordinator:
persistentStoreCoordinator];
}
```

```
- (void)applicationDidFinishLaunching:(UIApplication *) application {
  [self loadCoreData];
  viewController.managedObjectContext = self.managedObjectContext;
  [window addSubview:viewController.view];
  [window makeKeyAndVisible];
}
- (void)dealloc {
  [viewController release];
  [managedObjectContext release];
  [window release];
  [super dealloc];
}
@end
```

Listing 17-6   FruitStandViewController.h

```
#import <UIKit/UIKit.h>
#import <CoreData/CoreData.h>
@interface FruitStandViewController : UIViewController {
  NSManagedObjectContext * managedObjectContext;
}
@property (nonatomic, retain) NSManagedObjectContext *
managedObjectContext;
@end
```

Listing 17-7   FruitStandViewController.m

```
#import "FruitStandViewController.h"
@implementation FruitStandViewController
@synthesize managedObjectContext;
- (void)dealloc {
  [managedObjectContext release];
  [super dealloc];
}
@end
```

This task's code should be straightforward. The application's delegate, in application DidFinishLaunching, calls the loadCoreData method. This method loads the model, obtains the persistent data store from the Documents folder (creating it if nonexistent), and then initializes a new context from the persistent store coordinator. When the delegate loads FirstViewController, it also sets the view controller's context to the delegate's context. FirstViewController can then use the context to add, edit, and delete NSManagedObjects.

Adding Objects

All objects managed by a managed object context are NSManagedObject instances. An NSManagedObject is a class that implements the required behavior for a Core Data model object. You do not create NSManagedObject instances, but rather subclasses. These subclasses are usually created from the entities defined in an xcdatamodel file.

The easiest way to create a new managed object is through the NSEntityDescription's class method, insertNewObjectForEntityForName:inManagedObjectContext.

```
+ (id)insertNewObjectForEntityForName:(NSString *) entityName
inManagedObjectContext:(NSManagedObjectContext *) context
```

This method obtains an entity from the model, creates a new NSManagedObject based upon the entity, and inserts it in the current managed object context. For instance, the following creates a new Apple from the Apple entity used in this chapter's Try This xcdatamodel file:

```
Apple * apple = (Apple *) [NSEntityDescription insertNewObjectForEntity
ForName: @"Apple" inManagedObjectContext:self.managedObjectContext];
```

After inserting a new object, you can then set its properties, just as if it was a normal object. The following code sets the newly created Apple's radius:

```
apple.radius = [NSNumber numberWithFloat:(float) 2.4];
```

Saving Changes

An application's managed object context does not automatically save changes to a model's data. You must manually save the context to persist changes. For instance, when terminating an application, you might wish to check the context for changes and, if there were changes, save them.

```
if ([managedObjectContext hasChanges] && ![managedObjectContext
save:&error])
```

The context saves changes using its save method. This method persists the context's changes to its associated persistent data store. The method takes an error as a parameter and returns a Boolean indicating success or failure.

```
- (BOOL)save:(NSError **) error
```

You can also roll back all changes to a context using the rollback method. This method removes everything from something called the undo stack and removes all insertions and deletions, and restores all context-managed objects to their original state.

NOTE

An NSManagedObjectContext can have an NSUndoManager instance assigned to its undoManager property. An NSUndoManager manages undoing actions. When using Core Data, you can use this class to undo changes made to an application's NSManagedModelContext. For more information, refer to the NSUndoManager Class Reference.

Fetching Entities

Managed objects remain in the persistent data store until needed. You request objects from the persistent data store using NSFetchRequests. The NSFetchRequest wraps search criteria for retrieving data from the store. A fetch request consists of an NSEntityDescription, an optional NSPredicate, and an optional NSSortDescriptor.

NSFetchRequest

The NSFetchRequest class is how you query a persistent object store for its data. It uses an NSEntityDescription to know which entity to fetch. Listing 17-8 creates an NSFetchRequest and an NSEntityDescription, and assigns the description to the request. The NSManagedObjectContext then executes the request.

Listing 17-8 NSFetchRequest example

```
NSFetchRequest * myRequest = [[NSFetchRequest alloc] init];
NSEntityDescription * entDesc = [NSEntityDescription
entityForName:@"Orange" inManagedObjectContext:myContext];
[myRequest setEntity:entDesc];
NSError * error;
NSArray * fetchResults = [self.managedObjectContext
executeFetchRequest:myRequest
error:&error];
if(fetchResults == nil) {
  NSLog(@"an error occurred");
  [error release];
}
```

The code in Listing 17-8 first creates a new NSFetchRequest. It then creates an NSEntityDescription for the Orange entity existing in myContext. After creating the NSEntityDescription, it sets the request's entity to oranges and executes the request.

Notice Listing 17-8 selects all the oranges in myContext. Usually, you will desire limiting the results returned. One way you could do this is through the NSFetchRequest's fetchLimit property. This property limits the objects returned by a fetch request. However, this property does not distinguish which objects to exclude. Often, you will wish limiting results to only objects meeting certain criteria. For instance, you might want all oranges with a radius greater than three. The way you limit results based upon given criteria is through the NSPredicate class.

NSPredicate

The NSPredicate class restricts the data returned by an NSFetchRequest. It is similar to a SQL statement's WHERE clause. The easiest way to create a predicate is by using the predicateWithFormat class method.

```
+ (NSPredicate *)predicateWithFormat:(NSString *)format, ...
```

The code is similar to initializing an NSString with a format. You write the expression and include a substitution parameter, followed by one or more substitution values. For instance, you might create a predicate limiting entities to those with a radius greater than 2.1.

```
NSPredicate * predicate = [NSPredicate predicateWithFormat: @"radius > %@",
[NSNumber numberWithFloat:(float)2.1]];
```

Notice the preceding predicate does not tell you which entity the predicate is associated with; to make the association, you set the entity and predicate to the same fetch request.

```
[myRequest setEntity:entDesc];
```

```
[myRequest setPredicate: predicate];
```

Predicates can have more than one item in the substitution list. For instance, you might create the following predicate:

```
NSPredicate * predicate = [NSPredicate predicateWithFormat:
@"radius > %@ and variety like %@", [NSNumber numberWithFloat:
(float)2.1], @"Valencia"];
```

This predicate assigns 2.1 to the radius value and Valencia to the variety value. Notice the "like" keyword; there are many similarities between Apple's predicate syntax and SQL.

NOTE

Apple's predicate syntax is quite detailed. For more information on predicate syntax, see Apple's "Predicate Programming Guide."

NSSortDescriptor

By default, fetched objects are unsorted; sorting the objects requires an NSSortDescriptor instance. This class represents the sort order for a fetched object collection. The following statement creates and initializes an NSSortDescriptor that sorts fruit in ascending order based upon their radius:

```
NSSortDescriptor * myDesc = [[NSSortDescriptor alloc]
initWithKey:@"radius" ascending:YES];
```

A request can have more than one sort descriptor, so you add your NSSortDescriptors to an NSArray and then add the array to the NSFetchRequest using its setSortDescriptors method. The following creates an array and initializes it with the descriptor from the previous paragraph. It then sets the request's sort descriptors by passing the newly created array.

```
NSArray * myArray = [NSArray alloc] initWithObjects:myDesc, nil];
[myRequest setSortDescriptors:myArray];
```

NOTE

Although not covered in this chapter, you can predefine fetch requests, predicates, and sort descriptors in an application's xcdatamodel file. Then at runtime, you can fetch those predefined objects from the data model and use them in your code.

Deleting Entities

You use the NSManagedObjectContext's deleteObject method to delete objects from an application's managed object context. This method takes an NSManagedObject instance of the object to delete. You might pass an Orange instance to the method.

```
[myContext deleteObject: (NSManagedObject *) myOrange];
```

The managed object context is smart enough to mark the particular orange for deletion; remember, the context does not actually delete the object until code calls the context's save method.

Try This Adding, Fetching, and Deleting Entities

1. Open FruitStand in Xcode.

2. Open FruitStandViewController.h and import MyObjects.h. Suspend disbelief (it is an unrealistic example project) and add the following actions to FruitStandController: addFruitStand, listFruitStandContents, replaceApple, listApple, and deleteFruitStand (Listings 17-9 and 17-10).

3. Implement the methods like the code in the listings.

4. Open FruitStandViewController.xib in Interface Builder.

5. Add five buttons (Figure 17-11).

6. Connect each button to the appropriate actions in FruitStandViewController (Figure 17-12).

7. Save and exit Interface Builder.

8. Click Build And Go to run the application in the iPhone Simulator (Figure 17-13).

Listing 17-9   FruitStandViewController.h

```
#import <UIKit/UIKit.h>
#import <CoreData/CoreData.h>
#import "MyObjects.h"
@interface FruitStandViewController : UIViewController {
  NSManagedObjectContext * managedObjectContext;
}
```

(continued)

```
@property (nonatomic, retain) NSManagedObjectContext *
managedObjectContext;
- (IBAction) initFruitStand: (id) sender;
- (IBAction) listFruitStandContents: (id) sender;
- (IBAction) removeApple: (id) sender;
- (IBAction) deleteFruitStand: (id) sender;
- (IBAction) listApple: (id) sender;
@end
```

Listing 17-10   FruitStandViewController.m

```
#import "FruitStandViewController.h"
@implementation FruitStandViewController
@synthesize managedObjectContext;
- (IBAction) initFruitStand: (id) sender {
  FruitStand * stand = (FruitStand *) [NSEntityDescription
insertNewObjectForEntityForName:@"FruitStand"
inManagedObjectContext:self.managedObjectContext];
  stand.standName = [NSString stringWithFormat:
@"James's Grand Fruit Stand %i", random()/1000];
  Crate * crateOne = (Crate *) [NSEntityDescription
insertNewObjectForEntityForName:@"Crate"
inManagedObjectContext:self.managedObjectContext];
  Crate * crateTwo = (Crate *) [NSEntityDescription
insertNewObjectForEntityForName:@"Crate"
inManagedObjectContext:self.managedObjectContext];
  Orange * orangeA = (Orange *) [NSEntityDescription
insertNewObjectForEntityForName:@"Orange"
inManagedObjectContext:self.managedObjectContext];
  orangeA.radius = [NSNumber numberWithFloat:(float)4.2];
  Orange * orangeB = (Orange *) [NSEntityDescription
insertNewObjectForEntityForName:@"Orange" inManagedObjectContext:self.
managedObjectContext];
  orangeB.radius = [NSNumber numberWithFloat:(float)3.3];
  Apple * appleA = (Apple *) [NSEntityDescription
insertNewObjectForEntityForName:@"Apple"
inManagedObjectContext:self.managedObjectContext];
  appleA.radius = [NSNumber numberWithFloat:(float)1.9];
  Apple * appleB = (Apple *) [NSEntityDescription
insertNewObjectForEntityForName:@"Apple"
inManagedObjectContext:self.managedObjectContext];
  appleB.radius = [NSNumber numberWithFloat:(float) 2.4];
  [crateOne addFruitsObject:orangeA];
  [crateOne addFruitsObject:appleA];
  [crateTwo addFruitsObject:appleB];
  [crateTwo addFruitsObject:orangeB];
```

```
  [stand addCratesObject:crateOne];
  [stand addCratesObject:crateTwo];
  NSError *error;
  if (![[self managedObjectContext] save:&error]) {
    NSLog(@"Unresolved error %@, %@", error, [error userInfo]);
    [error release];
  }
}
- (IBAction) listApple: (id) sender {
  NSFetchRequest  * request =[[NSFetchRequest alloc] init];
  NSEntityDescription * entity = [NSEntityDescription
entityForName:@"Apple" inManagedObjectContext:self.
managedObjectContext];
  [request setEntity:entity];
  NSPredicate * predicate = [NSPredicate predicateWithFormat:
@"radius > %@", [NSNumber numberWithFloat:(float)2.1]];
  [request setPredicate:predicate];
  NSError *error;
  NSArray * fetchResults = [self.managedObjectContext
executeFetchRequest:request error:&error];
  if(fetchResults == nil) {
    NSLog(@"an error occurred");
  }
  NSEnumerator * enumerator = [fetchResults objectEnumerator];
  id setObject;
  while( (setObject = [enumerator nextObject]) != nil) {
    NSLog(@"got an apple with radius %f", [((Fruit *)setObject).radius
floatValue]);
  }
}
- (IBAction) listFruitStandContents: (id) sender {
  NSFetchRequest  * request =[[NSFetchRequest alloc] init];
  NSEntityDescription * entity = [NSEntityDescription entityForName:
@"FruitStand" inManagedObjectContext:self.managedObjectContext];
  [request setEntity:entity];
  NSError *error;
  NSArray * fetchResults = [self.managedObjectContext
executeFetchRequest:request
error:&error];
  if(fetchResults == nil) {
    NSLog(@"Unresolved error %@, %@", error, [error userInfo]);
    [error release];
  }
  NSEnumerator * standsEnumerator = [fetchResults objectEnumerator];
  id setStandObject;
  while( (setStandObject = [standsEnumerator nextObject]) != nil) {
    NSLog(@"****** FRUIT STAND **********");
```

(continued)

```
        FruitStand * stand = (FruitStand *) setStandObject;
        NSLog(@"stand name: %@", stand.standName);
        NSEnumerator * enumerator = [stand.crates objectEnumerator];
        id setObject;
        while( (setObject = [enumerator nextObject]) != nil) {
          NSEnumerator * innerEnumerator = [((Crate *) setObject).fruits
   objectEnumerator];
           id innerSetObject;
           NSLog(@"-------Crate------------");
           while( (innerSetObject = [innerEnumerator nextObject]) != nil) {
             Fruit * myFruit = (Fruit *) innerSetObject;
             if( [myFruit isKindOfClass:[Orange class]]) {
               NSLog(@"orange with radius: %f", [myFruit.radius floatValue]);
             }
             else {
               NSLog(@"apple with radius: %f", [myFruit.radius floatValue]);
             }
           } //innermost while
         } //outer while
         NSLog(@"*******************");
      } //outermost while
      [request release];
}
- (IBAction) removeApple: (id) sender {
   NSFetchRequest  * request =[[NSFetchRequest alloc] init];
   NSEntityDescription * entity = [NSEntityDescription
entityForName:@"Fruit" inManagedObjectContext:self.
managedObjectContext];
   [request setEntity:entity];
   NSSortDescriptor * sortDescriptorRadius = [[NSSortDescriptor alloc]
initWithKey:@"radius" ascending:NO];
   NSArray * sortDescriptors = [[NSArray alloc]
initWithObjects:sortDescriptorRadius, nil];
   [request setSortDescriptors:sortDescriptors];
   NSError *error;
   NSArray * fetchResults = [self.managedObjectContext
executeFetchRequest:request error:&error];
   if(fetchResults == nil) {
     NSLog(@"an error occurred");
     [error release];
   }
   NSEnumerator * enumerator = [fetchResults objectEnumerator];
   id setObject;
   while( (setObject = [enumerator nextObject]) != nil) {
     if( [(Fruit *)setObject isKindOfClass:[Apple class]]) {
       NSLog(@"removing an apple");
```

```objc
      [self.managedObjectContext deleteObject:(NSManagedObject
*)setObject];
      }
    else NSLog(@"found an orange, leaving");
  }
  NSError *error2;
  if(![self.managedObjectContext save:&error2]) {
    NSLog(@"Unresolved error %@, %@", error2, [error2 userInfo]);
    [error2 release];
  }
  [sortDescriptors release];
  [sortDescriptorRadius release];
  [request release];
}
- (IBAction) deleteFruitStand: (id) sender {
  NSFetchRequest  * request =[[NSFetchRequest alloc] init];
  NSEntityDescription * entity = [NSEntityDescription entityForName:
@"FruitStand" inManagedObjectContext:self.managedObjectContext];
  [request setEntity:entity];
  NSLog(@"deleting the fruit stand");
  NSError *error;
  NSArray * fetchResults = [self.managedObjectContext
executeFetchRequest:request
error:&error];
  if(fetchResults == nil) {
    NSLog(@"Unresolved error %@, %@", error, [error userInfo]);
    [error release];
  }
  NSEnumerator * enumerator = [fetchResults objectEnumerator];
  id setObject;
  while( (setObject = [enumerator nextObject]) != nil) {
    NSLog(@"deleting..");
    [self.managedObjectContext deleteObject: (NSManagedObject
*)setObject];
  }
  NSError *error2;
  if(![self.managedObjectContext save:&error2]) {
    NSLog(@"Unresolved error %@, %@", error2, [error2 userInfo]);
    [error2 release];
  }
}
- (void)dealloc {
  [managedObjectContext release];
  [super dealloc];
}
@end
```

(continued)

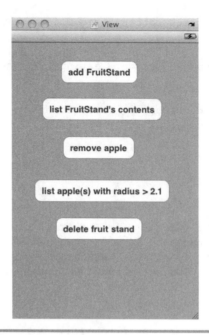

Figure 17-11 Adding five buttons to the canvas

Consider the application's behavior. Upon invoking the initFruitStand method in FruitStandViewController, the application creates a new FruitStand, two crates, two apples, and two oranges. It assigns an apple and orange to each crate. At the method's end, it persists the changes to the managedObjectContext by calling its save method. Multiple clicks result in multiple FruitStand instances being created. Although Core Data keeps the different instances separate internally, to make the example easier to view in the Debugger Console, you added a random number to the fruit stand's name.

Invoking the listFruitStandContents method creates an NSFetchRequest that selects all fruit stands from the persistent data store. The persistent store returns the fruit stands as an NSSet, and so the method enumerates through each fruit stand, selecting the stand's crates. The method then enumerates through each crate, listing each crate's contents. Each crate's contents are also an NSSet, so the method enumerates through the fruit also. Listing 17-11 is the Debugger Console's logging after invoking the initFruitStand method twice and then invoking the listFruitStandContents method.

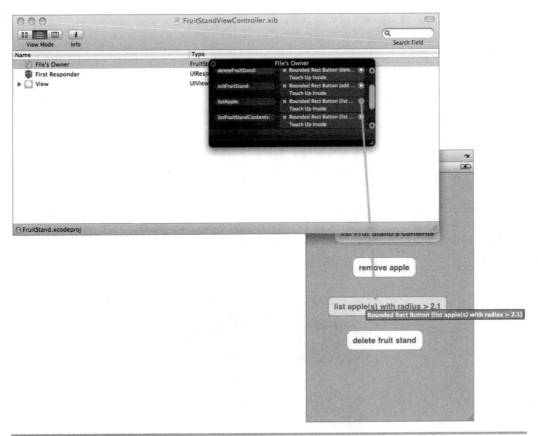

Figure 17-12 Connecting the five buttons to appropriate actions

---

Listing 17-11 The listFruitStandContents method's logging

```
2009-04-15 07:38:20.350 FruitStand[530:20b] ****** FRUIT STAND *********
2009-04-15 07:38:20.351 FruitStand[530:20b] stand name: James's Grand
Fruit Stand
1681692
2009-04-15 07:38:20.351 FruitStand[530:20b] -------Crate-----------
2009-04-15 07:38:20.352 FruitStand[530:20b] orange with radius: 4.200000
2009-04-15 07:38:20.352 FruitStand[530:20b] apple with radius: 1.900000
2009-04-15 07:38:20.353 FruitStand[530:20b] -------Crate-----------
2009-04-15 07:38:20.353 FruitStand[530:20b] apple with radius: 2.400000
2009-04-15 07:38:20.353 FruitStand[530:20b] orange with radius: 3.300000
2009-04-15 07:38:20.355 FruitStand[530:20b] *******************
```

(continued)

```
2009-04-15 07:38:20.356 FruitStand[530:20b] ****** FRUIT STAND **********
2009-04-15 07:38:20.356 FruitStand[530:20b] stand name: James's Grand
Fruit Stand
1714636
2009-04-15 07:38:20.357 FruitStand[530:20b] -------Crate------------
2009-04-15 07:38:20.357 FruitStand[530:20b] apple with radius: 1.900000
2009-04-15 07:38:20.357 FruitStand[530:20b] orange with radius: 4.200000
2009-04-15 07:38:20.358 FruitStand[530:20b] -------Crate------------
2009-04-15 07:38:20.358 FruitStand[530:20b] orange with radius: 3.300000
2009-04-15 07:38:20.358 FruitStand[530:20b] apple with radius: 2.400000
2009-04-15 07:38:20.359 FruitStand[530:20b] ********************
```

Notice in the example that you save immediately upon changing the managed object context. Sometimes this might not be the desired behavior. You can delay persisting changes to the context until the application terminates. There are also many life-cycle management

Figure 17-13   The application running in the iPhone Simulator

methods in NSManagedObjectContext that you might use—for instance, detectConflicts ForObject, refreshObject, processPendingChanges, insertedObjects, updatedObjects, and deletedObjects. For more information refer to the NSManagedObjectContext Class Reference.

The listApple method illustrates using a simple predicate. Upon invocation, the method creates an NSFetchRequest for an apple. It also creates an NSPredicate telling the request to only fetch apples with a radius greater than 2.1.

```
NSPredicate * predicate = [NSPredicate predicateWithFormat: @"radius > %@",
[NSNumber numberWithFloat:(float)2.1]];
```

After fetching the results as an NSSet, it loops through each id, casting it as an apple and then printing its radius.

The removeApple method illustrates deleting managed objects. Select the object(s) you are interested in, delete them, and, if you wish, save the changes to the managed context immediately.

```
[self.managedObjectContext deleteObject:(NSManagedObject *)setObject];
```

Listing 17-12 illustrates the logging after invoking initFruitStand followed by invoking removeApple.

Listing 17-12   Debugger Console logging after invoking initFruitStand and removeApple methods

```
2009-04-15 07:39:41.153 FruitStand[530:20b] found an orange, leaving
2009-04-15 07:39:41.153 FruitStand[530:20b] found an orange, leaving
2009-04-15 07:39:41.154 FruitStand[530:20b] removing an apple
2009-04-15 07:39:41.154 FruitStand[530:20b] removing an apple
2009-04-15 07:39:43.385 FruitStand[530:20b] ****** FRUIT STAND **********
2009-04-15 07:39:43.385 FruitStand[530:20b] stand name: James's Grand
Fruit Stand
1957747
2009-04-15 07:39:43.386 FruitStand[530:20b] -------Crate-----------
2009-04-15 07:39:43.386 FruitStand[530:20b] orange with radius: 3.300000
2009-04-15 07:39:43.387 FruitStand[530:20b] -------Crate-----------
2009-04-15 07:39:43.388 FruitStand[530:20b] orange with radius: 4.200000
2009-04-15 07:39:43.388 FruitStand[530:20b] *******************
```

The deleteFruitStand method also illustrates deleting managed objects. However, it also illustrates Cascade Delete. When you delete a fruit stand, you delete all its crates. Each crate deletes all its fruit. When using Cascade Delete, you can delete much data in a short time, so be certain this is the desired behavior.

Summary

In this chapter, you learned the basics of Core Data framework. After learning how to model your application's data objects, you learned how to insert, fetch, and delete instances from the data model. But you only scratched Core Data's surface in this chapter. There are so many ways to create an NSPredicate, so many ways to create an NSFetchRequest, and so many variations on the different ways of working with the managed object context that covering them all would result in a several-hundred-page book. To continue learning more about Core Data, refer to Apple's documentation.

Apple has heavily documented the Core Data framework. The first reference you should consult is Apple's Core Data Tutorial for iPhone OS. This document provides a tutorial on using the Core Data framework with a UITableView and the CFLocation objects. It is similar to this chapter's example tasks, only it expands upon them by presenting a slightly more difficult, but more realistic, example by loading data in a UITableView. Consult Apple's Creating a Managed Object Model with Xcode tutorial and also Xcode Tools for Core Data for more information on using Xcode's data modeler. Consult Apple's "Predicate Programming Guide" for more information on writing predicates. Finally, for a complete reference on Core Data, consult Apple's "Core Data Programming Guide."

Chapter 18

Multimedia

Key Skills & Concepts

- Playing system sounds
- Playing songs
- Using the Media Player to interact with a device's multimedia
- Playing video

U p until the release of the iPhone OS 3.0, the iPhone was a difficult platform for developing multimedia applications. The capabilities were there, as you could always resort to using low-level C APIs to program audio and video, but the higher-level APIs were strictly undocumented and off limits. And as for the multimedia on a device that was placed there by iTunes? Forget it, off limits. Any media you wished playing in your application had to either be packaged as part of your application or streamed from a server. That restriction changed with iPhone OS 3.0; now you can access and play a user's audio iTunes multimedia, making the iPhone and iPod touch the most programmable portable music players ever released.

In this chapter, you explore the basic multimedia capabilities of the iPhone and iPod touch. You first learn how to play system sounds and longer sounds. You then move to the Media Player framework, where you use the framework to select and play a user's iTunes audio multimedia. After learning to play iTunes media, you then learn how to play a video using the Media Player framework's video player.

Playing Sounds

Playing short sounds on an iPhone or iPod touch is easy. Simply load the song as a system sound, obtain the sound's id, and use the AudioServicesPlaySystemSound method to play the sound. Playing a longer sound using the AVAudioPlayer is not difficult, but a little more involved. However, there is one important limitation you must realize when using sound on your device using the AudioServicesPlaySystemSound function or AVAudioPlayer: Any media you play must be packaged as part of your application or must be streamed from a server. So, although these two classes are good for adding sound to your application or for developing an interface to a server that streams multimedia, they are not good classes for developing a music player. Instead, you should use the Media Player Framework, covered later in this chapter.

AudioServicesPlaySystemSound

The AudioServicesPlaySystemSound function plays a short system sound. Although security restrictions prevent your application from playing a device's OS system sounds, you can load and play your own short (30 seconds or less) sounds and play them using this function.

The AudioServicesPlaySystemSound function can only play a sound with the following format: .caf, .aif, or .wav. The sound plays at whatever audio level the device is set to, and the sound plays immediately upon its id being passed to the function. There is no pausing, rewinding, fast-forwarding, or other sound manipulation functionality. You load a sound, and the function plays it.

```
void AudioServicesPlaySystemSound (SystemSoundID inSystemSoundID);
```

The function takes a SystemSoundID as a parameter. A SystemSoundID is an unsigned integer that uniquely identifies the sound. You obtain a SystemSoundID by loading a sound into the AudioServicesCreateSystemSoundID function.

```
OSStatus AudioServicesCreateSystemSoundID (CFURLRef inFileURL,
SystemSoundID * outSystemSoundID);
```

The AudioServicesCreateSystemSoundID function takes a reference to the file's URL and the SystemSoundID to assign the value to. A CFURLRef is simply a lower-level pointer to a URL. You can ignore creating a CFURL (what the CFURLRef points to) and instead cast an NSURL as a CFURLRef. After obtaining a sound's URL, you pass it to the create system sound function. It assigns the value to the system sound ID variable you defined; you pass that ID to the system sound player function; and it plays the sound.

Ask the Expert

Q: What's a CFURLRef? What's an NSURL?

A: A CFURLRef is a reference to a CFURL object. A CFURL is part of the Core Foundation framework, meaning it is C, not Objective-C, and provides functions to create and parse URLs. An NSURL is a higher-level, Cocoa Objective-C class for working with URLs. It encapsulates a URL and provides many functions for manipulating URLs. Refer to the NSURL Class Reference for more information.

You can cast an NSURL * as a CFURLRef because of Apple's "toll-free bridging" functionality. The term "toll-free bridging" refers to certain Core Foundation types being interchangeable with their higher-level Cocoa counterparts. Remember, a pointer to an NSURL is equivalent to a CFURL reference.

TIP

You can use the AudioServicesPlaySystemSound to vibrate a user's iPhone. Pass the kSystemSoundID_Vibrate identifier constant to the function. Currently, only the iPhone can vibrate; this code does not do anything on an iPod touch.

```
AudioServicesPlaySystemSound(kSystemSoundID_Vibrate);A
```

AVAudioPlayer and AVAudioPlayerDelegate

The AVAudioPlayer plays sounds. The audio player does not have the limitations of the AudioSer vicesPlaySystemSound function. It can play any length sound, loop a sound, play multiple sounds at the same time, and allows control over a sound's volume. Methods you might use include prepareToPlay, play, pause, and stop. Each method's functionality should be intuitive. Notice that prepareToPlay and play return a BOOL, so you can evaluate if the call was successful.

- (BOOL)prepareToPlay
- (BOOL)play
- (void)pause
- (void)stop

You can initialize an AVAudioPlayer with data or a URL. The initWithData:error: function initializes an audio player using data encapsulated in an NSData object. The initWithContentsOfURL:error: initializes an audio player using the sound file referenced by the URL. That sound file can be in your application's bundle, or it can be a resource on a server and streamed. If streamed, note that the prepareToPlay method discussed previously takes more importance, as it buffers the content and helps lessen a user's wait when playing an external resource.

- (id)initWithData:(NSData *) data error:(NSError **) outError
- (id)initWithContentsOfURL:(NSURL *) url error:(NSError **) outError

Properties you might use include the currentTime, data, delegate, duration, playing, volume, and numberOfLoops. The currentTime property returns the playback in seconds as an NSTimeInterval. The duration property returns a sound's duration in seconds as an NSTimeInterval. The volume returns the player's playback gain as a float between 0.0 and 1.0. The playing property returns a BOOL, while the numberOfLoops property returns an unsigned int. There are also more advanced properties, such as numberOfChannels and peakPowerForChannel. For a more complete listing of AVAudioPlayer's properties and methods, refer to the AVAudioPlayer Class Reference.

An AVAudioPlayer's delegate property refers to an audio player's AVAudioPlayerDelegate protocol. As with all protocols, you implement a custom class that adopts the protocol. Protocol methods you might implement are listed in Table 18-1.

Method	Description
- (void) audioPlayerBeginInterruption: (AVAudioPlayer *) player	Responds to an interruption to an audio player.
- (void) audioPlayerDecodeErrorDidOccur: (AVAudioPlayer *) player error: (NSError *) error	Responds to a decoding error.
- (void) audioPlayerDidFinishPlaying: (AVAudioPlayer *) player successfully: (BOOL) flag	Responds to a sound finished playing.
- (void) audioPlayerEndInterruption: (AVAudioPlayer *) player	Responds to an interruption.

Table 18-1 AVAudioPlayerDelegate methods

Try This Playing a Sound and an MP3

1. Create a new View-based Application and name it Avplayer.

2. From the Resources folder, add the mp3, charleston1925_64kb.mp3, to the application's Resources folder. Also add the burp_2.aif file.

3. Add the AudioToolbox.framework to the application's frameworks. Also add the AVFoundation.framework. Remember, you add a framework by choosing File | Add | Existing Frameworks, and then navigating to the framework. Remember to select the framework for the iPhone OS version you are compiling for. For instance, in my project, I navigated to iPhoneSimulator3.0.sdk/System/Library/Frameworks to find the frameworks.

4. Open AvplayerViewController.h and import the AudioToolbox and AVFoundation header files (Listing 18-1). Have the class adopt the AVAudioPlayerDelegate protocol.

5. Add a SystemSoundID as a variable to AvplayerViewController; name it burpSoundID. Also add an AVAudioPlayer as a variable and name it player.

6. Add two IBActions to AvplayerViewController named playSound and playSong. Do not forget to add the actions to AvplayerViewController's header and implementation (Listing 18-2). Don't implement the actions yet, you do that in step nine. Save the application.

7. Open AvplayerViewController.xib in Interface Builder and add two buttons. Connect one button to playSound and one button to playSong. Label both buttons appropriately.

8. Save and exit Interface Builder.

9. Implement playSound, playSong, and viewDidLoad. Also implement the audioPlayerDid FinishPlaying:successfully: method from the AVAudioPlayerDelegate protocol.

10. Click Build And Go. Tap the button connected to playSong to begin playing the song. After the song starts playing, tap the button connected to playSound, and the iPhone Simulator belches simultaneously (Figure 18-1).

This task is straightforward; first, you loaded the sound and obtained its id. As system sounds are 30 seconds or less, loading it into memory and keeping it there should not tax your device's memory. Notice you do not load the longer song into memory until you actually play it in the playSong method, as it takes more memory.

You initialize the system sound in the viewDidLoad method. Don't let the one line of code be intimidating; it's actually doing something quite simple. It gets the path to the file, creates an NSURL using the path, casts it as a CFURLRef, and creates a system sound from the resource.

The playSong method creates a new AVAudioPlayer instance every time the application calls it. If an error occurs, the method logs the error; otherwise, it plays the song. When the song is finished playing, it calls the audioPlayerDidFinishPlaying:successfully: method and releases the player.

(continued)

Figure 18-1 The finished application in the iPhone Simulator

Listing 18-1 AvplayerViewController.h

```
#import <UIKit/UIKit.h>
#import <AudioToolbox/AudioToolbox.h>
#import <AVFoundation/AVFoundation.h>
@interface AvplayerViewController : UIViewController
<AVAudioPlayerDelegate> {
  SystemSoundID burpSoundID;
  AVAudioPlayer * player;
}
- (IBAction) playSound: (id) sender;
- (IBAction) playSong: (id) sender;
@end
```

Listing 18-2   AvplayerViewController.m

```
#import "AvplayerViewController.h"
@implementation AvplayerViewController
- (void) viewDidLoad {
  AudioServicesCreateSystemSoundID((CFURLRef)[NSURL fileURLWithPath:
[[NSBundle mainBundle] pathForResource:@"burp_2" ofType:@"aif"]],
&burpSoundID);
}
- (IBAction) playSound: (id) sender {
  AudioServicesPlaySystemSound (burpSoundID);
}
- (IBAction) playSong: (id) sender {
  NSError *error = nil;
  player = [[AVAudioPlayer alloc] initWithContentsOfURL:
[NSURL fileURLWithPath:[[NSBundle mainBundle] pathForResource:
@"charleston1925_64kb" ofType:@"mp3"]] error:&error];
  player.delegate = self;
  if(error != NULL) {
    NSLog([error description]);
    [error release];
  }
  [player play];
}
- (void) audioPlayerDidFinishPlaying: (AVAudioPlayer *) theplayer
successfully:(BOOL)flag {
  [theplayer release];
}
- (void)dealloc {
  [player release];
  [super dealloc];
}
@end
```

NOTE

The mp3 song is entitled The Charleston, and is a digital copy of the 1925 recording.
I obtained the mp3 from the Internet Archive's 78RPMS & Cylinder Recordings Collection.
The mp3 is licensed under the Creative Commons Commercial license. The burp_2.aif is
also public domain. Hopefully, I am not violating any software patents by playing burp
sounds on a mobile device...

Media Player Framework

Before iPhone OS 3.0, a device's multimedia loaded by iTunes was off limits for application developers. The Media Player framework released with OS 3.0 removes that restriction by providing several classes that work with a device's iTunes-loaded multimedia.

NOTE
Running the Media Player audio applications in this chapter require installing the application on an iPod touch or iPhone running iPhone OS 3.0 or later.

Media Data Classes

An MPMediaLibrary class represents a device's multimedia library loaded from iTunes. An MPMediaItem object represents every multimedia item in the media library. The MPMediaItem class contains metadata such as title, artist, and length about a media item.

When working with the MPMediaLibrary, you usually execute an MPMediaQuery that returns an MPMediaItemCollection. Although the Media Player framework offers several methods for accessing a device's media programmatically, another way is by using an MPMediaPickerController. An MPMediaPickerController is a class that presents a view much like the current iPod application. A user can then select one or more media items, and the picker returns an MPMediaItemCollection.

After selecting the media items to play, you pass them to an MPMusicController to play. The MPMusicController class is responsible for playing music, rewinding, forwarding, and other playback functionality.

MPMediaItem and MPMediaItemCollection

An MPMediaItem encapsulates a single audio multimedia element in a device's iTunes multimedia collection. The MPMediaItem contains one method for obtaining a media item's properties, the valueForProperty: method.

```
- (id)valueForProperty:(NSString *)property
```

The valueForProperty: method takes a constant representing the property for which to obtain a value. Notice that the method returns an id; this means the function's return value is tied to the property constant passed to the method. Listing 18-3 lists the properties you might pass to the valueForProperty: method.

Listing 18-3 Media Item properties

```
NSString *const MPMediaItemPropertyPersistentID;
NSString *const MPMediaItemPropertyAlbumTrackNumber;
NSString *const MPMediaItemPropertyAlbumTrackCount;
```

```
NSString *const MPMediaItemPropertyDiscNumber;
NSString *const MPMediaItemPropertyDiscCount;
NSString *const MPMediaItemPropertyArtwork;
NSString *const MPMediaItemPropertyLyrics;
NSString *const MPMediaItemPropertyPodcastTitle;
```

You can also use user-defined properties. These properties have a variable value, depending upon a user's multimedia collection use. Listing 18-4 lists the user-defined properties.

Listing 18-4   User-defined properties

```
NSString *const MPMediaItemPropertyPlayCount;
NSString *const MPMediaItemPropertySkipCount;
NSString *const MPMediaItemPropertyRating;
NSString *const MPMediaItemPropertyLastPlayedDate;
```

The MPMediaItemCollection class is a collection of media items. You obtain a collection's media items through its items property. This property returns an NSArray of MPMediaItem objects. Other properties include count, mediaTypes, and the representativeItem properties. The count property returns a count of the collection's multimedia items as an NSUInteger. You use the mediaTypes property and representativeItem property to obtain a collection's media types.

Selecting Multimedia

Before playing multimedia, a user must select the media items. The easiest way to allow a user to do this is through the MPMediaPickerController. Similar to the UIImagePickerController, the view it controls is hidden from developers. Also, like the image picker, you can define a delegate for the media picker. That delegate, the MPMediaPickerControllerDelegate, responds to a user's interaction with the media picker.

MPMediaPickerController

The MPMediaPickerController class manages the media picker view. Like the UIImagePickerController, you present this controller's view as a modal view that overlays the currently displaying view.

```
[self presentModalViewController:mediaController animated:YES];
```

You can initialize a media picker to only display certain media types using the initWithMediaTypes method. This method takes an MPMediaType; valid types are MPMediaTypeMusic, MPMediaTypePodcast, MPMediaTypeAudioBook, and MPMediaTypeAnyAudio. Notice there is no MPMediaTypeVideo; you cannot select or play an iTunes-loaded video.

You can also initialize a media picker to allow a user to select multiple items by setting the allowsPickingMultimediaItems property to YES. If you don't set this property, its default value is NO.

MPMediaPickerControllerDelegate

A media picker requires an MPMediaPickerControllerDelegate if it is to do anything interesting. An MPMediaPickerControllerDelegate has two methods you implement when adopting this protocol: the mediaPicker:didPickMediaItems: and mediaPickerDidCancel: methods.

```
- (void) mediaPicker: (MPMediaPickerController *)mediaPicker
didPickMediaItems: (MPMediaItemCollection *) mediaItemCollection

- (void) mediaPickerDidCancel: (MPMediaPickerController *) mediaPicker
```

The mediaPickerDidCancel: method responds to a user canceling the media picker, while the mediaPicker:didPickMediaItems: method responds to a user clicking the Done button after selecting media in the media picker.

Playing Multimedia - MPMusicPlayerController

A user will probably wish to play multimedia after selecting it. You play an MPMediaItemsCollection using the MPMusicPlayerController. This class is responsible for playing audio media items. There are two player types to choose from: an iPodMusicPlayer and applicationMusicPlayer. An iPodMusicPlayer replaces an iPod's state, while an applicationMusicPlayer is independent of a user's iPod. For instance, if you are using an iPodMusicPlayer and set it to shuffle mode, the user's iPod application will be in shuffle mode the next time he or she uses it. When using the applicationMusicPlayer, this does not happen because it does not modify the iPod's state.

You initialize a music player's media collection using the setQueueWithQuery:, setQueueWithItems:, or setQueueWithItemCollection: methods. The set with query method takes an MPMediaQuery, the set with items method takes an NSArray of MPMediaItems, and the set with collection method takes an MPMediaItemCollection.

You can initialize a media player's state using the repeatMode and shuffleMode properties. If you do not set these properties, your player's state is the user's iPod application state. Other properties you can use to obtain information about a media player are the nowPlayingItem, currentPlaybackTime, and playbackState properties. The nowPlayingItem property is an MPMediaItem that represents the currently playing media item. The currentPlaybackTime is an NSInterval containing the now-playing item's playback location in seconds. The playbackState property returns the music player's playback state as an MPMusicPlaybackState. Valid values for these states include MPMusicPlaybackStateStopped, MPMusicPlaybackState Playing, MPMusicPlaybackStatePaused, MPMusicPlaybackStateInterrupted, MPMusicPlayback StateSeekingForward, and MPMusicPlaybackStateSeekingBackward.

Methods you can use to control a media player are play, pause, stop, beginSeekingForward, beginSeekingBackward, endSeeking, skipToNextItem, skipToBeginning, and skipToPreviousItem.

The play, pause, and stop methods should be self-explanatory. The beginSeekingForward and beginSeekingBackward methods are for fast-forwarding and rewinding, respectively, while the endSeeking method stops fast-forwarding or rewinding. The skipToNextItem, skipToPreviousItem, and skipToBeginning methods should also be self-explanatory.

The MPMusicPlayerController has no delegate protocol for responding to its events. Instead it provides two notifications: the MPMusicPlayerControllerPlaybackStateDidChange and MPMusicPlayerControllerNowPlayingItemDidChange notifications. The first notification posts when an MPMusicPlayerController's playback state changes. The second notification posts when an MPMusicPlayerController's now-playing media item changes. By using these two notifications, your application can respond to the media player's state, as the next example task illustrates.

Try This ## Using the Media Picker and Media Player

1. Create a new View-based Application; name it iPodSongs.

2. Add the Media Player framework (MediaPlayer.framework) to the project's frameworks.

3. Add the player_stop.png, player_pause.png, player_begin1.png, player_play.png, player_rew.png, player_fwd.png, and player-end.png images from the Resources folder to the project's Resources folder.

4. Open iPodSongsViewController and add four IBOutlets: three for UILabels and one for a UIView. Name the outlets currentTitle, currentArtist, currentLengthInSeconds, and volumeView.

5. Add an IBAction named selectSongs. Don't implement selectSongs yet. Add an IBAction named changeState (Listings 18-5 and 18-6).

6. Save. Open iPodSongsViewController.xib in Interface Builder. Create a button and connect its Touch Up Inside event to the selectSongs method.

7. Create five buttons and add an image to each button (Figure 18-2). Assign each button a unique tag in the Inspector. Connect the five buttons to the changeState action.

8. Add three labels to the canvas. Also add a UIView to the view's canvas and connect it to the volumeView outlet.

9. Connect the three labels to the currentTitle, currentArtist, and currentLengthInSeconds outlets.

10. Exit Interface Builder and return to iPodSongsViewController.

11. Create a new Objective-C class that is a subclass of NSObject named MyMediaPickerDelegate and have it adopt the MPMediaPickerControllerDelegate protocol (Listings 18-7 and 18-8). Don't forget to import the MediaPlayer header file.

(continued)

Figure 18-2 The application's canvas in Interface Builder

12. Open iPodSongsViewController and add properties for the MyMediaPickerDelegate, MPMediaLibrary, and MPMusicPlayerController. Name the properties mediaPickerDelegate, mediaLib, and player.

13. Add a variable for MPVolumeView named mpVolumeView.

14. Be certain that iPodSongsViewController imports MyMediaPickerDelegate and do not forget to synthesize the three properties.

15. Return to MyMediaPickerDelegate and implement the didPickMediaItems delegate methods.

16. Return to iPodSongsViewController and implement the selectSongs and changeState methods.

17. Implement the viewDidLoad method and the songsPicked method, pay particular attention to the NSNotification.

18. Click Build And Go. The application runs, displays the control, and allows selecting multimedia. Upon tapping Done, the music player starts playing and displays the currently playing item in the labels (Figure 18-3).

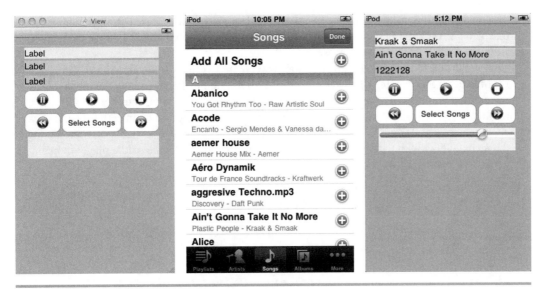

Figure 18-3   The application running on an iPod touch

This is perhaps the coolest application in this entire book. The user interface isn't pretty, but the application works well as a simple music player. In fact, I like it more than my iPod touch's Music application, as I can quickly select all the songs I am interested in and then play them. I have used the application several times for over an hour each time while exercising, so the application works.

In the viewDidLoad method, notice the code for initializing a volume control. Although the MPVolumeView class provides a sizeThatFits method, in my opinion, it is better to do it the way presented here. Simply add a UIView as a subview, size it to the desired size, and then add the volume view to the subview. Easy, and it is guaranteed to size correctly.

```
mpVolumeView = [[MPVolumeView alloc] init];
[mpVolumeView setFrame:[self.volumeView bounds]];
[self.volumeView addSubview:mpVolumeView];
```

As the MPMediaPlayerController does not have a delegate, you made the iPodSongsViewController a listener for the MPMusicPlayerControllerNowPlayingItemDid ChangeNotification event. When a player's now-playing item changes, the player fires this event. You set the songChanged method as the method called when the event fires. After being called, the songChanged method obtains the now-playing item and updates the view's labels.

The changeState method handles any one of the five control buttons being tapped. Because each button has a different tag, the method can distinguish which button fires the Touch Up Inside Event and handle the message appropriately. In a real-world application, you would

(continued)

disable the buttons as appropriate. For instance, when paused, the Pause button should be disabled and only the Play button enabled. However, here, the extra code would have detracted from the example's intended purpose.

In addition to the player's notification, you created your own notification in MyMediaPickerDelegate. Upon selecting an MPMediaItemCollection using the media picker, this notification is fired. The songsPicked method in iPodSongsViewController responds to this notification. The method takes the NSNotification as a parameter; remember, notifications can contain an object. Here, that object is the selected MPMediaItemCollection. After initializing the media player with the collection, the songsPicked method tells the media player to begin generating playback notifications and then starts playing.

Listing 18-5   iPodSongsViewController.h

```
#import <UIKit/UIKit.h>
#import <MediaPlayer/MediaPlayer.h>
#import "MyMediaPickerDelegate.h"
@interface iPodSongsViewController : UIViewController {
  MyMediaPickerDelegate * mediaControllerDelegate;
  MPMediaLibrary * mediaLib;
  IBOutlet UILabel * currentTitle;
  IBOutlet UILabel * currentArtist;
  IBOutlet UILabel * currentLengthInSeconds;
  MPMusicPlayerController * player;
  IBOutlet UIView * volumeView;
  MPVolumeView * mpVolumeView;
}
@property (nonatomic, retain) MyMediaPickerDelegate *
mediaControllerDelegate;
@property (nonatomic, retain) MPMediaLibrary * mediaLib;
@property (nonatomic, retain) UILabel * currentTitle;
@property (nonatomic, retain) UILabel * currentArtist;
@property (nonatomic, retain) UILabel * currentLengthInSeconds;
@property (nonatomic, retain) MPMusicPlayerController * player;
@property (nonatomic, retain) IBOutlet UIView * volumeView;
- (IBAction) selectSongs : (id) sender;
- (IBAction) changeState: (id) sender;
@end
```

Listing 18-6   iPodSongsViewController.m

```
#import "iPodSongsViewController.h"
@implementation iPodSongsViewController
@synthesize mediaControllerDelegate;
@synthesize mediaLib;
```

```objc
@synthesize currentTitle;
@synthesize currentArtist;
@synthesize currentLengthInSeconds;
@synthesize player;
@synthesize volumeView;
int currentItem = 0;
- (void) viewDidLoad {
  [MPMediaLibrary defaultMediaLibrary];
  [[NSNotificationCenter defaultCenter] addObserver:self selector:
@selector(songsPicked:) name:@"SongsPicked" object:nil];
  [[NSNotificationCenter defaultCenter] addObserver:self selector:
@selector(songChanged) name:
@"MPMusicPlayerControllerNowPlayingItemDidChangeNotification"
object:nil];
  mpVolumeView = [[MPVolumeView alloc] init];
  [mpVolumeView setFrame:[self.volumeView bounds]];
  [self.volumeView addSubview:mpVolumeView];
}
- (void) songsPicked: (NSNotification *) notification {
  player = [MPMusicPlayerController applicationMusicPlayer];
  player.repeatMode = MPMusicRepeatModeNone;
  player.shuffleMode = MPMusicShuffleModeOff;
  [player setQueueWithItemCollection:(MPMediaItemCollection *)
[notification object]];
  [player beginGeneratingPlaybackNotifications];
  [player play];
}
- (void) songChanged {
  MPMediaItem * tempMediaItem = (MPMediaItem *)player.nowPlayingItem;
  [self.currentTitle setText:[tempMediaItem valueForProperty:
MPMediaItemPropertyTitle]];
  [self.currentArtist setText: [tempMediaItem valueForProperty:
MPMediaItemPropertyArtist]];
  [self.currentLengthInSeconds setText: [NSString
stringWithFormat:@"%i",
[tempMediaItem valueForProperty:MPMediaItemPropertyPlaybackDuration]]];
}
- (IBAction) changeState: (id) sender {
  NSInteger num = ((UIControl*)sender).tag;
  switch (num) {
    case 1: [player pause]; break;
    case 2: [player play]; break;
    case 3: [player stop]; break;
    case 4: [player skipToPreviousItem]; break;
    case 5: [player skipToNextItem]; break;
  }
}
```

(continued)

```
- (IBAction) selectSongs: (id) sender {
  MPMediaPickerController * mediaController =
[[MPMediaPickerController alloc] init] ;
  mediaController.allowsPickingMultipleItems = YES;
  mediaController.delegate = [[MyMediaPickerDelegate alloc] init];
  [self presentModalViewController:mediaController animated:YES];
}
- (void)dealloc {
  [[NSNotificationCenter defaultCenter] removeObserver:self];
  [mediaControllerDelegate release];
  [player stop];
  [mpVolumeView release];
  [super dealloc];
}
@end
```

Listing 18-7 MyMediaPickerDelegate.h

```
#import <Foundation/Foundation.h>
#import <MediaPlayer/MediaPlayer.h>
@interface MyMediaPickerDelegate : NSObject <MPMediaPickerController
Delegate> {
}
@end
```

Listing 18-8 MyMediaPickerDelegate.m

```
#import "MyMediaPickerDelegate.h"
@implementation MyMediaPickerDelegate
- (void) mediaPicker: (MPMediaPickerController *) mediaPicker
didPickMediaItems: (MPMediaItemCollection *) mediaItemCollection {
  NSArray * mediaItems = [mediaItemCollection items];
  NSEnumerator * enumer = [mediaItems objectEnumerator];
  id myObject;
  while (myObject = [enumer nextObject]) {
    MPMediaItem * tempMediaItem = (MPMediaItem *) myObject;
    NSLog(@"Title: %@", [tempMediaItem valueForProperty:
MPMediaItemPropertyTitle]);
    NSLog(@"id: %@", [tempMediaItem valueForProperty:MPMediaItemProperty
Artist]);
    NSLog(@"id: %i", [tempMediaItem valueForProperty:
MPMediaItemPropertyPersistentID]);
```

```
    NSLog(@"----------------------");
  }
  [mediaPicker.parentViewController dismissModalViewControllerAnimated
:YES];
  [mediaPicker release];
  [[NSNotificationCenter defaultCenter] postNotificationName:
@"SongsPicked" object: mediaItemCollection];
}
- (void) dealloc {
  [[NSNotificationCenter defaultCenter] removeObserver: self];
  [super dealloc];
}
@end
```

MPMoviePlayerController

The MPMoviePlayerController plays video bundled as part of your application. It can also stream video from a server. However, despite its name, it cannot use video loaded on a user's device by iTunes.

The MPMoviePlayerController presents a modal, full-screen video when it plays. You can only minimally modify its appearance using properties. What you can change are a movie player's background color, a movie's scaling, and the controls presented to the user when playing a movie. You change a movie's background color using the backgroundColor property. You change a movie's scaling using the scalingMode property, and you change the controls presented using the movieControlMode property.

The backgroundColor property changes the movie player's background color when playing a movie. For instance, when you watch a video using the Video application on an iPod touch, the background is black. If you wish, you can change that color using this property.

The scalingMode property changes a movie's scaling. Valid values for scalingMode are MPMovieScalingModeNone, MPMovieScalingModeAspectFit, MPMovieScalingModeAspect Fill, and MPMovieScalingModeFill.

The movieControlMode property determines the visible controls when a movie plays. For instance, when playing a movie using the Video application, if you tap the screen, it presents a control showing the volume, a control showing the location in the video, a scaling control, and a Done button. You can modify which control a player presents using this property. Valid values are MPMovieControlModeDefault, MPMovieControlModeVolumeOnly, and MPMovie ControlModeHidden.

You initialize a movie player using the initWithContentURL: method. This method takes an NSURL to the movie's location. This location must be within your application's sandbox or available via an Internet server (it's a URL). After initializing the player, you call the prepareToPlay and play methods. If you wish to be notified that the player has stopped playing, you register as a notification listener, listening for the player's MPMoviePlayerPlay backDidFinishNotification notification.

Try This Play a Video

1. Create a new View-based Application called MoviePlayer. Add the Media Player framework to the application.

2. Add the movie short.3gp from the Resources folder to the project's Resources folder.

3. Open MoviePlayerController and add an MPMoviePlayerController as a property; name it moviePlayer (Listings 18-9 and 18-10). Do not forget to import the MediaPlayer.

4. Add a method called playingDone and an IBAction called playMovie to MoviePlayerView Controller. Implement both methods the same as in Listing 18-10. Also implement the viewDidLoad method.

5. Save or build. Open MovieplayerViewController.xib in Interface Builder.

6. Add a button to the canvas and connect it to the playMovie action. Save and exit Interface Builder.

7. Click Build And Go.

Like the music player, you register to listen to the finished playing event in the viewDidLoad method. Notice that unlike the previous task, you didn't place the event's name in quotations. This omission was intentional. The event and the event's NSString name are the same, and you can use either. The viewDidLoad method also initializes the movie player with the short.3gp movie's location. In a real-world application, loading a movie when a view loads is probably not a good idea, as movies are usually quite large.

When a user taps the button, the movie player begins playing the movie in landscape mode (Figure 18-4). Upon tapping the Done button, the user returns to the application's view in portrait mode. The controller also receives the notification that the player stopped playing and releases the player.

Listing 18-9 MovieplayerViewController.h

```
#import <UIKit/UIKit.h>
#import <MediaPlayer/MediaPlayer.h>
@interface MovieplayerViewController : UIViewController {
  MPMoviePlayerController * movieplayer;
}
@property (nonatomic, retain) MPMoviePlayerController * movieplayer;
-(IBAction) playMovie: (id) sender;
- (void) playingDone;
@end
```

Figure 18-4 The application running in iPhone Simulator

Listing 18-10 MovieplayerViewController.m

```
#import "MovieplayerViewController.h"
@implementation MovieplayerViewController
@synthesize movieplayer;
- (void) viewDidLoad {
  [[NSNotificationCenter defaultCenter] addObserver:self selector:
@selector (playingDone) name:MPMoviePlayerPlaybackDidFinishNotification
object:nil];
}
- (IBAction) playMovie: (id) sender {
  movieplayer = [[MPMoviePlayerController alloc] initWithContentOfURL:
[NSURL fileURLWithPath:[[NSBundle mainBundle] pathForResource:@"short"
ofType:@"3gp"]]];
  [movieplayer play];
}
```
(continued)

```
- (void) playingDone {
  [movieplayer release];
  movieplayer = nil;
}
- (void)dealloc {
  [[NSNotificationCenter defaultCenter] removeObserver:self];
  [movieplayer release];
  [super dealloc];
}
@end
```

Summary

In this chapter, you learned how to play system sounds, sounds, a device's audio multimedia loaded from iTunes, and video. You first played a system sound. System sounds are 30 seconds or less, and are designed as audible alerts. You also played an MP3 using the AVAudioPlayer. The AVAudioPlayer is for playing longer sounds, including your application's multimedia, such as MP3s. However, the audio player is limited to sounds bundled with your application or streamed from a server. It cannot play iTunes-loaded multimedia.

The newer media player can play iTunes multimedia, provided it is audio. You learned how to use the media player and how to use a controller to select music and a player to play it. After learning about the Media Player framework's newer features, you then learned about its movie player. Despite being part of the Media Player framework, you can only play video bundled as part of your application or video streamed from a server.

Index